JANE AUSTEN

JANE AUSTEN

Woman and Writer

JOAN REES

823
7
AUSTEN

ST. MARTIN'S PRESS
NEW YORK

ROBERT HALE & COMPANY
LONDON

St. Martin's Press, Inc.
175 Fifth Avenue
New York, N.Y. 10010

Library of Congress Catalog Card Number 76–2166

Robert Hale & Company
Clerkenwell House
Clerkenwell Green
London EC1R oHT

ISBN 0 7091 5523 9

PRINTED IN GREAT BRITAIN BY
CLARKE, DOBLE & BRENDON LTD.
PLYMOUTH

Contents

Illustrations

PICTURE CREDITS

The kind permission of the owners as listed for
the reproduction of the illustrations is gratefully
acknowledged.

Acknowledgments

In a book which owes so much to quotations from Jane Austen's letters, for I have tried to make her speak for herself as much as possible, I have first to thank the Oxford University Press for the many passages taken from the *Letters of Jane Austen to her sister Cassandra and Others*, so helpfully and thoroughly edited by Dr R. W. Chapman that scarcely a question is left unanswered. Other quotations have been taken from the *Letters of Jane Austen* edited by Lord Brabourne. I am also grateful for the quotations I have been enabled to make from Jane Austen's *Minor Works*, Oxford University Press, edited by R. W. Chapman and B. C. Southam, 1972.

For their generous permission for the use of other material, I would like to thank most gratefully: Mrs Margaret Austen-Leigh, *Jane Austen, Her Life and Letters* by W. & R. A. Austen-Leigh, and the invaluable *Austen Papers, 1704–1856*, edited by R. A. Austen-Leigh; Penguin Books Ltd., The Penguin English Library edition of the Novels of Jane Austen, and Alfred Cobban, *A History of Modern France*, Vol. 2 (2nd edition 1965); Archon Books, Howard Babb, *Jane Austen's Novels, The Fabric of Dialogue*, 1967 (reprinted from the original publication in 1962 by Ohio University Press); The Bodley Head, J. H. & Edith Hubback, *Jane Austen's Sailor Brothers*, John Lane, 1906; Routledge & Kegan Paul Ltd. and in USA Barnes & Noble, B. C. Southam, *Jane Austen, The Critical Heritage*, 1968; © Oxford University Press, B. C. Southam, *Jane Austen's Literary Manuscripts*, 1964; Malcolm Bradbury, *Jane Austen's Emma*, and E. F. Shannon and the Modern Language Association of America, *Emma, Character and Construction*, both essays reprinted in *Emma, A Casebook* ed. David Lodge, Macmillan, 1968; Chatto & Windus Ltd. and in USA the Oxford University Press, A. Walton Litz, *Jane Austen, A Study of her Artistic Development*, 1965; Curtis Brown Ltd., © 1937 W. H. Auden, *Letter to Lord Byron* reprinted from *Collected Longer*

Poems, in USA by permission of Random House, Inc.; J. M. Dent Ltd., and in USA, Curtis Brown Ltd., Edna Nixon, *Mary Wollstonecraft*, 1971; Chatto & Windus, © V. S. Pritchett, *George Meredith and English Comedy*, in USA Alfred A. Knopf, Inc. 1969; the Literary Estate of Virginia Woolf and the Hogarth Press for quotations from her *Collected Essays*, in USA Harcourt Brace Jovanovich, Inc.

For several quotations listed in the References from the Annual Reports and from Caroline Austen's *My Aunt Jane Austen*, and for the provision of some of the illustrations, I am most appreciative of the assistance of the Jane Austen Society. For those of her admirers unaware of it, I would like to take this opportunity of drawing attention to the untiring work of the Jane Austen Memorial Trust in the preservation of her Chawton home, which contains so many evocative reminders of her life and work.

I am also most grateful for helpful conversations with Jane Aiken Hodge, B. C. Southam and T. F. Carpenter, for the efficient and friendly service of the London Library; and would like to conclude with thanks to my mother, Mrs Alice Rees, for her invaluable typing assistance, and to my husband, Frank Cyprien, for painstaking reading and patience.

J.R.

For John F. Gibson
my agent, guide, and friend

"Nobody, who has not been in the interior of a family, can say what the difficulties of any individual of that family may be."

Emma

ONE

Prelude

Early in the morning of Thursday 24th July 1817, Cassandra Austen, a handsome, pale woman in her forties, watched sadly from the window of a little house in College Street, Winchester, as the body of her only sister, Jane, was carried to the cathedral for burial. The ceremony had to be completed early, before the customary service began, and in attendance were three of Jane's brothers, Edward, Henry, and Frank, and her nephew, James Edward, the son of her eldest brother. No one was present outside the family.

The extent to which both the life of Jane Austen, and the record of that life, were shaped by her family can hardly be over-estimated. Her first brief memorial was written by her favourite brother, Henry; a more substantial account, aided by notes provided by his sisters, and with some letters, was produced more than fifty years later by her nephew, James Edward, who still remembered her vividly. This was followed by further letters and notes prepared by her great-nephew, Lord Brabourne, who was born after her death, but whose mother was her favourite niece, Fanny, later Lady Knatchbull. Among many useful works by Austen descendants, there is the valuable Life published in 1913 by her great-nephew William and his son Richard, and every subsequent biographer has relied to a large extent on family productions.

A major source of information about her life is Jane's own correspondence, but even here, of 153 letters published in R. W. Chapman's finely edited volume, only eighteen were addressed outside the family. Moreover, the letters as we have them were passed through the medium of the family filter. Ninety-four of the letters were written to Jane's devoted sister, Cassandra, and before passing these on to Lady Knatchbull, Cassandra completely destroyed some and deleted from those remaining many passages which she considered unsuitable to be seen by any eyes other than her own. In her turn, no doubt

Fanny, Lady Knatchbull, also made her own sacrifices and deletions. Comparing his mother's letters from her Aunt Jane with her diary entries of letters received, her son, Lord Brabourne, concluded that at least twenty-five letters must have been destroyed.

As the years went by and the family began to realize Jane's great literary significance, so the temper of the age had changed. The clear light of the eighteenth century which had irradiated her, was not always acceptable to the Victorians, and Fanny, that much loved niece, was later able to write of her aunts in these terms: "They were not rich & the people around with whom they chiefly mixed, were not at all high bred, or in short anything more than *mediocre* & *they* of course tho' superior in *mental powers* and *cultivation* were on the same level as far as *refinement* goes . . . if it had not been for Papa's marriage which brought them into Kent, & the kindness of Mrs Knight who used often to have one or the other of the sisters staying with her, they would have been, tho' not less clever & agreeable in themselves, very much below par as to good Society and its ways."[1] It seems fairly certain that this writer never expected her letter would be published.

The memorial which was originally placed in Winchester Cathedral makes no mention of Jane Austen's works:

The benevolence of her heart, the sweetness of her temper, and the extraordinary endowments of her mind obtained the regard of all who knew her, and the warmest love of her intimate connections. Their grief is in proportion to their affection they know their loss to be irreparable, but in their deepest affliction they are consoled by a firm though humble hope that her charity, devotion, faith and purity, have rendered her soul acceptable in the sight of her redeemer.

Fifty-five years were to pass before the second tablet was added, containing the words, "To Jane Austen known to many by her writings". This inscription concludes with a quotation from the book of Proverbs: "She openeth her mouth with wisdom; and in her tongue is the law of kindness", not perhaps the most aptly chosen comment on one of the most gently malicious of witty writers. It is very likely that Jane may have had the curse and the blessing of her own quick tongue principally in mind when she wrote her prayer: "May we now, and on each return of night, consider how the past day has been spent by us, what have been our prevailing thoughts, words and actions during it, and how far we can acquit ourselves of evil."[2]

The first biographical notice of Jane Austen provided by her favourite brother, Henry, prefaced the posthumously published edition of *Northanger Abbey* and *Persuasion* in 1817. Henry can be both forgiven and applauded for his idealized portrait, but no careful reader of his sister's novels and letters can believe that "though the frailties, foibles, and follies of others could not escape her immediate detection, yet even on their vices did she never trust herself to comment with unkindness. . . . Faultless herself, as nearly as human nature can be, she always sought, in the faults of others, something to excuse, to forgive or forget. Where extenuation was impossible, she had a sure refuge in silence. She never uttered either a hasty, a silly, or a severe expression."[3] We may believe she never uttered a silly one.

While at a distance of fifty years, her nephew Edward presents a livelier character, he too depicts an almost improbably perfect aunt, never turning "individuals into ridicule" and "as far as possible from being censorious or satirical".

Aided by the recollections of his sisters, Edward recalls his aunt's habits of work in his *Memoir*:

> . . . most of the work must have been done in the general sitting-room, subject to all kinds of casual interruptions. She was careful that her occupation should not be suspected by servants, or visitors, or any persons beyond her own family party. She wrote upon small sheets of paper which could easily be put away, or covered with a piece of blotting paper. There was, between the front door and the offices, a swing door which creaked when it was opened; but she objected to having this little inconvenience remedied, because it gave her notice when anyone was coming.[4]

Edward goes on to say that no intruder ever noticed any signs of impatience or irritability in the writer. But was it possible that she was invariably contented to break the flow of composition to help in the household, or pour drops for her mother, or that she was always able to tuck her work away placidly, without some degree of profound frustration?

Unfortunately, no authentic portrait of Jane Austen exists, apart from a small sketch by her sister which seems to have been drawn towards the close of her life, with her mouth unhappy, her fine dark eyes circled and shadowed, perhaps already showing the marks of her fatal illness. In the engraving made from this for the *Memoir*, the features have been flatteringly softened and blurred, losing in the process much of their reality. Allowing for its lack of technical proficiency, Cassandra's drawing seems to retain more of the tension and intelligence of her sister's character, and shows a remarkable resemblance to the portrait of her brother Frank, which can be seen at Chawton House.

Outside the family circle, opinions about Jane Austen the woman are practically negligible. From Mary Russell Mitford, whose mother was once a neighbour of the Austens, there are a couple of second-hand comments, in sharp contrast and not particularly reliable. "Mamma says that she was *then* the prettiest, silliest, most affected, husband-hunting butterfly she ever remembers."[5] Rather unconvincingly, this silly creature, according to Miss Mitford, later "stiffened into the most perpendicular, precise, taciturn piece of single blessedness that ever existed, and that, till *Pride and Prejudice* showed what a precious gem was hidden in that unbending case, she was no more regarded in society than a poker or a firescreen. . . . The case is very different now: she is still a poker—but a poker of whom everybody is afraid."[6]

In 1870, Fulwar William Fowle, the nephew of Jane's friend Martha Lloyd, writing to Caroline Austen, remembered, "Your dear Aunt Jane I can testify to as being the most attractive, animated, delightful person her Biographer has represented her. . . . The last time I ever saw her was at Steventon, when she was on a visit to your Mother. . . . She was a very sweet reader. She had just finished the first Canto of Marmion. . . . When Mr W. Digweed was announced it was like the interruption of some pleasing dream."[7]

Apart from this, there is only the comment of Sir Egerton Brydges, who admired her girlhood looks but thought her cheeks a little too full. When he became aware of her talent, this pedestrian fellow-writer wished he had taken more notice of her.

It is a wish that must be shared. For, in spite of the Austen family's achievement in preserving so many memories and so much biographical material, it must always be a source of regret that there are no less guarded and possessive, more deeply discerning and objective descriptions of Jane Austen— left to us, for example, by a group of friends, such as those who loved John Keats, whose impressions and opinions have helped to build a portrait of a living man.

Much as Jane Austen loved and was loved by her family, so that any account of her life must be to a considerable extent a family chronicle, it may not be wrong to read some personal feeling into Emma's remark to Mr Knightley: "Nobody, who has not been in the interior of a family, can say what the difficulties of any individual of that family may be."[8]

Jane Austen was received with joy into her family on 16th December 1775. Her happy father wrote to his half-brother's wife, "You have doubtless been for some time in expectation of hearing from Hampshire, and perhaps wondered a little we were in our old age grown such bad reckoners but so it was, for Cassy certainly expected to have been brought to bed a month ago: however last night the time came, and without a great deal of warning, everything was soon happily over. We have now another girl, a present plaything for her sister Cassy and a future companion."[9] Their father was prophesying about his two daughters with more truth than he can have realized. For the two little girls, who were such contented and inseparable playmates, grew up to share with each other their deepest and most intimate adult relationship.

When Jane arrived, the Austen family was already a large one, and four years later, Cassandra Austen gave birth to Charles, her last child. Her first born son was James, ten years older than Jane, followed a year later by George, who was never able to share in the life of his family. No details are known of George's disability, fits are mentioned, and some degree of mental and perhaps physical handicap may be surmised, but this second son never came home from his period of wet-nursing in the village, which all the children underwent, and survived to a good age to be a constant source of expense to his far from well-off family.

Two more healthy sons were born in 1768 and 1771, Edward and Henry, and then, at last, in 1773, the Austens were delighted to welcome their first daughter, named for her mother, Cassandra. Another son, Francis, usually known in the family as Frank, and sometimes as Fly, was born before the arrival of Jane, the second and last daughter.

For nearly four years, Jane was the baby of a family including three intelligent and handsome brothers a good deal her senior. Since her mother was always busy and preoccupied, to a great extent Cassandra supervised and mothered her little sister, and from the very beginning, the sisters were unusually close.

At this time, Jane's father, George Austen, was the Rector of Steventon and Deane. The Steventon living had been presented to him by a distant cousin, Thomas Knight of Godmersham in Kent. Mr Knight had leased his Steventon Manor House and most of his land to the Digweed family, and to a certain extent, the Rector tended to be regarded as the lord of the manor. The presentation of the neighbouring living at Deane had been purchased for the Rector by his Uncle Francis in 1773. But the total from the two livings provided only a modest income on which to raise and educate a family of boys, and besides supervising with some energy the farm attached to the rectory which produced a useful additional revenue, Mr Austen, who as a young man had been a teacher at his old school at Tonbridge, accepted a limited number of boarding pupils who were educated in the company of his sons.

George Austen was descended from a Kentish family whose prosperity, originating from generations of workers engaged in the manufacture of woollen cloth, enabled later members of the family to enter the legal and medical professions. George's father, William Austen, was a doctor, but unfortunately he died when his only son was just six years old, also leaving his widow with her son, William Hampson Walter, by her first marriage, and two little girls, Philadelphia and Leonora. She herself died not long after her husband.

His father's brother, Francis, a large, shrewd, prosperous Sevenoaks lawyer, took care of the orphaned boy, and as the purchase of the Deane living shows, maintained in him a kindly lifelong interest. Thanks to his uncle, George received a good education at Tonbridge school, obtaining a scholarship to St John's College, Oxford, where he later became a Fellow. He was ordained in 1760, and in 1764 at Walcot Church in Bath, he married Miss Cassandra Leigh. The young Austens were a good looking pair. George, with his regular features and bright hazel eyes, had been known at Oxford as "the handsome proctor",[10] and Cassandra was a slim striking girl, justly proud of her distinguished aristocratic nose.

Cassandra's father was also a parson, and his elder brother, Dr Theophilus Leigh, who was Master of Balliol College for more than half a century, had a reputation as a notable wit. Mrs Thrale mentioned him in a letter to Dr Johnson, delighted by his "gaiety of manners and youthful vivacity" at eighty-six years of age.[11] The Leigh family was descended from the Sir

Thomas Leigh who was Lord Mayor of London at the time of the accession of Elizabeth I, and whose grand-daughter Alice married and was deserted by Robert Dudley, son of the great Queen's favourite. The ancestral home of Stoneleigh Abbey was still in the family. Another famous ancestor was Sir Thomas White, founder of George Austen's old college of St John's, which gave to his sons the useful privilege of "Founder's kin".

Cassandra was also much attached to her sister Jane, wife of Dr Edward Cooper, Vicar of Whaddon near Bath, and her brother James Leigh, who had adopted the additional name of Perrot on inheriting some property. James was devoted to his wife Jane, and since they were wealthy and had no children, the needy Austens cherished some expectations from them. There was also a mentally handicapped brother, Thomas.

Cassandra Austen was sharp and humorous, a descriptive and amusing letter writer, with a facility for writing verse. She and her husband seem to have been well matched, and to have shared a happy married life. She was a practical woman, not too proud to cut up the scarlet riding habit that formed part of her trousseau for clothes for her boys, her busy hands always making and mending, and a keen supervisor of her own little herd of Alderney cows, her dairy, her baking, and brewing.

With so much activity, schoolboys coming and going, the work of the parish and farm, visits to the villagers, Steventon Rectory, where Jane spent the first twenty-five years of her life, formed a self-contained little world.

Steventon was, and remains, a small and rather straggling North Hampshire village, some seven miles from Basingstoke. It is set in attractive, if unexciting countryside, green and peaceful, with gentle hills, the occasional more distant view, the thick hedgerows busy with birds and carpeted with flowers. Nothing now remains of the Rectory except its pump which, a reviewer recently noted, resembles quite remarkably other, less literary pumps. Nevertheless, it serves as a useful marker to the pleasant situation of the Austens' home.

In 1826, the Old Rectory was destroyed, and a new one built, which can still be seen across the road although a Rectory no longer. From his Victorian viewpoint, Edward tells us that Jane's old home "was considered unworthy . . . the rooms were finished with less elegance than would now be found in the most ordinary dwellings. No cornice marked the junction of wall and ceiling; while the beams which supported the upper floors projected into the rooms below in all their naked simplicity, covered only by a coat of paint or white-wash."[12]

Jane's niece, Anna Lefroy, who loved the old Rectory, sketched and described it: a square Georgian house, sheltered by trees, the front door flanked by two pairs of casement windows, with five above on the first floor, three dormers rising from the roof, and two solid chimneys. Of the interior, Anna wrote:

The dining—or common sitting-room looked to the front and was lighted by two casement windows. On the same side the front door opened into a smaller parlour, and visitors, who were few and rare, were not a bit the less welcome to my grandmother because they found her sitting there busily engaged with her needle, making and mending. In later times . . . a sitting-room was made upstairs: "the dressing-room", as they were pleased to call it, perhaps because it opened into a smaller chamber in which my two aunts slept. I remember the common-looking carpet with its chocolate ground, and painted press with shelves above for books, and Jane's piano, and an oval looking glass that hung between the windows.[13]

The Rectory was approached by a gravelled carriage drive, and the informal garden, where vegetables mingled with the flowers, had a sundial and a finely turfed sloping terrace down which, like Catherine Morland, the youngest and most ingenuous of her heroines, Jane no doubt rolled as a child. The family kept a carriage, although probably, like Mr Bennet's, the horses had also to do duty on the farm.

About half a mile away, standing back from the road in a fine position opposite the Manor House, is the Church of St Nicholas, which is probably as peaceful today as it was when the Austen family officiated and worshipped there. It is a tiny thirteenth-century church, dignified and simple, with white-washed walls and dark beams. In the intervening period it has been changed only slightly by the addition of the steeple, which now surmounts the square tower, and a memorial window to Jane Austen.

Attending this little church to hear their father preach in company with their neighbours must have seemed like an extension of family worship to the Austens. This was not a time of spiritual conflict, and religion sat lightly upon most ministers of the church. The ministry was a profession rather than a vocation, and apart from a University degree, no special theological qualifications and certainly no sense of divine mission were required. "Pluralism was common . . . and a large number of Church people regarded a 'living' as just that—a house and income to live on rather than as a sphere of duty."[14]

Although Mr Austen had two parishes to look after, together they were made up of less than three hundred souls. The duties were not arduous, but he was a conscientious man who took them seriously. In his own family, the Christian faith was an unquestioned source of help and strength. Two of his sons were ordained to follow in their father's footsteps, Frank was once noted as "the officer who kneeled at church"[15] and Jane's prayers, her letters at the time of her father's death, and Cassandra's moving letter to Fanny after Jane herself had died, reveal a firm untroubled faith, and a settled conviction of the existence of life after death.

Nevertheless, Jane Austen was to grow up without any undue reverence for the clergy, and no doubt her father, who wrote his own sermons, enjoyed with his family such critical lines as these from one of their favourite poets, Cowper, in which among other faulty patterns of preacher, he describes those that:

> . . . mount the rostrum with a skip,
> And then skip down again; pronounce a text;
> Cry—hem : and, reading what they never wrote,
> Just fifteen minutes, huddle up their work,
> And with a well-bred whisper close the scene![16]

Mr Austen's sound scholarship was reflected both in his work for the ministry and as a teacher, and he seems to have inspired the interest and enjoyment in learning of his children and his pupils. But the most notable of his charges, the little son of Warren Hastings, was too young to have profited by his instruction.

George Hastings had been sent home from India on the death of his mother, and it was one of the unhappinesses of Cassandra Austen's early married life that when he was only six he succumbed to the so called "putrid sore throat",[17] which was most likely to have been diphtheria. "She always declared that his death had been as great a grief to her as if he had been a child of her own."

Mr Austen's connection with Warren Hastings arose from his sister Philadelphia's friendship with the first Mrs Hastings, and her kindness to the great Governor-General after his wife's death. While Uncle Francis had helped to establish his nephew in life by providing him with a good education and a living, his efforts on behalf of Philadelphia had been to buy her a passage to India in the hopes that she would find herself a husband in that land where life was hard and women scarce. A neat illustration of the difference between what were then considered appropriate provisions for boys and girls.

Suitable young ladies did not remain unattached for long in India, and soon after her arrival in 1752, Philadelphia married Tysoe Saul Hancock, at that time surgeon at Fort St David in Madras. Their only daughter Eliza, always called Betsy by her father, was born in 1761. Warren Hastings was her godfather, a role he carried out with unfailing care and generosity.

Probably fearful of the effects of the Indian climate on their charming and delicate little girl, the Hancocks returned to England. But before long, Mr Hancock realized they were living above their means, and the only practical course, leaving his wife and child at home, was for him to return to India.

No doubt this was in the nature of a relief to Philadephia, for Mr Hancock, more than twenty years her senior, whom she can scarcely have married for love, was an irritable, pessimistic, ailing man. Even today, his letters home make uncomfortable reading, especially as he begins to realize the unlikelihood of his ever seeing his family again, and frets against the intolerable delays in the mail.

"My dear Betsy," he writes, "Your letter of 17th September 1770 was more than one year old when I received it, for it did not arrive till the 23rd September 1771."[18] In response to his wife's gift of a waistcoat, he rages: "I should be the most ridiculous Animal upon Earth could I put any finery upon such a Carcase as mine worn out with age and diseases".[19]

A little later, he assures her, "While I can crawl on the face of the Earth, I will do my utmost to make you easy when it shall have pleased Providence to release you from the Remembrance of an old Wretch."[20]

Perhaps he was being unjust to himself, for a young protegé, Philip Dormer Stanhope, paints a happier picture of "a most agreeable companion, and who though upwards of fifty years of age still retains all the fire and pleasantry of youth."[21]

Mr Hancock died in November 1775, and by this time the loss of her husband can hardly have made much difference to Philadelphia's life. She was completely wrapped up in her daughter, and although her husband's estate was only sufficient to pay his debts, the generous trust of £10,000 provided by Hastings left her reasonably secure. When she wanted advice, she turned to her brother, George.

Eliza spent many happy hours of her young life at Steventon, but when she was seventeen, and Jane was only three, her mother took her off to the continent, first to Brussels and then to Paris to finish her education. During the years that followed, she remained for her cousins a glamorous inhabitant of a remote and glittering world.

"Indeed I am almost ashamed to say what a racketing life I have led, but it was really almost unavoidable, Paris has been remarkably gay this year on account of the birth of the Dauphin. This event was celebrated by illuminations, fire works, balls, etc. The entertainment of the latter kind given at court was amazingly fine. The Court of France is at all times brilliant, but on this occasion the magnificence was beyond conception. . . ."[22]

The fairy-tale story of Eliza's life seemed to have achieved its perfect happy ending when in 1781 came the news that she had married a French aristocrat with the romantic name of Jean Gabriel Capotte, Comte de Feuillide. "The whole study of his life seems to be to contribute to the happiness of mine", she wrote contentedly.[23]

Mr George Austen was not so pleased. It seemed to him the connection meant his sister and niece giving up all their friends, their country, and he feared their religion. Perhaps he also detected the storm clouds gathering in France.

Jane's two eldest brothers were the next to enter on a wider scene. James, an earnest, serious boy, though not without humour, was enabled to enter St John's College, Oxford, on a Founder's Kin scholarship in 1779 at the very early age of fourteen.

Edward, who was not so academically minded, was to become the protegé of Mr Thomas Knight and his wife of Godmersham Park in Kent and Chawton House in Hampshire. This was the son of the benefactor who had given Mr Austen his Steventon living, and he and his beautiful wife, who had been Catherine Knatchbull, to their great disappointment, had remained childless. On a visit to Steventon, they had taken a liking to the good humoured little boy, and asked if he could go to stay with them. Unwilling for the boy to miss his lessons, Mr Austen hesitated, but the practical Cassandra, no doubt foreseeing future benefits for her son, gained his permission:

"I think, my dear, you had better oblige your cousins and let the child go."[24]

The experiment was a success. Edward spent more and more time at Godmersham with the Knights, who became as fond of him as if he were their own son, and adopted him as their heir. His attractive character and sound business sense made him thoroughly worthy of his good fortune, and he was always to remain an affectionate son to his own parents.

When she returned from her spell of being nursed in the village, Jane's earliest years must have been spent happily. Although the two eldest boys were only occasionally at home, there was the constant companionship of Cassandra, before long a baby brother, and Henry and Frank to admire, both working hard with their father.

Henry was regarded as the most handsome of a family of handsome boys, and although not the steadiest, as the gaiest and most brilliant. He was always to be the brother closest to Jane. Frank was a sturdy, independent lad, neat, accurate, and precise. At the age of seven, he purchased for a guinea and a half a chestnut pony which was named Squirrel, but usually known as Scug. During the next two years, Frank became a familiar sight in the neighbourhood, riding Squirrel about the countryside, hunting, "jumping everything that the pony could get its nose over", and finally selling it for a guinea more than he had paid.[25]

Mrs Austen's affection for her pretty sister Jane, who had married Dr Edward Cooper, the Rector of Whaddon near Bath, ensured that the two families kept in touch, and the Austen children saw a good deal of their cousins, Edward and Jane. It seems probable that the two girls accompanied their mother on her visits to her sister, and that from her childhood, Jane was associated with the city of Bath which was later to play so important a part in her life and work.

Probably it was Mrs Cooper's decision to send her Jane to school that influenced Mr and Mrs Austen to let their own daughters go with her. They may also have been glad of some extra room for Mr Austen's pupils at the time. The school was at Oxford and run by Mrs Cawley, Dr Cooper's sister, the widow of a Principal of Brasenose College.

The two little girls set off from Steventon in 1782, when Jane was only six. No doubt Mrs Austen thought it best to keep them together, although Jane was very young to be sent away. She was so fond of her sister that she would have fretted without her. As Mrs Austen said: "If Cassandra were going to have her head cut off, Jane would insist on sharing her fate."[26]

As it happened, these words came unhappily near to the truth. After a period in Oxford, Mrs Cawley moved to Southampton, and the girls went with her. While they were there, both Cassandra and Jane became seriously ill with an infectious disease which again was probably diphtheria. Cassandra's case was slight, but Jane's grew steadily more alarming. No doubt hoping for the best and anxious to keep her pupils' custom, Mrs Cawley failed to notify their parents. Luckily, their cousin Jane, upset and afraid, had the good sense to write home, and immediately the two anxious mothers hurried to Southampton. Mrs Austen stayed to nurse her girls back to health, while her sister returned to Bath with her own daughter. Tragically, when she reached home, it was found that Mrs Cooper had herself contracted the disease, and after a short illness, she died. Little Jane Austen had been very close to death, and clearly the incident might have ended fatally for them all.

After such an unfortunate experience, it seems strange that the parents should have entrusted their daughters to boarding school again. But once more, it may have been as companions for the now motherless Jane Cooper. This time, they selected the romantically situated Abbey School at Reading, run by a Mrs Latournelle, who had what must have been to the children the intriguing disability of a cork leg. In spite of this, she was an active and energetic woman, if with few qualifications for teaching. From the domestic point of view, the school was admirably run; the educational regime was far from taxing; discipline was sufficiently relaxed for the girls to be permitted a meal with their brothers at a local inn; and no doubt they enjoyed the period, from summer 1785 till the spring of 1787 that they spent there.

Later, Jane Austen was to be scathing on the subject of female education. For example, Charlotte Palmer's from *Sense and Sensibility* : "over the mantlepiece still hung a landscape in coloured silks of her performance, in proof of her having spent seven years at a great school in town to some effect".[27] But it is likely that a girl of Jane's keen intelligence at least made the best possible use of whatever was to be gleaned there. No doubt some history, some selected English literature, dancing, needlework, and the rudiments of French.

When she and Cassandra returned home for ever, their real education with their father and their brothers began. By this time, Jane was eleven, a bright eyed and aware young girl, used to the company of her elders, with the assurance a child quickly gains from being sent away from home; a keen sense of humour and a tendency to laugh at the wrong people at the wrong times; her brief experience already including several changes of scene and companions, and recovery from a dangerous illness.

James had taken his degree, travelled to France, and was shortly to return to St John's as a Fellow. As well as his father, James was to be responsible for guiding Jane's literary taste. He himself enjoyed writing and at Oxford edited and wrote the best part of a periodical called *The Loiterer*, in which later Henry was also to collaborate. This aimed at giving "a rough but not entirely inaccurate Sketch of the Character, the Manners, and the Amusements of Oxford at the close of the eighteenth century".[28] Later in the family chronicles, James seems to emerge as a rather melancholy fellow, but *The Loiterer* shows him to have had some talent and wit.

Instead of the university, the Knights had decided that Edward would derive more benefit from a grand tour of the continent, which was to take him as far south as Rome. Henry was preparing to enter St John's College as a scholar in 1788 at the age of seventeen, while young Frank had already departed to the Royal Navy Academy at Portsmouth where, as soon as he was old enough, Charles was to follow him.

When he was only fourteen, Frank sailed to the East Indies on the *Perseverence*. The letter his father wrote to him on the eve of his departure, which he treasured to the end of his exceptionally long life—he died at the age of 91—gives a good idea of the quality of the relationship between George Austen and his children. After a good deal of sensible advice, he ends: "I have nothing to add but my blessing and best prayers for your health and prosperity, and to beg you would never forget you have not upon earth a more disinterested and warm friend than your truly affectionate father."[29]

While the girls had been away at school, Eliza de Feuillide, expecting her first and only child, had returned to England with her mother for her confinement. They settled in Orchard Street, and in 1786 Eliza gave birth to a son, christened Hastings in honour of her own famous godfather. Hastings was to prove a delicate child, prone to convulsions.

Although she was fond of her little boy, Eliza was young and gay, and never overburdened by her responsibilities.

As to me I have been for some time past the greatest rake imaginable & really wonder how such a meagre creature as I am can support so much fatigue, of which the history of one day will give you some idea, for I only stood from two to four in the Drawing Room & of course loaded with a great hoop of no inconsiderable weight, went to the Dutchess of Cumberland's in the evening, & from thence to Almacks where I staid till five in the morning.[30]

From her portrait, it can be seen that this "meagre creature" was an exceptionally attractive young woman, quick, petite, pert, with a tiny tip-tilted nose, and great slanting eyes. Her sojourn in France had endowed her with a good deal of confidence and chic, and altogether, she was quite enchanting.

Her cousin and Jane's, Philadelphia Walter, with whom she had always affectionately if intermittently corresponded, writes in judgment:

The Countess has many amiable qualities, such as the highest duty, love and respect for her mother: for whom there is not any sacrifice she would not make, & certainly contributes entirely to her happiness: for her husband she professes a large share of respect, esteem and the highest opinion of his merits, but confesses that Love is not of the number on her side, tho' still very violent on his: her principles are strictly just, making it a rule never to bespeak anything she is not quite sure of being able to pay for directly, never contracting debts of any kind. Her dissipated life she was brought up to—therefore it cannot be wondered at, but her religion is not changed.[31]

One of Eliza's passions was the stage. Although the Austen family had enjoyed amateur dramatics before, never had they been entered into with the verve and enthusiasm that Eliza inspired in the Christmas of 1787. The Rectory barn was fitted up like a theatre, and two plays, Which is the Man? and Bon Ton, were acted. No doubt, as well as taking starring parts, Eliza was a key figure in the direction. She had two handsome male cousins to order about; it seems very likely they were strongly attracted to her; and in the absence of her husband, young though they were, she probably had no objections to flirting mildly with them both. Much later, she was to write of her reluctance to "give up dear Liberty, & yet dearer flirtation,"[32] and in the excitement of these Christmas plays, well aware of her own attractions, it is improbable that Eliza made no attempt to exert them. Jane was too young to take part in the plays, and participated only as an eager spectator. When, many years later, she introduced the play acting as a crucial incident in *Mansfield Park*, she must have remembered the plays at Steventon, and how at rehearsals, the real life drama was apt to intrude upon the representations enacted upon the amateur stage.

At this time, there was beginning in London the long drawn out trial for the impeachment of Eliza's old friend and god-father, Warren Hastings. This was to last a wearying eight years before Hastings was acquitted in 1795, and its course was keenly followed by the strongly partisan members of the Austen family. Mr and Mrs Hastings were staying in St James's Place, and Eliza saw them frequently.

She and her mother were beginning to make plans to rejoin the Comte de Feuillide. Her little boy was giving cause for concern, and she was also worried about the news coming from France. There had been widespread rioting and unrest due to the King's request for new taxes; the convocation of the Estates General in the next year had been announced, which was to lead inevitably to the revolution; and ten years of depression was culminating in a disastrously bad harvest. Frivolous though she may have been, Eliza realized there was cause for alarm.

Before she left in September 1788, she visited the Austen brothers at Oxford. "My cousin James met us there, & as well as his brother was so good as to take the trouble of showing us the lions. We visited several of the colleges, the museum etc. & were very elegantly entertained by our gallant relations at St John's . . . I do not think you would know Henry with his hair powdered and dressed in a very *tonish* style, besides he is at present taller than his father."[33] She conjures up a vivid picture—a warm July day in Oxford, the two scholarly young men, one serious, one gay, both attracted by their butterfly of a cousin, both knowing her married and out of their reach, both rivalling each other for her attention. But by the next Christmas, she was back in France, and the amateur dramatics, *The Sultan* and *High Life Below Stairs* this year, had to take place without her.

At about the same time as their brothers were entertaining Eliza at Oxford, Jane and Cassandra were visiting Uncle Francis Austen at Sevenoaks in Kent. While they were there, they met Philadelphia, and this not entirely sympathetic observer records the following impressions:

As it's pure Nature to love ourselves I may be allowed to give the preference to the Eldest who is generally reckoned a most striking resemblance of me in features, complexion & manners. . . . The youngest (Jane) is very like her brother Henry, not at all pretty & very prim, unlike a girl of twelve: but it is hasty judgement which you will scold me for. . . .

I continue to admire my amiable likeness the best of the two in every respect: she keeps up conversation in a very sensible & pleasing manner. Yesterday they all spent the day with us, & the more I see of Cassandra the more I admire her—Jane is whimsical & affected.[34]

In what way, one wonders, did young Jane tease or needle her rather humourless elder cousin?

Now that Jane and Cassandra were settled at Steventon, studying, and helping their mother in the daily domestic chores, two neighbouring families, the Lloyds and the Lefroys, began to play a major part in their lives. Mrs Nowes Lloyd was a widow with three daughters a little older than the Austen girls, Eliza, Martha, and Mary. On the death of her husband, who had been Rector of Enborne, near Newbury, in 1789, Mrs Lloyd moved into the parsonage at Deane, which she was to occupy for the next three years. Her own childhood had been far from happy, since her mother, the beautiful Mrs Craven, had so notoriously ill-treated her daughters, that they had all taken the extremely brave step in those days of running away from home. Stories of this unnatural mother were still told in the family, where life was now so very different.

The Lloyds were related by marriage to the Leigh family, and Thomas Craven Fowle, one of their cousins, had studied as a boarding pupil at Steventon in 1779, and remained a friend. He was present at one of the earlier acting parties in 1784, when *The Rivals* was produced, and was later to fall in love with Cassandra.

Mrs Lloyd's eldest daughter, Eliza, was soon to marry her first cousin, Thomas's elder brother, Fulwar Craven Fowle, the Vicar of Kintbury, and it was with the two younger girls, particularly Martha, that Jane and Cassandra became such firm friends.

The pretty village of Ashe lies two miles west of Deane, and after the death of Dr Russell, the grandfather of Mary Russell Mitford, the new Rector appointed in 1783 was the Reverend Isaac Lefroy. Only thirty-eight years old when he arrived in the neighbourhood, the Rector had an attractive wife, a little daughter, Jemima Lucy, and a baby son, John Henry George. Other children followed, Christopher in 1785, and Benjamin in 1791. Anne Lefroy was the sister of the writer, Sir Egerton Brydges, who recalling Jane as a girl said, "she was very intimate with Mrs Lefroy and much encouraged by her".[35] Anne Lefroy, whom her brother described as one of the most amiable and elegant women he ever knew—universally beloved and admired, took a great interest in her intelligent and lively young neighbour, while as many a young girl does, Jane found particular satisfaction in this affectionate friendship with a mature and elegant woman.

Eliza de Feuillide's sojourn in France did not last long, and by January 1791 she is writing to Philadelphia from an address in Margate, which she hoped would benefit the health of both her frail son and her mother, who was suffering painfully now from the cancer of the breast which was soon to kill her.

Philadelphia Hancock died early in 1792 to the great distress of her daughter. The Comte de Feuillide travelled to England to comfort his wife, later taking her to Bath, "from which I derived little amusement, perhaps more owing to the state of my spirits, than anything else".[36] It must have been a melancholy time for Eliza, mourning her mother; her only son's health so uncertain; and with her husband "a strong *Aristocrate* or Royalist in his heart",[37] preoccupied by the disturbing news from revolutionary France. By June 1792, he was obliged to return to Paris, having learned that unless he did so he would be considered as an emigrant, and his entire property forfeited. In his absence, Eliza decided to spend the remainder of the summer with her good friends at Steventon where she hoped "the quiet and good air will be of great service to my health which indeed stands much in need of some such restorative".[38]

At Steventon, change and romance were in the air. First to marry was the fortunate Edward, whose lovely nineteen-year-old bride was the daughter of Sir Brook Bridges, a neighbour of the Knights, of Goodnestone in Kent. To begin with, the young couple moved into a modest house called Rowling, not far from Godmersham. James, who had by now taken holy orders and was curate at Overton, not far from home, married Anne Mathew, whose parents, General Mathew and Lady Jane, daughter of the second Duke of Ancaster, rented Laverstoke House. Anne was five years older than James, "prettyish, with a brown skin, large dark eyes, and a good deal of nose".[39]

The third marriage from Steventon Rectory, due to the recent death of her father, was of Jane Cooper, the cousin and schoolfriend of the Austen girls, who had taken part in the Steventon Christmas dramatics. Jane married Captain Williams of the Royal Navy, whose presence in the family was later to prove of assistance to Jane's sailor brothers.

During this summer of 1792 which Eliza spent at Steventon, her cousin Jane was sixteen and judging from the mention of a Club Ball at Basingstoke and another pair of private balls in the neighbourhood, which she attended with Cassandra, she was already, as the phrase went, 'out'.

Writing to Philadelphia, Eliza tells her:

> Cassandra & Jane are both very much grown (the latter is now taller than myself) and greatly improved as well in manners as in person, both of which are now much more formed than when you saw them. They are I think equally sensible, and both so to a degree seldom met with, but still my heart gives the preference to Jane, whose kind partiality to me indeed requires a return of the same nature. Henry is now rather more than six foot high, I believe: He also is much improved, and is certainly endowed with uncommon abilities, which indeed seem to have been bestowed, tho' in a different way upon each member of this family—As to the coolness which you know had taken place between H. & myself, it has now ceased, in consequence of due acknowledgments on his part, and we are at present on very proper relation-like terms; you know that his family design him for the Church.[40]

One doubts if either the coolness or the reconciliation escaped the sharp eyes of Jane.

Eliza was a sadder companion now and occasionally unwell, but her gaiety still bubbled up at times, and her presence in the house must have made a welcome diversion for Jane, who was always fond of her. Hastings became "the plaything of the whole family"[41] and with Eliza chattering to her son and to the invaluable Madame Bigeon, her personal maid who was his second mother, the household's knowledge of spoken French must have improved. It seems likely that Jane read some French with her cousin at this time, and that Eliza, who was musical, helped her with her piano playing. Later in her letters, Jane seems to suggest that music held little charm for her, but she was a reasonable performer and practised with diligence. She was also exceedingly fond of dancing, and no one can enjoy dancing without some appreciation of music.

Her music books which can be seen at Chawton House, as well as dances and popular songs, contain sonatas by Arne, Handel, and Haydn. She was, however, acutely sensitive to noise, and some of the amateur—and even professional—performances she was forced to endure were probably painful on that account alone.

At the beginning of 1792, Mrs Lloyd and her two unmarried daughters moved to the village of Ibthrop, near Hurstbourne Tarrant, some seventeen miles from Steventon. But their removal made little difference to the friendship between the families. In their place, James and his wife moved into Deane Parsonage, James acting now as his father's curate. Both Mrs James and Mrs Edward were already expecting their first babies. When Mary Lloyd left, Jane gave her a little needlework case which she had made and embroidered, together with this message written in a minute hand:

> This little bag, I hope will prove
> To be not vainly made;
> For should you thread and needles want,
> It will afford you aid.
>
> And, as we are about to part,
> 'Twill serve another end:
> For, when you look upon this bag,
> You'll recollect your friend.[42]

Jane and Cassandra had now been home from school for five years. During this time, under the direction of her father and her two clever brothers, James and Henry, Jane had been doing a great deal of reading, and she had the unsupervised run it seems of her father's library of more than 500 books. She read sermons; she read history; she was steeped in Shakespeare and Dr Johnson; Cowper and Crabbe were her favourite poets; she liked works of travel; like many people of her generation she was to be much influenced by Gilpin who was writing on landscape and the picturesque. But above all, she read novels: the works of the greater writers, Fielding, Richardson, Sterne, and Smollett; the many popular novels of sensibility and horror; and surely with particular interest and curiosity, the first book of Miss Fanny Burney, *Evelina*. Her knowledge of Richardson, in particular, her nephew says, "was such as no one is likely again to acquire".[43] She was a reader of wide tastes, easily captivated by the printed word.

Later, giving her advice to her niece Caroline, she was to

say that she wished at sixteen she had read more and written less. No doubt she regretted that her reading had not been more methodical and disciplined. Yet probably nothing was of greater value to her future development than her early and continuous writing practice.

Encouraged by her family, she wrote freely and extensively: the jog-trot verse for charades at which her mother excelled; funny sketches for family performances; comical pieces which she read aloud in her expressive and attractive voice. The best of the pieces were applauded, revised, and carefully copied into three note books, entitled, *Volume the First*, *Volume the Second*, and *Volume the Third*. They were written between 1787 and 1793, her twelfth to her seventeenth years.

Published in the volume of *Minor Works* edited by R. W. Chapman and B. C. Southam, certainly some of the Juvenilia of Jane Austen are deserving of wider attention. As might be expected, some of them are extremely funny. Anyone who has laughed at *The Young Visiters* is likely to be amused by *Love and Freindship*. They are of particular interest in their author's development as a writer, and they prove the unusually early emergence of her critical faculty.

She read nothing without passing judgment upon it and evaluating it. Much of what she read, she found ludicrous and she made fun of it. In these early pieces, she takes most often as her butt the popular novels of sensibility, shooting at them with the same unerring aim she was later to use in *Northanger Abbey* against the Gothic novel.

The end of the eighteenth century was a very prolific period for the production of the popular novel, and the writers of the novel of sensibility had begun to stretch their medium to the verge of the absurdity which was finally to ensure its extinction. Of the two great English novelists of the eighteenth century, Fielding and Richardson, undoubtedly Richardson inspired the greatest crop of imitators, and the sentiments in particular of his *Clarissa* led to the novel that extolled above every other virtue that of sensibility. From the continent, Goethe's *Sorrows of Werther*, and Rousseau's *La Nouvelle Heloise* were similarly influential.

In *The Popular Novel in England*, Joyce M. S. Tompkins has conducted a valuable survey of the many works published from 1770–1800,[44] a great number of which it is safe to say Jane Austen had read. From her earliest years to the end of her life, she enjoyed reading novels, as her vigorous defence in *Northanger Abbey*, and the following letter to Cassandra make clear: "I have received a very civil note from Mrs Martin, requesting my name as a subscriber to her library which opens January 14. . . . As an inducement to subscribe, Mrs Martin tells me that her collection is not to consist only of novels, but of every kind of literature. . . . She might have spared this pretension to *our* family, who are great novel-readers and not ashamed of being so. . . ."[45]

Like every novel reader, Jane must have enjoyed some more than others. Although she satirized it, there can be no doubt, for example, that she thoroughly enjoyed *The Mysteries of Udolpho*. But no novel, whether of horror or of sensibility escaped her critical vigilance. It is hard to believe that some of their worst excesses can ever have been taken seriously, but it is true to say that when she wrote her own burlesques, Jane Austen scarcely needed to exaggerate. With the slender information available about these years of her adolescence, the Juvenilia provide the best means of hearing her own already very individual young voice.

Among the more important pieces in *Volume the First*, the opening item, dedicated by the author to Martha Lloyd, "for your late generosity to me in finishing my muslin Cloak",[46] is *Frederic & Elfrida*. This 'novel' in five tiny chapters romps through a bizarre collection of incidents and characters, including: the hero and heroine who wait more than eighteen years before they marry; the good natured Charlotte, who unable to hurt either of their feelings, accepts two suitors, then after sitting down to "Supper on a young Leveret, a brace of Partridges, a leash of Pheasants and a Dozen of Pigeons",[47] perhaps understandably drowns herself next morning; and the pair of lovers, who insist on marriage in spite of their tender years, "Rebecca being but 36 & Captain Roger little more than 63".[48]

A passage which smiles at the romantic attitude to nature, has a curious echo of Coleridge's "Kubla Khan", which had still to be written:

Frederic & Elfrida . . . proposed to her to take a walk in a Grove of Poplars which led from the Parsonage to a verdant Lawn enamelled with a variety of variegated flowers & watered by a purling Stream, brought from the Valley of Tempé by a passage under ground.

In this Grove they had scarcely remained above 9 hours, when they were suddenly agreeably surprized by hearing a most delightfull voice. . . .[49]

Jack and Alice is a longer narrative in nine chapters. Already Jane Austen is beginning to practise the turn of phrase that was later to give her work such terseness and point: "In Lady Williams every virtue met. She was a widow with a handsome Jointure & the remains of a very handsome face."[50] Satiric use is made of the well worn convention of allowing a character to interrupt the flow of a novel with a lengthy recital of his 'life and adventures'. For a heroine, Alice has the unromantic quality of an addiction to wine, and there is an hilarious absurdity in a quarrel scene about the merits of a red complexion which shows that Jane Austen had soon realized her skill with dialogue.

Henry and Eliza opens with a favourite and hackneyed situation, the discovery of a foundling child, but never before so described:

As Sir George and Lady Harcourt were superintending the Labours of their Haymakers, rewarding the industry of some by smiles of approbation, & punishing the idleness of others, by a cudgel, they perceived lying closely concealed beneath the thick foliage of a Haycock, a beautifull little Girl not more than 3 months old.

Touched with the enchanting Graces of her face & delighted with the infantine tho' sprightly answers she returned to their many questions, they resolved to take her home &, having no Children of their own, to educate her with care & cost.[51]

Amelia Webster is a very short exercise in the form of telling a story by means of letters. Although she was to attempt this several times, Jane soon realized the many disadvantages of the method, in particular the restriction to the first person, the absence of all but reported dialogue, and she is already making fun of it.

I have found a very convenient old hollow oak to put our Letters in; for as you know we have long maintained a private Correspondence. It is about a mile from my House & seven from yours. You may perhaps imagine that I might have made choice of a tree which would have divided the Distance more equally—I was sensible of this at the time, but as I considered that the walk would be of benefit to you in your weak & uncertain state of Health, I preferred it to one nearer your House. . . .[52]

Also in letter form is *The Three Sisters*, in which young

Jane takes a very realistic look at certain attitudes towards marriage. As Auden puts it, she had already begun to:

> Describe the curious effects of "brass"
> Reveal so frankly and with such sobriety
> The Economic basis of society.[53]

Moreover, she perceives there are many more motives for marriage than just "brass"—vanity, desire for position, fear of spinsterhood, and even the spiteful triumphing at the expense of others.

The frequently overwritten accounts of sickroom and death-bed scenes are caustically dealt with in a piece carefully entitled, "A Beautiful Description of the Different Effects of Sensibility on Different Minds".

> Sir William is constantly at her bedside. The only repose he takes is on the Sopha in the Drawing room, where for five minutes every fortnight he remains in an imperfect Slumber, starting up every Moment & exclaiming "Oh! Melissa, Ah! Melissa," then sinking down again, raises his left arm and scratches his head. . . . I am usually at the fire cooking some little delicacy for the unhappy invalid—Perhaps hashing up the remains of an old Duck, toasting some cheese or making a Curry which are the favourite dishes of our poor friend.[54]

Volume the Second opens with two more lengthy works, *Love and Freindship* and *Lesley Castle*. In these, the young Jane Austen can be seen practising staying longer on the wing, in itself a necessary gift of authorship.

Love and Freindship is dedicated to Madame La Comtesse de Feuillide, and was written in June 1790 when Jane was fourteen. It would be entertaining to have Eliza's opinion of it. In *Jane Austen's Literary Manuscripts*, B. C. Southam has described it as a "work of precocious genius". He also points out that at this tender age, Jane did not scruple to write about "deformity, injury, death, drunkenness, child-bearing, and illegitimacy"[55]—he might also have added adultery, murder, and theft—in works presumably designed to entertain her family in the Rectory.

Written as a series of letters, as well as a comical and sharp attack on the sentimental novel, *Love and Freindship* again convincingly demonstrates many of the absurdities of the form. Laura, the lovely heroine and writer of the letters, has the exotic origins so beloved of the romantic novelists, here efficiently disposed of in a neat little paragraph: "My Father was a native of Ireland & an inhabitant of Wales; My Mother was the natural Daughter of a Scotch Peer by an italian Opera-girl—I was born in Spain & received my Education at a Convent in France."[56]

Writing of her adventures to the daughter of an old friend, Laura describes her sudden marriage to Edward, a perfect stranger who appeared out of the night at her parents' Welsh cottage, having missed his way on a journey from Bedford-shire to Middlesex! Edward's father and sister having dis-approved of this hasty union, he and Laura take shelter with his friends, Sophia and Augustus.

> Never did I see such an affecting Scene as was the meeting of Edward and Augustus.
> "My Life! my Soul!" (exclaimed the former)
> "My Adorable Angel!" (replied the latter) as they flew into each other's arms. It was too pathetic for the feelings of Sophia and myself—We fainted Alternately on a Sofa.[57]

In the course of the absurdly complicated plot, Augustus and Edward are imprisoned in Newgate, while their wives, too full of sensibility to endure the sight of their sufferings, travel far away to Scotland. There, after several none too respectable adventures, thrown from their latest refuge, Laura and Sophia walk away into the countryside, after a mile and a half, sitting down to rest. "The place was suited to meditation.—A Grove of full-grown Elms sheltered us from the East—. A Bed of full-grown Nettles from the West.—Before us ran the mur-muring brook & behind us ran the turn-pike road."[58]

Before long, the girls are disturbed by a phaeton overturn-ing in the road behind them. Predictably enough, they arrive at the scene of the accident to discover the dead body of Augustus, and just in time for Edward's expiry. While Sophia faints every moment, in the mingled manner of Hamlet, Ophelia, and Tilburina in Sheridan's *Critic*, Laura runs mad. "Look at that Grove of Firs—I see a Leg of Mutton—They told me Edward was not Dead; but they deceived me—they took him for a Cucumber."[59]

Poor Laura, who has by now lost her parents, and her husband, is fated to watch the mournful end of Sophia from a cold contracted while she was lying "in the open Air as the Dew was falling", in a swoon. With her dying words, Sophia implores: "Beware of swoons Dear Laura. . . . A frenzy fit is not one quarter so pernicious; it is an exercise to the Body & if not too violent, is I dare say conducive to Health in its consequences—Run mad as often as you chuse; but do not faint—."[60]

On her travels again, the now solitary Laura enters a stage coach on its way from Stirling to Edinburgh, only to find herself sharing it with her husband's family, her own old friends, and Gustavus and Philander, her cousins. After a great deal of explanation in the manner of the speedy conclusion to so many very complicated plots, all the loose ends are carefully knotted, and we leave Laura rather ungraciously in possession of £400 a year from her father-in-law, "in a romantic Village in the Highlands of Scotland".[61]

Lesley Castle, which was written two years later in 1792, is also told through the medium of letters, but this time to and from several correspondents, enabling some of the same characters and incidents to be described from widely differing points of view. Although the story is still farcical and remains incomplete, Jane is beginning to broaden her experiments, and to seek ways of gaining in character drawing and flexibility. A strong criticism of social hypocrisy is maintained throughout the whole of this short work:

> During our visit, the Weather being remarkably bad, and our party particularly stupid, she was so good as to conceive a violent partiality for me, which very soon settled in a downright Freindship, and ended in an established correspondence. She is probably by this time as tired of me as I am of her; but as she is too polite and I am too civil to say so, our letters are still as frequent and affectionate as ever, and our Attachment as firm and sincere as when it first commenced.[62]

Miss Charlotte Luttrell, one of the correspondents, is an original creation of whom one would like to have more. The great business of her life is food, and her letters abound in culinary details. "We spent a very pleasant Day, and had a very good Dinner, tho' to be sure the Veal was terribly underdone, and the Curry had no seasoning. I could not help wishing all dinner-time that I had been at the dressing it. . . ."[63] *Lesley Castle* was dedicated to Jane's brother Henry, and an additional paragraph presumes he would value the work at one hundred guineas.

Just before she was sixteen, Jane completed *The History of England from the reign of Henry the 4th to the death of Charles the 1st*, "by a partial, prejudiced, & ignorant Historian".[64] The work seems to have been inspired by her reading of Goldsmith's *History of England*, and was a joint production with Cassandra who provided water colour portraits of twelve of the monarchs. Dedicated to Cassandra, it commences with an attractive N.B.: "There will be very few Dates in this History."[65] This (which is a thrust at Goldsmith's singular lack of dating), together with the strong views Catherine Morland later expressed in *Northanger Abbey*, suggest that Jane Austen enjoyed her history somewhat selectively, more for the drama of the characters than for the politics.

"The quarrels of popes and kings, with wars or pestilences, in every page; the men all so good for nothing, and hardly any women at all—it is very tiresome . . .", grumbles Catherine.[66]

There is nothing tiresome about Jane's witty little history. It is very funny; her satiric spirit is well in evidence; no traditionally cherished hero is taken too seriously; and it appears she knew her Horace Walpole, for that much disputed monarch, Richard III, is supposed "a very respectable Man".[67]

The Tudors come off badly. Henry VII is "a Monster of Iniquity and Avarice";[68] the only merit of Henry VIII was "his not being *quite* so bad as his daughter Elizabeth".[69] Rather surprising, Anne Boleyn gets a good notice, but her daughter is quickly toppled from her pedestal and becomes, "that disgrace to humanity, that pest of Society, Elizabeth."[70]

Perhaps because of the Stuart loyalties of Jane's mother's family, the Leighs, who had sheltered Charles I at Stoneleigh Abbey, the heroine of the history is undoubtedly Mary, Queen of Scots. "I now most seriously do assure my Reader that she was entirely innocent; having never been guilty of anything more than Imprudencies into which she was betrayed by the openness of her Heart, her Youth, & her Education."[71]

James I "was of that amiable disposition which inclines to Freindships," says Jane rather knowingly, going on to illustrate her point with a "Sharade on a Carpet" . . . "& in such points was possessed of a keener penetration in Discovering Merit than many other people".[72]

In conclusion, Charles I features as an "amiable Monarch . . . born to have suffered Misfortunes equal to those of his lovely Grandmother".[73]

Apart from some little pieces headed *Scraps*, the last item in *Volume the Second* is *A Collection of Letters*. Since this is dedicated to Miss Cooper, it was written before Jane Cooper's marriage in 1792. It is chiefly interesting for its satiric comment on the snobbish character of Lady Greville, who is a formidable combination of Lady Catherine de Bourgh and Mrs Norris.

Volume the Third contains only two works. The first, *Evelyn*, is dedicated to Miss Mary Lloyd and dated 6th May 1792.

A. Walton Litz in *Jane Austen: A Study of her Artistic Development* points out, "*Evelyn* is distinguished from the other Juvenilian burlesques by Jane Austen's concentration on one aspect of the cult of sensibility . . . [a grotesque distortion of true benevolence] so intense and steadily maintained that we must look for reasons behind it."[74] This might also be said to be one of the principal themes of Fanny Burney's *Camilla* (1796) in which the unwise benevolence of Sir Hugh Tyrold is the mainspring of much of the action.

There is also some satire at the expense of the Gothic or horror novel:

> If we consider his situation indeed, alone, on horseback, as late in the year as August, and in the day, as nine o'clock, with no light to direct him but that of the Moon almost full, and the Stars which alarmed him by their twinkling, who can refrain from pitying him? No house within a quarter of a mile, and a Gloomy Castle blackened by the deep shades of Walnuts and Pines, behind him. He felt indeed almost distracted with his fears. . . .[75]

The last work, *Catharine or The Bower*, comprising some 14,000 words, is the longest of the Juvenilia, and is written, not in letters, but as a straightforward narrative. Although the dedication to her sister is humorous, nonetheless, it also indicates in its mocking and ironic way that by now Jane Austen as a writer had serious intentions for the future.

To Miss Austen

Madam

Encouraged by your warm patronage of The beautiful Cassandra, and The History of England, which through your generous support, have obtained a place in every library in the Kingdom, and run through threescore Editions, I take the liberty of begging the same Exertions in favour of the following Novel, which I humbly flatter myself, possesses Merit beyond any already published, or any that will ever in future appear except such as may proceed from the pen of Your Most Grateful Humble Servt

Steventon August 1792

The Author[76]

It would appear that the story was planned as a simple account of the introduction to life and love of the orphaned Catharine, who has been brought up by her aunt, known alternatively throughout the narrative as Mrs Percival or Mrs Peterson—an Edgar Wallace-like slip which is most untypical of the author. Faced with life's tendency to be at sixes and sevens, Mrs P retreats into hypochondria, and is particularly fearful of the wiles of young men. The bower, a shady arbour which Catharine has built at the end of her aunt's garden as a shelter from the boredom and trials of her home, is an important motif throughout the story—a symbol of Catharine's girlish and romantic dreams.

The following account of the fate of one of Catharine's friends, which follows so closely the career of her Aunt Philadelphia Hancock, is an interesting case of Jane Austen's drawing upon her knowledge of a family experience.

The eldest daughter had been obliged to accept the offer of one of her cousins to equip her for the East Indies. . . . Her personal Attractions had gained her a husband a soon as she had arrived at Bengal, and she had now been married nearly a twelvemonth. Splendidly, yet unhappily married. United to a Man of double her own age, whose disposition was not amiable, and whose Manners were unpleasing, though his Character was respectable.[77]

The action is slight—the arrival of friends to the quiet household; a ball (always an event of significance and purpose in Jane Austen's novels) which Catharine is first unable to attend because of toothache, but later joins to cause a stir in the company of the uninvited son of her aunt's friends; and the precipitate departure of first the ardent young man, and then his family. At this point, still in midstream, the story is left uncompleted.

Among the Juvenilia, *Catharine* offers the clearest prophesy of what is to come. Less rooted in literary criticism than the rest, *Catharine* indicates the development of Jane Austen's narrative style; the characterization is growing out of the caricature, becoming more careful and consistent; some of the basic themes of the later novels are beginning to emerge; and already there can be heard Jane Austen's individual tone of voice.

"They entered the small vestibule which Mr Dudley had raised to the dignity of a Hall."[78] ". . . they continued conversing together on almost every subject, for Stanley seldom

dwelt long on any, and had something to say on all. . . ."[79]
"Queen Elizabeth, said Mrs Stanley who never hazarded a
remark on History that was not well founded, lived to a good
old age, and was a very Clever Woman."[80]

There is a remarkable little scene in which Catharine's
warm hearted and passionate denouncement of the treatment
of the elder Miss Wynne is commented upon with unconscious
irony by her superficial friend, Camilla. "Well, I cannot
conceive the hardship of going out in a very agreeable Manner
with two or three sweet Girls for Companions, having a
delightful voyage to Bengal or Barbadoes or wherever it is,
and being married soon after one's arrival to a very charming
Man immensely rich—. I see no hardship in all that."[81]

Anyone who has ever considered that Jane Austen was
unaware of the problems of her age, and in particular the
plight of impoverished middle-class women, will do well to
reflect on the implications of this sophisticated paragraph
from a girl of sixteen.

The date of the writing of *Lady Susan* is open to conjecture.
It exists in a fair copy made, as the watermarks of some of
the paper attests, in or after 1805, and some critics have
assumed it was written around this date. From his meticulous
study of the manuscripts, B. C. Southam judges it to have been
written some time during 1793–4.[82] Certainly in spirit it seems
to belong more to the Juvenilia than to the first group of
three finished novels. In her later work, Jane Austen was
never again to tackle such a wide range of characters and
situations. She was never again to be so extravagant. "I
murdered my father at a very early period of my Life, I have
since murdered my Mother, and I am now going to murder
my Sister,"[83] writes one of her young ladies, who is certainly
not a character to be expected from the pen of the cosy Aunt
Jane figure still cherished by some admirers. Unmistakably,
her youthful experiments had helped her to define her future
limitations.

Never again was she to attempt to describe such a totally
immoral character as Lady Susan, the charming, intelligent,
beautiful, but frivolous and callous widow, who lives for
flirtation and flattery and cruelly ill-treats her only child. This
quite considerable story of more than 30,000 words, with
something of the tone of a Restoration comedy, is told in a
series of letters which enables the fullest insight to be given
into Lady Susan's deplorable motives and practised social
hypocrisy. It has been suggested that her character was based

on that of Mrs Craven, the notorious grandmother of the three Lloyd sisters.

Lady Susan has no scruples about adultery; she is prepared to force her daughter to marry a man she dislikes, and she herself despises, yet in the end to marry him; she is quite untroubled by the prospect of getting into debt—on placing her daughter in school, she declares gaily, "the price is immense, & much beyond what I can ever attempt to pay";[84] she sponges on other people's hospitality, and in recompense sows discord in their family life; she is without loyalty; she is deceitful and untruthful; and her cynical view of marriage is indissolubly bound up with money.

This thoroughly unpleasant yet superficially fascinating character is presented in several ways; the evidence of her own letters, the severe judgment of her sister-in-law, the infatuated regard of the young man who falls in love with her—her sister-in-law's brother, and the confidences of Mrs Johnson, her equally reprehensible London friend.

The novel shows a great advance on Jane's previous attempts at epistolary narration. The several different viewpoints and moral standards employed build up a depth and richness of texture, and assist the speedy progression of the action.

Unlike Jane's later leading ladies, and perhaps because she is a villain and not a heroine, Lady Susan learns nothing through the experiences she encounters in the tale, and she is rewarded by a silly, but young, rich, and titled husband. Undoubtedly, she is set to progress to further adventures, while her daughter is vindicated and happily united to the young man who had once been deluded by her mother.

The series of forty-one letters is abruptly terminated by a brisk piece of narrative. Perhaps the young author had tired of her tale, or of the letter writing technique, although there is evidence that *Sense and Sensibility* and even perhaps *Pride and Prejudice* started life in this form.

These early works of Jane Austen can be seen as both exercises in technique and a repository of ideas to which she was to return throughout her writing life.

Among some examples, the first is the simple one of naming her characters, and she is already using Emma, Fanny, Anne, Georgiana, Marianne, and Willoughby.

Both in their characters and their relationship to each other, Catharine and Camilla Stanley of *Catharine* bear a striking resemblance to the warm hearted and agreeable ingenue, Catherine Morland of *Northanger Abbey* and Isabella Thorpe, her shallow and affected friend, while Camilla's insistence on status is also reminiscent of the similar preoccupation of *Persuasion's* Mary Musgrove.

In *Frederic and Elfrida*, written some time between Jane's twelfth and fifteenth years, the "different excellencies of Indian & English Muslins"[85] are compared in a manner which forestalls Henry Tilney's knowledgeable appraisal in *Northanger Abbey*. "I always buy my own cravats, and am allowed to be an excellent judge; and my sister has often trusted me in the choice of a gown. I bought one for her the other day, and it was pronounced to be a prodigious bargain by every lady who saw it. I gave but five shillings a yard for it, and a true Indian muslin."[86]

In *Love and Freindship*, the girls who dismiss the claims of a suitor because they are, "convinced he had no soul, that he had never read the *Sorrows of Werther*, and that his Hair bore not the slightest resemblance to Auburn",[87] are later echoed in *Sense and Sensibility* by the romantic Marianne Dashwood when she considers the worthy young man who has aroused her sister's esteem and affection.

Oh! mama, how spiritless, how tame was Edward's manner of reading to us last night! I felt for my sister most severely. Yet she bore it with so much composure, she seemed scarcely to notice it. I could hardly keep my seat. To hear those beautiful lines which have frequently almost driven me wild, pronounced with such impenetrable calmness, such dreadful indifference![88]

In later life, Jane Austen was both an amused recorder and a patient sufferer of other people's hypochondria. Yet before she was twenty, she had already identified not only the symptoms of imaginary suffering, but also its applications in society, as a weapon of selfishness and as a form of escape.

For Mrs Percival of *Catharine*, ill-health is an escape, while for Mr Johnson of *Lady Susan* it an effective means of thwarting the caprices of his wife. "He had heard I imagine by some means or other, that you were soon to be in London, & immediately contrived to have such an attack of the Gout, as must at least delay his journey to Bath, if not wholly prevent it. I am persuaded the Gout is brought on, or kept off at pleasure; it was the same, when I wanted to join the Hamiltons to the Lakes; & three years ago when *I* had a fancy for Bath, nothing could induce him to have a Gouty symptom."[89]

Already in these early works, Jane Austen deals with the theme of snobbery, the rigid ladder of society, and the position of the characters upon it, which recurs throughout the six novels. Mary Wynne in *Catharine* finds herself in the position of governess, that Jane Fairfax in *Emma* was so eloquently to compare with the slave trade, and which perhaps Jane Austen may even have dreaded for herself.

The dependence of the bereaved Wynne family is basically similar to that of the Dashwood family in *Sense and Sensibility*, later developed with such ironic brilliance when in their famous duologue, his wife, somewhat in the manner of Lady Macbeth's screwing up her husband's courage to the sticking place, persuades Mr John Dashwood that far from a present of three thousand pounds, all the help his late father had in mind for his mother and sisters was "looking out for a comfortable small house for them, helping them to move their things, and sending them presents of fish and game, and so forth, whenever they are in season".[90]

While she was writing her impressive early pieces, from the ages of twelve to sixteen, Jane Austen must have been a disconcerting young girl. Much of the work is based on her reading, but it also demonstrates her acute sensitivity to the fine differences of human relationships, her wit and humour, and her exceptional intelligence, all qualities which must have been observable in her life. It is not surprising that Philadelphia Walter was nonplussed. Yet it is clear from the dedications which almost invariably preface these early works that Jane never lacked encouragement and admiration in her family circle. Dedications are made to each of her brothers, to her sister, her parents, Mary and Martha Lloyd, and her cousins Eliza de Feuillide and Jane Cooper. Although Jane must have worked hard, clearly she had great fun creating these high-spirited, comical, and sometimes outrageous pieces. Altogether, the years when she was growing up must have been happy ones.

Eliza quotes in her letters that Jane and Cassandra are "two of the prettiest girls in England"[91] . . . "perfect Beauties & of course 'gain hearts by dozens' ".[92]

There were balls and visits, to the Lloyds at Ibthrop, Edward's home at Rowling, Gloucestershire, and Southampton. Cassandra was falling in love with Thomas Fowle, and Jane undoubtedly was thinking about romance.

This is a rather touching example of her, as Elizabeth Jenkins puts it, "larking about in her father's register",[93] and completing the specimen form of the Entry of Publications of Banns for "Henry Frederick Howard Fitzwilliam of London and Jane Austen of Steventon," and of the Entry of the Marriage itself between Jane Austen of Steventon once more, but this time to the more prosaic Arthur William Mortimer of Liverpool. As Elizabeth Jenkins points out, "the hypothetical gentleman whose banns were to be published, bore the names afterwards given to Henry Crawford, Frederick Wentworth, the Mr Howard who was to marry Emma Watson, and Fitzwilliam Darcy".

In contrast to this general air of happiness, Jane's late teens were disturbed by two family tragedies. In 1795, Anne Austen, the wife of her brother James, died at the age of thirty-six, leaving him with Anna, their three year old daughter. And for trying to protect a neighbour from the consequence of her crime of laying down arable land in lucerne, sainfoin, and clover "with the object of producing a famine",[94] Eliza's husband, Jean Gabriel Capotte, Comte de Feuillide, was tried in Paris, condemned to death, and on the same day, 22nd February 1794, suffering the fate of Louis XVI, Marie Antoinette, and so many of his fellow aristocrats and friends, he was guillotined.

TWO

The Years of Promise

"Bliss was it in that dawn to be alive,
But to be young was very Heaven!"[1]

With these words, Wordsworth spoke for the many hopeful young idealists who had been inspired by the driving principles of the French Revolution, and believed that the creeds outworn were being vanquished by the inspiring concepts of liberty, equality, and fraternity. Many signs pointed in that same direction. America had asserted its independence and could now be regarded as a free as well as a brave new world. In Britain, the slave trade was condemned and within a few years would be abolished. Workers were beginning to consider their powers and their rights. The first slow steps were being taken on the long path to political reform. All over Europe, there was a flowering of artistic and intellectual life. In England, the Romantic movement in literature was taking shape, with such great figures as Blake, Wordsworth, and Coleridge generating the ideas and poetry that were to inspire their successors in the next generation, Byron, Shelley, and Keats. William Godwin had published his influential work *Political Justice* and Mary Wollstonecraft, who was to become his wife, had published *A Vindication of the Rights of Woman.* Inevitably as time went by, much of the bright hopefulness was slowly dimmed and extinguished by the terrible events of the Revolution, the Imperial ambitions of Napoleon, and the economic effects of the long war with France which, at the same time, accelerated some of the trends.

It is hard to say how much of this ferment reached the quiet village of Steventon, but it is inconceivable that Jane Austen, as has sometimes been assumed, lived completely cocooned from all the vital currents of her own age.

There is no evidence that she had read the works of Mary Wollstonecraft, whose life, because of her lower social position and poverty, was so much harder than Jane's own, and whose opinions were so much more radical. Yet it is significant that this passage about Bath from a recent biography seems almost as relevant to Jane as to Mary Wollstonecraft herself.

The scenes she witnessed in the streets, the public assembly rooms, the pleasure grounds, the concert halls and theatres were in themselves an education. Here was a display of the pleasures of high society where women dominated the scene, the un-married seeming to have but one care, to ensnare a rich husband. Here was England's fashionable marriage market. It was a way of life so artificial that she could not witness it without wonder and revolt. Where lay the possibilities of happiness in such a system, she asked herself, at least for any woman with a mind of her own?[2]

In the poorest classes of society, there has never been any argument about whether women should work. If they and their families were to eat, women had to work, and on the farms, in the great and lesser houses, in the textile and cloth-ing trades and, as the industrial revolution proceeded, in many other manufactories, there were always endless grinding hours of poorly paid work available to them. Leisure was only a problem to the middle and upper classes. Just how much of a problem it could be is nowhere better illustrated than in the terrible frustrations of the life of Florence Nightingale before she began her great work in nursing and administra-tion.

"Half occupied, always interrupted, with much leisure but little time to themselves and no money of their own, these armies of listless women were either driven to find solace and occupation in religion, or, if that failed, they took, as Miss Nightingale said, to that perpetual day-dreaming which is so dangerous."[3]

The money-making opportunities available to needy women of the middle classes were few indeed. Foremost among them was marriage, but for a secure and attractive match, a girl without a portion was at a disadvantage. For a woman pre-pared to capitalize on her charms, there were the higher reaches and more sophisticated branches of prostitution. For the talented, there were the theatre and music. For the reason-ably educated, there were the usually dreaded roles of governess and companion, or, depending on available capital, the possi-bility of starting a school. And there was the profession which had once been a male prerogative, but to which women were steadily infiltrating, that of writing. In her unique career, the beautiful Lady Blessington was brilliantly successful in the spheres of prostitution, marriage, and writing. But she was never accepted by the ladies in polite society.

Some of the many novels by ladies which appeared in the years before and after the beginning of the nineteenth century, were certainly "a methodising of daydreams".[4] But many of them were competent exercises in meeting the demands of the novel readers of the day, and some were genuinely gifted. Gradually, too, women were gaining entry into other branches of the profession, reviewing, translating, pamphleteering, editing, and writing for and on behalf of children. Most of their names and works are now generally forgotten, but they were the energetic pioneers in one of the first professions into which women, against great odds and by their talent and determination, forced their admission.

At the beginning of Jane Austen's career, professional women writers were still regarded with suspicion. Some notable figures, for example, Fanny Burney, with the help of her father's wide circle of cultured friends, Dr Johnson, and royal patronage: and Maria Edgeworth, with the encouragement and collaboration of her dynamic father and her works on education as well as her novels, had already done much to claim respect for women writers, yet all Jane Austen's books, except that which appeared posthumously, were published anonymously.

Nonetheless, she clearly wrote with publication in mind, which already established her for her age as an emancipated woman, and far from "methodising day-dreams", she made her own quiet revolution in the novel, and must be considered the first great woman writer in the English language.

Two general and related criticisms have frequently been levelled against the deliberately circumscribed world depicted in Jane Austen's novels. First, it is rightly said, her characters belong exclusively to the middle class, her own class, of society, and she failed to portray the lives and problems of the lower orders. Neither did she attempt to describe the lives of the aristocracy, but for that she is not so often criticised. Secondly, it is deplored that the stirring events of the years through which she lived, including the French Revolution and the Napoleonic wars, made not the slightest impact on her work.

In fact, this knowledge of her limitations was one of Jane Austen's great strengths. In the course of her reading, she had

D

recognized constantly the absurdity of writing on any subject imperfectly comprehended. Perhaps her most striking contribution to a new conception of the novel was that she was, first and foremost, concerned with the truth. In each of her novels, like so many veils, illusions, distortion, hypocrisy, prejudice, insincerity, are gradually drawn aside, until the truth is revealed.

This innate core of reality could only have been damaged by the intervention of characters or events drawn without knowledge or experience. It has been said, for example, that in the lifelike rendering of domestics, Jane Austen has been outshone by Emily Eden who drew the characters of her servants with a "brilliance of touch and a knowledge of flunkeyana which Thackeray might have envied".[5] But they are observed purely from the outside, with an unmistakable hint of patronage, and one wonders what an expert like Mrs Margaret Powell would think of them.

Even in the twentieth century, when social life in Britain must be regarded at least as far more democratic than that of the Regency, few subjects involve more sensitive and delicate hazards than the representation of one class by a member of another.

Writing on this, Virginia Woolf, who it must be hoped was joking, declared: "Unfortunately, however, life is so formed that literary success invariably means a rise, never a fall, and seldom, what is far more desirable, a spread in the social scale. The rising novelist is never pestered to come to gin and winkles with the plumber and his wife."[6]

Jane Austen's meticulous avoidance of such details saved her from falling into what may be called the gin and winkles trap.

The French Revolution and the Napoleonic wars formed the political background to Jane Austen's adult life. Her cousin's husband was guillotined by the revolutionaries, and two of her brothers saw long and dangerous active service at sea. That she realized she had neither the scope, knowledge, nor imagination to write about these events is no evidence that she was not concerned and anxious about them. She must have been.

Not irrelevant to this point perhaps, is the success and widespread popularity achieved during the Second World War by *Pride and Prejudice*, in its original form as a novel, and as a film, and there is much to be said for the view expressed by V. S. Pritchett.

Our perfect novelist of comedy, Jane Austen, is often presented as an example of the felicity of living in a small, cosy world, with one's mind firmly withdrawn from the horror outside. This has always seemed to me untrue. I think of her as a war novelist, formed very much by the Napoleonic wars, knowing directly of prize money, the shortage of men, the economic crisis and change in the value of capital. . . . Militancy and vigilance are the essence of comedy.[7]

In the years of her early twenties, in spite of the war and her anxiety for her brothers, Jane Austen's life was full of promise. She was aware of her own literary talent, and in spite of her lack of privacy, she was managing to find sufficient time to produce a considerable volume of satisfactory and exciting work. In 1795, she was writing a novel presented as a series of letters and entitled *Elinor and Marianne*. This was read aloud to the family and enjoyed, but she was not satisfied with the form, which she was to recast. Critical as she was of all she read, Jane Austen never failed to apply the same keen judgment to her own work.

Her best friend and sister, Cassandra, was in love and engaged; her own social life was busy and gay; and an interesting young Irishman, Thomas Lefroy, was staying with his aunt at Ashe. In the new year of 1796, Cassandra was on a visit and spending her birthday at the home of her fiancé's brother, the Rev. Fulwar Fowle, and his wife Elizabeth, at Kintbury. For Cassandra, this must have been both an anxious and happy time, for her lover, Thomas Fowle, who was far from wealthy and whose present living at Allington was apparently insufficiently remunerative for him to hazard marriage, had decided to go abroad to seek his fortune. Pinning his hopes on the patronage of his influential relative, Lord Craven, who had the attractive living of Ryton in Shropshire in his gift, Thomas evidently believed that a spell as chaplain in Lord Craven's regiment would bring him a step nearer this preferment. Perhaps, too, he hoped there might be money-making opportunities in the West Indies.

Cassandra was a patient girl and prepared to wait, but it must have been with a sad heart that she bade her Thomas farewell on his long voyage to distant lands, with little idea of when she might expect the relief and happiness of his return. She stayed at Kintbury until after his departure, and while she was there, she received two letters from her sister, Jane.

These are the first of the preserved letters which from January 1796 until a few weeks before her death in 1817 recall the day to day events of Jane Austen's life. Unfortunately, there are much regretted gaps, but her readers can only be grateful that Jane and her sister spent so many months apart, or so much more would have gone unrecorded.

As Dr Chapman reported, his edition of the *Letters* was greeted by a "chorus of disappointment and hostility". He quotes in particular Harold Nicolson's dismissal of her "appalling gentility of style and aspect", a wit "old-maidish and disagreeable", a mind "like a very small, sharp pair of scissors".[8] Later, Harold Nicolson was to revise this view considerably, and in 1956 in an address to the Jane Austen Society, although still a qualified admirer, concluded that the letters "furnish important documentary evidence of the habits, thoughts, and feelings of a distinct class in English society at the outset of the nineteenth century . . ." and "reveal so much of what was most honest and most admirable in her character and mind".[9]

Professor Garrod described the letters as "a desert of trivialities punctuated by occasional oases of clever malice;"[10] E. M. Forster found in them nothing but "officers, dances, officers, giggling, balls";[11] Marvin Mudrick declared them a "bustle of news-bits with irony gleaming like a knife blade among them".[12]

They are, in fact, natural, spontaneous, often hurried bulletins, passing in most cases between two close and affectionate sisters and sometimes intended to be read aloud to the rest of the family. Jane herself makes the best comment on them when she writes, "I have now attained the true art of letter-writing, which we are always told is to express on paper exactly what one would say to the same person by word of mouth. I have been talking to you almost as fast as I could the whole of this letter."[13]

In a uniquely satisfying way, therefore, it is possible to eavesdrop on Jane Austen talking to her sister for the best part of twenty years. In this time, she passes from an eager young woman on the threshold of life to a mature artist greeting the onset of death with dignity at the comparatively early age of forty-one. The chronicle inevitably includes a wealth of unimportant details, but as will be seen, much else besides, which throws light on Jane Austen's character, and on her attitudes towards her life and her work. There are no personal revelations, confidences, or confessions, no anxious searchings after self-identity, no agonies of doubt, nor would one expect there to be. Any such matters, if in fact they were discussed, would have been talked over quietly by the sisters in the intimacy of their small shared bedroom. But since Jane and Cassandra were essentially private people who understood each other so well, it is most likely that even between themselves, they left much to be inferred. Her letters show their author looking out attentively at the world without egotism, without illusions, but with the calm assurance of faith.

The more particularly biting comments have often been quoted as damaging evidence of heartlessness. Usually the same five or six extracts are selected—not an untoward number in twenty years of correspondence—invariably including poor Mrs Hall of Sherborne, "brought to bed yesterday of a dead child, some weeks before she expected, owing to a fright. I suppose she happened unawares to look at her husband."[14] In isolation, this seems to be a strikingly cold and callous remark, an unfeeling inability to resist an inappropriate joke. But who knows how many laughs the sisters had previously shared about Mr Hall's unfortunate appearance? The same thought also applies to the Miss Debarys, to whom Jane was "as civil as their bad breath would allow me."[15] Nonetheless, however charitably one views them, it is hard to reconcile the writer of such comments with the woman who never trusted herself "to comment with unkindness".

But for all the touches of malice, there are many more instances of good natured humour and fun. Some of the impressions gathered from the novels, for instance, that Jane Austen disliked children, can be effectively dispelled in the letters by her obvious affection for her ever growing family of nephews and nieces, as she declined from a daughter and sister into an aunt.

Jane Austen's first full-length biography was written by her nephew, and one of the most influential of her Victorian critics, Richard Simpson, ended his extended review of this work with the following words, "Might we not borrow from Miss Austen's biographer the title which the nephew bestows upon her, and recognise her officially as 'dear Aunt Jane'?"[16]

This seems to have started an "Aunt Jane" tradition, which reinforced by the frequently applied term of spinster has tended to freeze an image of Jane Austen at a particular stage in her life, and probably by no means that by which she would have chosen to be remembered. Three of her books were written when she was only just an aunt, and far from an old maid, a sparkling attractive young woman, if not in love already, with every prospect of falling in love and getting married. For some reason, the designation of spinster is usually faintly disparaging, but there is no evidence that Jane Austen ever pitied herself as a single woman. She was to die unmarried, but Fanny Burney was to find happiness in marriage at approximately the same age as Jane was at her death, and she went on to produce a son. Moreover, at a time when so many wives died in childbirth, girls who had been passed over in their youth, often found themselves in demand later on. All Jane's brothers were to lose their first wives, and four of them were to marry again. Few women of forty feel themselves too old for marriage and, until her last illness, there is no reason to suppose that Jane Austen had totally discounted the possibility.

When she was twenty, marriage must have seemed inevitable. While not so strikingly fine featured as Cassandra, the younger sister was a most appealing girl. Her brother Henry, looking back at the time of her death, wrote: "Her carriage and deportment were quiet, yet graceful. Her features were separately good. Their assemblage produced an unrivalled expression of that cheerfulness, sensibility, and benevolence, which were her real characteristics. Her complexion was of the finest texture. It might with truth be said, that her eloquent blood spoke through her modest cheek. Her voice was extremely sweet."[17]

Henry, whose written style does not live up to his reputation for conversational brilliance, remembered his sister throughout the whole course of her life. Her nephew, Edward, who was to recall her many years later, draws on his memories of Jane as a respected figure in her thirties: "In person she was very attractive; her figure was rather tall and slender, her step light and firm, and her whole appearance expressive of health and animation. In complexion she was a clear brunette with a rich colour; she had full round cheeks, with mouth and nose small and well formed, bright hazel eyes, and brown hair forming natural curls close round her face."[18]

The two descriptions form an attractive picture, to which must undoubtedly be added the shining light of a rare intelligence, and the constant hint of merriment in the humorous hazel eyes.

At the time Jane's letters start, she makes repeated references to a considerable number of what were probably at the time eligible young men. Whether she herself was considered eligible is a different story. In spite of her personal appeal, with her talent still unrevealed and no fortune to speak of, probably not.

The society in which Jane moved at this time has been well summarized.

> In the outer circle of their neighbourhood stood the houses of three peers—those of Lord Portsmouth at Hurstbourne, Lord Bolton at Hackwood, and Lord Dorchester at Greywell. The owners of these places now and then gave balls at home, and could also be relied upon to bring parties to some of the assemblies at Basingstoke. Hardly less important than these magnates were the Mildmays of Dogmersfield and the Chutes of the Vyne. . . . Then came other squires—Portals at Freefolk, Bramstons at Oakley Hall, Jervoises at Herriard, Harwoods at Deane, Terrys at Dummer, Holders at Ashe Park—with several clerical families and other smaller folk.[19]

Jane attended balls in Kent, when she stayed there with her brother, and the Lefroys and the Lloyds continued to hold their leading places in her life. Another family with whom both she and Cassandra were on specially close terms were the confusingly named Bigg-Withers. Because of an inheritance, Mr Bigg had added Wither to his own name and that of his only son Harris, while his daughters retained the simple Bigg. They lived at a substantial manor house at Manydown Park, between Steventon and Basingstoke, where Jane and Cassandra often spent a night or two before and after the Basingstoke balls. The youngest sister, Alethea, two years Jane's junior, was to remain unmarried and to stay at Manydown with her father until his death; while her two elder sisters both married. Elizabeth's marriage was sadly brief, as her husband, the Rev. William Heathcote, died after four years in 1802. Catherine was to become in 1808 the second wife of the Rev. Herbert Hill of Streatham, the uncle of the poet and writer, Robert Southey. These three women became and remained close friends of both Jane and Cassandra.

In those young days, Jane, who loved dancing, never lacked partners, and though she tends to joke about them in her letters, there must have been some among so many to whom she was in some degree attracted. We hear of Charles Fowle; two Mr Watkins; two fellow students of Henry's at Oxford, John Warren, and Benjamin Portal, who had "handsome eyes"; John Lyford—not a favourite partner; Richard Buller; John and Earle Harwood; three of the Digweed brothers from Steventon Manor; and there is a tantalizing reference to Edward Taylor of Bifrons in Kent, "We went by Bifrons, and I contemplated with a melancholy pleasure the abode of him, on whom I once fondly doated".[20] When Edward married his cousin Charlotte some years later, Jane commented, "Those beautiful dark Eyes will then adorn another Generation at least in all their purity".[21]

But the young man who first seriously engaged Jane Austen's feelings was Thomas Lefroy. The Austen family has tended to minimize the effect of this young man's impact on her life, but it probably had considerable significance. Tom was the nephew of Jane's beloved Anne Lefroy. He was a few months younger than herself, and she describes him as "a very gentle-manlike, good-looking, pleasant young man".[22] His portrait shows him to have had a sensitive, humorous face, with frank eyes under well defined brows, and a full, finely shaped mouth. An interesting photograph also exists of him as a powerful old man of ninety with a stubborn jaw.

The attractive rectory at Ashe was well adapted for the giving of private balls, as the dividing doors between the morning and dining rooms could be thrown back to allow ample room for dancing, and Mrs Lefroy was an accomplished hostess. Jane jokingly reports to Cassandra: ". . . I am almost afraid to tell you how my Irish friend and I behaved. Imagine to yourself everything most profligate and shocking in the way of dancing and sitting down together."[23] He was teased about her, and at a later ball, to which Jane was looking forward with impatience, she rather expected to "receive an offer from my friend in the course of the evening. I shall refuse him, however, unless he promises to give away his white coat."[24] Since she had declared his white morning coat to be his one fault, it seems likely she was prepared to accept him.

"At length," she writes, "the day is come on which I am to flirt my last with Tom Lefroy, and when you receive this it will be over."[25] One gathers she means the day, not the flirtation.

This letter was written on 16th January 1796, and soon afterwards Tom must have left the neighbourhood. It is not known whether he proposed and was refused, but it is much more likely that his expected offer never came. Evidently, Tom needed to marry money, and fond though Mrs Lefroy was of Jane, it is very possible that she warned her young nephew against an impetuous attachment perhaps based on only a fleeting attraction.

From September 1796 until April 1798, there is a gap in the letters, and nothing more is heard of Tom, and his possible comings and goings, until November 1798, when Jane reports a visit of Mrs Lefroy to her sister, "of her nephew she said nothing at all . . . and I was too proud to make any enquiries; but on my father's afterwards asking where he was, I learnt that he was gone back to London in his way to Ireland, where he is called to the Bar and means to practise."[26]

Pride is not a word or a concept Jane Austen would have employed lightly, and suggests that she had maintained a deep interest in the affairs of Tom Lefroy for the considerable time in a young woman's life of almost three years. He was soon to marry in Ireland, where he later became Chief Justice, and lived until 1869. When questioned about this early affair towards the end of his life, he was to say that he had been in love with Jane Austen, but it was a boyish love. So, of course, is any young love not given a chance to develop. But whatever were her deepest feelings, this inconclusive love affair must have left Jane, like any girl who has permitted herself to reveal a preference for a young man in public, in some measure rebuffed, disappointed, and hurt.

In 1796, when Cassandra was engaged and Jane was dwelling on the merits of Tom Lefroy, another complicated romantic drama was being played in the Austen family. It is impossible to doubt that this situation provided Jane with both insights and ideas. James Austen was now a widower, and his bright little daughter Anna, spent a good deal of time with her grandparents and aunts. Clearly, it was desirable that he marry again. Henry Austen, who had attained his Master's degree, had not, as was expected, entered the church, but, already a lieutenant in the Oxford Militia, was considering making soldiering his career. He was now twenty-five years of age and still unmarried. Both young men had been attracted by the Comtesse de Feuillide, their fascinating, out-of-reach cousin. But now, Eliza was free.

Apart from his desire for her, James must have thought the match mutually suitable. They had both lost partners and were both left with a single child to raise. James was only four years her junior, so they were near enough of an age. For Henry, not yet launched on his career, especially to his mother, it semed foolish to burden himself with a wife, never in robust health, ten years his senior, and with a sickly child.

Family tradition records that Eliza, who made no bones about her love of flirting, tantalized them both. After dangling James in a state of uncertainty for some months, she declared she could never accept to be a parson's wife, which no doubt had the effect of deflecting Henry from his preordained course. But in spite of the long-standing physical attraction between them, neither would Eliza say yes to Henry.

Although there is no reason to question its sincerity, a letter in Henry's ponderous and pompous style had been despatched the year before to Warren Hastings, congratulating him on his acquittal, which suggests that the suitor was already hopefully drawing himself to the notice of Eliza's godfather.

Engaged as you must be by those who are more relatively though not more abstractedly interested in this late decision than myself, I dare not take up more of your leisure, for intruding on any part of which I already owe an apology, though I have none to offer except that the many instances of your kindness shown to me have long since justified the sincerity of that respect and esteem with which I now take the liberty of subscribing myself.[27]

Eliza was a bird of paradise, loving nothing better than "dear Liberty, & yet dearer flirtation",[28] and she was hard to trap. Less self-confident than his younger brother, James admitted the hopelessness of his case, and cast about again more modestly, weighing the relative merits of two Marys: Mary Lloyd, whose good looks had been marred by small pox, and Mary Harrison of Andover.

Perhaps because they were already old friends on terms of comfortable familiarity, James asked Mary Lloyd to be his wife, and their engagement and marriage in November 1796 was welcomed by the whole family. On learning of the engagement, Mrs Austen wrote generously: "Had the Election been mine, you, my dear Mary, are the person I should have chosen for *James's wife*, *Anna's Mother*, and *my Daughter*; being as certain as I can be of anything in this uncertain world, that you will greatly increase and promote the happiness of each of the three. . . . I look forward to you as a real Comfort to me in my old age, when Cassandra is gone into Shropshire, & Jane—the Lord knows where."[29]

Eliza's comment was made to their cousin, Phila Walter: "Jane seems much pleased with the match, and it is natural she should be having long known & liked the lady. . ." .[30]

Henry also made a determined effort to live without Eliza, and thought he had fallen in love with yet another Mary, Miss Mary Pearson, daughter of Sir Richard Pearson, R.N., an officer of Greenwich hospital. For a brief while, there was an engagement, and Jane, who, together with her brother Frank, was staying with Edward at Rowling at the time, was expecting to take Miss Pearson home with her to Steventon for a visit. One way and another, the method of her return home from this particular sojourn in Kent seems to have occasioned Jane a good deal of perplexity, complicated by the proposed collec- of Miss Pearson en route. Frank was going up to town to join his new ship, the *Triton*, and Jane thought of travelling with him. But she was dissuaded from what might have been a rash step "for if the Pearsons were not at home, I should inevitably fall a sacrifice to the arts of some fat woman who would make me drunk with small beer".[31] She was also "in great distress" being unable to determine whether to present a Rowling servant with "half a guinea or only five shillings when I go away".[32] A tipping predicament that haunts single women with modest incomes even today.

In the event, Mary Pearson was never fated to visit Henry's family, which was perhaps just as well, as Jane, who had evidently met her in London, writes cautiously, "If Miss Pearson should return with me, pray be careful not to expect too much beauty. I will not pretend to say that on a *first view* she quite answered the opinion I had formed of her. My Mother, I am sure, will be disappointed if she does not take great care. From what I remember of her picture, it is no great resemblance."[33]

Before much longer, the affair was at an end. Eliza reports somewhat complacently to Phila: "Our cousin Henry Austen has been in Town: he looks thin & ill. I hear his late intended is a most intolerable flirt, and reckoned to give herself great airs."[34] Nonetheless, it may well be that Henry's brief inconstancy had helped her to a decision. In May 1797, she writes approvingly: "I suppose you know that our cousin Henry is now Captain, Paymaster, & Adjutant. He is a very lucky young man & bids fair to possess a considerable share of riches & honours. I believe he has now given up all thoughts of the Church, & he is right for he certainly is not so fit for a parson as a soldier. . . ."[35]

By December of the same year, Henry's persistence had at last prevailed, and Eliza informs her Godfather: "I have consented to a Union with my Cousin Captn Austen who has the honour of being known to you. He has been for some time in Possession of a comfortable Income, and the excellence of his Heart, Temper, and Understanding, together with steady attachment to me, his affection for my little Boy, and disinterested concurrence in the disposal of my Property in favour of this latter, have at length induced me to an acquiescence which I have withheld for more than two years."[36]

Not surprisingly, Mrs Austen was far from pleased, yet this agreeable, if somewhat superficial, couple seems to have been well suited and to have made each other happy.

As well as James and Henry, Jane's brother Edward had also been undergoing a change in his own comfortable life. His patron, Mr Thomas Knight, had died in 1794, leaving Edward his heir, after the death of his wife. Three years later, Mrs Knight decided to offer her splendid home and estates at Godmersham and Chawton, and a handsome income to go with them, to Edward, his wife, and their ever growing family, which by 1797 already included their eldest daughter Fanny and three sons. At first, knowing how fond Mrs Knight was of her home, Edward affectionately rejected her generous offer. But she was able to convince him that she was firmly decided upon the wisdom of her plan. "Many circumstances attached to large landed Possessions, highly gratifying to a Man, are entirely lost on me at present; but when I see you in the enjoyment of them, I shall, if possible, feel my gratitude to my beloved Husband redoubled, for having placed in my hands the power of bestowing happiness on one so very dear to me."[37]

Mrs Knight moved to a small house, White Friars, near Canterbury, and continued to take the greatest interest in her adopted son and his family. From now on, when Jane and Cassandra went into Kent, they were to stay in the luxury of the classical mansion finely situated amid the attractive scenery of Godmersham Park.

As it happened, the elder sister was to stay there more often than the younger, perhaps because tragedy had now entered Cassandra's life. She had been looking forward happily to Tom Fowle's return from the West Indies and making clothes for their approaching marriage, when suddenly she received the news that her fiancé had died of yellow fever in St Domingo just a few weeks before he was due to embark for England. There are no letters between Jane and Cassandra around this date, but it can be imagined that this sad blow, which was to make such a difference to Cassandra's life, drew the sisters even closer together. The one person in the world who could give any comfort to Cassandra at that terrible time must have been Jane.

Once more, the voice that comments on this family sorrow is Eliza's. "This is a very severe stroke to the whole family, & particularly to poor Cassandra for whom I feel more than I can express. Indeed I am most sincerely grieved at this event & the pain which it must occasion our worthy relations. Jane says that her sister behaves with a degree of resolution & propriety which no common mind could evince in so trying a situation."[38]

It seems that, although she was only twenty-four at the time, Cassandra never again contemplated marriage, and to a great extent immersed herself in the domestic life and the children of Edward, who had always been her favourite brother. Tom Fowle had left Cassandra a legacy of £1,000, and Lord Craven, with whose regiment he had sailed away so hopefully, had declared too late, that he would never have let him go to so dangerous a climate had he known of his engagement.

As far as Jane was personally concerned recently, the matter of the greatest importance was that she had been writing another book. It was entitled *First Impressions*, she had worked on it from October 1796 until August 1797, and there was a great deal about it that thoroughly pleased her. It had been read aloud to the family, and everyone had liked it. Mr Austen was clearly impressed by it, as in November 1797, he wrote offering it to Cadell, the publisher.

Unfortunately, although Jane's father was a perceptive critic, he was no businessman, and not surprisingly in view of his hesitant and modest letter, the matter was not taken up. Jane's first attempt at publication had failed, and Cadell had lost the chance of being the first of the many publishers of the work that was eventually to take shape as *Pride and Prejudice*.

Unfortunately, no manuscript remains of *First Impressions* and it is not possible to say how far the book we know was altered from the original on which it was based. But the work is so infused with youth and optimism, so "light, and bright, and sparkling"[39] that clearly much of the inspiration and the tone of the young Jane of this period remains.

In the last months of 1797, probably for her own health, and perhaps to make a change for Cassandra, Mrs Austen took her daughters to Bath, to stay at No 1 the Paragon with her

brother, Mr James Leigh Perrot and his wife. Later, Jane was
to recall that when they arrived it was a wet and gloomy
November day. But they had a good circle of acquaintances
there at the time, including Mrs Lefroy and her daughter, and
apparently not downhearted by the lack of response from
Cadell, Jane took the opportunity to begin the work of trans-
forming *Elinor and Marianne* into the novel we know now as
Sense and Sensibility.

According to a note left by Cassandra on the dating of these
early novels, it was about this time too that her sister began
a new work, originally entitled *Susan*, and later renamed
Northanger Abbey.[40]

In many ways, this is the novel closest to the writings of
Jane's girlhood, satirizing as it does certain aspects of the
novels of sensibility, and the Gothic novels of Mrs Radcliffe
and her school. Some critics have preferred to treat *Northanger
Abbey* as its author's first completed novel, in spite of the
evidence provided by Cassandra.

It does, however, seem very likely that the work was begun
in Bath, where Jane was surrounded by all the scenes she
describes so vividly, and that her visit remained fresh in her
memory as she continued to write. Certainly *Northanger
Abbey* as it exists today was subjected to much less later
revision than *Sense and Sensibility* and *Pride and Prejudice*.
For when Jane came to consider it again, nearly twenty years
later, she found there were inherent difficulties involved in
bringing this particular novel up to date. Above all, the Gothic
novel was by then out of fashion, and almost equally important, Bath itself had undergone great change. Rather than
make any radical alterations, she contented herself by prefacing the work with a modest apology for its lack of
topicality, realizing perhaps that its merits made it timeless.

At the time of her death, she was still hesitating about
bringing it out. Revisions there were, but in so far as it
remains the nearest to her youthful original, then *Northanger
Abbey* may be fairly regarded as Jane Austen's first novel. But
perhaps because of the lack of response from Cadell, Jane
Austen was not to offer this sprightly and original work for
publication immediately.

They returned to Steventon from Bath, and it is evident
that Mrs Austen had not been cured of whatever it was from
which she suffered. Since she went on to attain the age of
eighty-seven it is not uncharitable to assume that it was
nothing very serious. But her condition must have imposed

additional burdens of duties and patience on both her daughters. As was to be expected, Jane met the situation, which was to continue intermittently for the rest of her life, with good sense and humour. But at times she must have been irritated, and a typical complaint runs: "My mother continues hearty; her appetite & nights are very good, but her Bowels are still not entirely settled, & sometimes she complains of an Asthma, a Dropsy, Water in her Chest & a Liver Disorder."[41]

While Mrs Austen coddled her health, in 1798 there were two deaths in the family. In April, Jane had the responsibility of writing the letter of condolence to Philadelphia Walter on the death of her father, Mr Austen's half brother, who had been in failing health for some time. "But the very circumstance which at present enhances your loss, must gradually reconcile you to it the better:—the Goodness which made him valuable on Earth, will make him Blessed in Heaven."[42]

The second death on 9th August of the same year was both violent and tragic. Lady Williams, formerly Jane Cooper, the little cousin who had gone to school with Jane and Cassandra, while driving herself in her whiskey—a light two-wheeled one-horse carriage—was in collision with a runaway dray horse, thrown out into the road, and killed instantly. This sad end to a happy and successful young life must have made a deep impression on her Austen cousins, who had taken the place of her own family when her parents had died, and from whose home less than six years before she had been married.

Following Jane's letter to Philadelphia Walter in April 1798, there is a gap in her correspondence until October, when she begins a long series of letters to Cassandra. But some time during this summer, she evidently met and was paid some attention by a young Fellow of Emmanual College, Cambridge, who was a friend of Mrs Lefroy, Samuel Blackall. While not in love with her, he seems to have been seriously interested in Jane, none the less perhaps because it is unlikely she gave him much encouragement, as this was during the period when she may still have been hoping for some development of her friendship with Tom Lefroy.

Some while after his departure, Blackall wrote to Mrs Lefroy: "I am very sorry to hear of Mrs. Austen's illness. It would give me particular pleasure to have an opportunity of improving my acquaintance with that family—with a hope of creating to myself a nearer interest. But at present I cannot indulge any expectation of it."[43]

Jane had no illusions about the strength of purpose of this lukewarm admirer: "It will all go on exceedingly well, and decline away in a very reasonable manner. There seems no likelihood of his coming into Hampshire this Christmas, and it is therefore most probable that our indifference will soon be mutual, unless his regard, which appeared to spring from knowing nothing of me at first, is best supported by never seeing me."[44]

Nothing more is heard of Mr Blackall in the correspondence until Jane reports his marriage to a Miss Lewis at Clifton in a letter written to her brother Frank fifteen years later. So Mr Blackall had certainly been in no great hurry to wed. "I would wish Miss Lewis to be of a silent turn & rather ignorant, but naturally intelligent & wishing to learn;—fond of cold veal pies, green tea in the afternoon, & a green window blind at night."[45]

In the autumn of 1798, Mr and Mrs Austen and their two daughters paid a visit to Edward, now newly established in his handsome home at Godmersham. The house, of course, had been long familiar to them, but it must have given the parents the greatest satisfaction to know that their early sacrifice of their son had led to such good fortune and happiness. Elizabeth had recently given birth to another son, William, so when the party returned home, Cassandra was left behind to continue her visit and help in the household.

The journey back was not without event, as soon after arriving at the Bull and George Inn at Dartford, where they were to spend the night, Jane discovered that "my writing and dressing boxes had been by accident put into a chaise which was just packing off as we came in, and were driven away towards Gravesend on their way to the West Indies. No part of my property could have been such a prize before, for in my writing box was all my worldly worth, 7l., and my dear Harry's deputation. Mr Nottley immediately despatched a man and horse after the chaise, and in half an hour's time I had the pleasure of being as rich as ever; they were got about two or three miles off."[46]

By the third and last day, Mrs Austen was beginning to feel the effects of so much travelling, and on her arrival home at Steventon, she took to her bed with twelve drops of laudanum prescribed by her physician, Mr Lyford, as a composer, and was to remain in an invalid state for the next few weeks, leaving Jane to act, it appears most competently, as housekeeper.

Sketch of Jane Austen by her sister Cassandra

Sketch of Steventon Rectory by Anna Lefroy

The Old North Front of Stoneleigh Abbey before 1836

"I am very grand indeed; I had the dignity of dropping out my mother's laudanum last night. I carry about the keys of the wine and closet, and twice since I began this letter have had orders to give in the kitchen."[47]

On 17th November, Jane records for her sister the visit of Mrs Lefroy, recently returned from Bath, and the information obtained from her on this occasion about Tom and Mr Blackall. Whatever her feelings, she continues her letter lightly, among other snippets, with news of her mother's praise for her housekeeping: "I really think it my peculiar excellence, and for this reason—I always take care to provide such things as please my own appetite. . . . I am very fond of experimental housekeeping, such as having an ox-cheek now and then; I shall have one next week, and I mean to have some little dumplings put into it, that I may fancy myself at Godmersham."[48]

By this time, Mr Austen had laid down his carriage, and Jane seems unenthusiastic about the forthcoming Basingstoke ball, no longer as well supported as formerly, "dis-convenience and dis-inclination to go have kept pace together".[49]

She had sent some designs to her three-year-old nephew George, known at that time as "itty Dordy", and makes the significant comment: "Perhaps they would have suited him as well had they been less elaborately finished; but an artist cannot do anything slovenly."[50] The letter ends with a most important piece of news, James's second wife, Mary, had given birth to a fine little boy, James Edward, the nephew who was to be his famous aunt's first biographer.

In her next letter, Jane tells her sister of the books the family has been buying and reading. Naturally, they were all interested in *Fitz-Albini*, the latest production of Egerton Brydges, Mrs Lefroy's brother, although they had apparently heard little good of it and Jane did not approve of the purchase of "the only one of Egerton's works of which his family are ashamed. . . . There is very little story, and what there is is told in a strange, unconnected way. There are many characters introduced, apparently merely to be delineated. We have not been able to recognize any of them hitherto, except Dr. and Mrs. Hey and Mr. Oxenden, who is not very tenderly treated . . ."[51]

In December, there was good news of Frank, who was safe and well at Cadiz, which was a relief to all the family and probably had a good effect on Mrs Austen's health. "My mother made her *entrée* into the dressing-room through crowds

E

of admiring spectators yesterday afternoon, and we all drank tea together for the first time these five weeks. She has had a tolerable night, and bids fair for a continuance in the same brilliant course of action today."[52]

By this time there are already hints in the letters that Mary Lloyd, who had been such a good friend, was not proving quite such a favourite as a sister-in-law, and no doubt many of the tactful excisions made by Cassandra were tart little comments about Mrs James. "Mary does not manage matters in such a way as to make me want to lay in myself. She is not tidy enough in her appearance; she has no dressing gown to sit up in; her curtains are all too thin, and things are not in that comfort and style about her which are necessary to make such a situation an enviable one."[53]

Although throughout the letters Jane wrote to her sister there is a good deal of discussion on clothes, the theme is generally how best to contrive to make a reasonable appearance on a very small allowance. It does not seem that either of the sisters was personally vain, and in his biography, Edward suggests that they were both a trifle on the dowdy side in later years.

At this time only twenty-three years of age, Jane writes: "I have made myself two or three caps to wear of evenings since I came home, and they save me a world of torment as to hair-dressing, which at present gives me no trouble beyond washing and brushing, for my long hair is always plaited up out of sight, and my short hair curls well enough to want no papering."[54] It seems a pity that Jane's naturally curly brown hair was pushed so soon under a cap, and a modern expert who examined a lock of it recently confirms that "within the last three years of her life Jane Austen did little to tend to her hair and that brushing, and combing, and handling were minimal".[55]

On Christmas Eve, there was more good news to relate to Cassandra of the sailor brothers. Charles's wish to be transferred to a frigate would be considered by the Admiralty, and Frank was to be promoted. Within a few days it was confirmed that Frank was to command the sloop *Petterel*. Jane had been staying at Manydown for the Basingstoke Ball.

Of the gentlemen present you may have some idea from the list of my partners—Mr. Wood, G. Lefroy, Rice, a Mr. Butcher (belonging to the Temples, a sailor and not of the 11th Light Dragoons), Mr. Temple (not the horrid one of all), Mr. Wm.

Orde (cousin to the Kingsclere man), Mr. John Harwood, and Mr. Calland, who appeared as usual with his hat in his hand, and stood every now and then behind Catherine and me to be talked to and abused for not dancing. We teased him, however, into it at last. I was very glad to see him again after so long a separation, and he was altogether rather the genius and flirt of the evening.[56]

It is possible that the tantalizing Mr Calland, who did not want to dance, contributed a little to that memorable and disdainful first appearance in *Pride and Prejudice* of Mr Darcy. Jane herself danced all twenty dances without any fatigue, and the black cap she had trimmed according to Cassandra's suggestions was a success.

Another ball followed early in the New Year of 1799 at Kempshott Park, the home of Lord and Lady Dorchester. This time, Jane wore what she calls a mamalone cap, which was probably the fashionable Mamelouk cap, a creation somewhat resembling a fez which, like other items of dress based on Egyptian costumes, was in vogue after Nelson's great victory of the Nile. Jane views her performance at this particular ball dispassionately. "I do not think I was very much in request. People were rather apt not to ask me till they could not help it; one's consequence, you know, varies so much at times without any particular reason."[57]

It appears she had not been at her best, suffering from a cold and what she describes as a weakness in her eyes. From time to time, her eyes continued to trouble her, which lends some force to the argument that the visual descriptions in her novels are rare and lacking in detail simply because she lived in the hazily defined world of the shortsighted. No doubt too, any defect of vision was likely to deteriorate in one who lived to read and write in an age of small type-faces and poor and flickering artificial light.

While Mary had lost ground, Martha Lloyd had grown in favour, and on this occasion kindly shared with Jane her put-you-up bed in the nursery at Deane which "did exceedingly well for us, both to lie awake in and talk till two o'clock, and to sleep in the rest of the night".[58]

For the first time in her letters, Jane mentions her novel: "I do not wonder at your wanting to read 'First Impressions' again, so seldom as you have gone through it, and that so long ago."[59]

Jane had been disappointed that her "particular little

brother", Charles, had not managed to get home in time for the Kempshott Ball, but he did manage to spend a few days with his family. He was now a young man of twenty, and his sister reports: "Martha writes me word that Charles was very much admired at Kintbury, and Mrs Lefroy never saw any one so much improved in her life, and thinks him handsomer than Henry."[60]

On 21st January, he caught the night coach to Deal to take up his new appointment. There was some doubt as to whether this would be on the *Tamar* or the *Endymion*, and Charles was very pleased to find himself on the frigate the *Endymion* under the command of Sir Thomas Williams, the widower of his cousin Jane, who had been knighted for his part in the capture of the French frigate *Le Tribune* when commanding the *Unicorn*, in which Charles was serving at the time in 1796.

As young sailors, the two Austen brothers had the unique experience of serving in one of the greatest periods in the history of the British Navy. It was true that the conditions for the men, many of whom were pressed into service, were often appalling, with bad quarters, poor and inadequate food, and pitiful pay. Particularly during periods of inactivity, discontent bubbled up to the surface, leading in 1797 at Spithead and the Nore to serious mutinies. Yet when they were engaged in battle with the enemy, these same ill-treated men displayed the utmost loyalty and courage. Under the brilliant leadership of admirals such as Lord Hood, Lord Howe, Sir John Jervis, and above all, Nelson, the French Fleet was rendered practically ineffective and the British Navy maintained ceaseless and vigilant control of the seas. This, and all it implied in continuing trading and combating the threat of invasion, was a key factor in the eventual victory over France and the dominant figure who emerged in 1799 and remained to inspire and to terrorize Europe for the next fifteen years, Napoleon Bonaparte.

For Frank and Charles Austen these must have been exciting times, and both young men were brave, ambitious, and proud to be serving their country in the greatest navy in the world. Jane Austen was always to take the keenest interest both in her brothers' individual careers and in naval matters in general. Some of the most sympathetic of her characters were to be sailors.

In a letter written on 21st January, Jane is beginning to look forward to her sister's return to Steventon. She expected this in March, but since there is no further correspondence until

May, perhaps Cassandra came home earlier. Before then, Jane had carried out her plan of visiting Martha at Ibthrop.

At Godmersham, just before Christmas, Edward, who perhaps in this particular took after his mother, had suffered a spell of bad health. Also like his mother, Edward was to live to a good old age, in his case, eighty-four.

Jane had written, "Poor Edward! It is very hard that he, who has everything else in the world that he can wish for, should not have good health too."[61]

A change of air had been prescribed and at first Brighton had been proposed. Since his mother was also convalescent, Edward had evidently suggested that she might share the benefit and accompany him and his family with her daughters.

"I assure you that I dread the idea of going to Brighton as much as you do, but I am not without hopes that something may happen to prevent it",[62] was Jane's comment on this proposal. It is not clear why the sisters were so prejudiced against Brighton, and it is unlikely that Jane had ever visited the town, made fashionable and notorious by the extravagance of the Prince Regent. Probably it had by then already featured in *First Impressions* as the Mecca of Lydia Bennet, and the scene of her elopement and disgrace.

In Lydia's imagination, a visit to Brighton comprised every possibility of earthly happiness. She saw with the creative eye of fancy, the streets of that gay bathing place covered with officers. She saw herself the object of attention, to tens and to scores of them at present unknown. She saw all the glories of the camp; its tents stretched forth in beauteous uniformity of lines, crowded with the young and the gay, and dazzling with scarlet; and to complete the view, she saw herself seated beneath a tent, tenderly flirting with at least six officers at once.[63]

In the event, the idea of Brighton was abandoned and instead it was decided that Edward, Elizabeth, their two eldest children, Fanny and Edward, and Mrs Austen accompanied by only Jane should go to Bath. This time Cassandra stayed at home to look after her father and attend to the housekeeping.

The visit was made in some style, with two of the Godmersham servants to supplement the local staff. Once more they arrived on a miserable day, stopping in the Paragon for news of Mrs Austen's brother, and meeting a gentleman in a buggy "who, on minute examination, turned out to be Dr. Hall—and Dr. Hall in such very deep mourning that either his mother, his wife, or himself must be dead".[64]

They were very pleased with their rooms in the handsome house with a little black kitten running about the staircase, which Edward had rented at 13 Queen Square, and may still be seen, in a convenient part of the city with a pleasant view. Edward lost no time in getting down to business: "He drinks at the Hetling Pump, is to bathe tomorrow, and try electricity on Tuesday,"[65] while Mrs Austen seems to have been on the mend without any treatment. Jane herself was preoccupied with various shopping commissions, among them some decorations for Cassandra's caps. Fruit was all the vogue, but flowers were cheaper . . . "besides, I cannot help thinking that it is more natural to have flowers grow out of the head than fruit".[66]

Apart from Mr and Mrs Leigh Perrot, they had plenty of acquaintances staying in the city, "so that we need not immediately dread absolute solitude; and there is a public breakfast in Sydney Gardens every morning, so that we shall not be wholly starved".[67] Besides her shopping, the usual round of Bath activities, and some local engagements, Jane enjoyed some pleasant walks, but she seems anxious that the stay should not be too prolonged, and it may be suspected that she was thrown too much in the company of her mother, and was a little bored. It seems unlikely that with such a full house and the presence of two affectionate and lively children aged five and six to whom she devoted a good deal of her time, she was able to do any work, yet a reference to *First Impressions* suggests she had brought the manuscript with her: "I would not let Martha read 'First Impressions' again upon any account, and am very glad that I did not leave it in your power. She is very cunning, but I saw through her design; she means to publish it from memory, and one more perusal must enable her to do it."[68] Clearly publication of this favourite work was still in Jane's mind.

There are many examples of her crisp distinctive style in the series of letters from Bath: "I am quite pleased with Martha and Mrs Lefroy for wanting the pattern of our caps, but I am not so well pleased with your giving it to them. Some wish, some prevailing wish, is necessary to the animation of everybody's Mind, and in gratifying this you leave them to form some other which will not probably be half so innocent."[69]

"Dr. Gardiner was married yesterday to Mrs. Percy and her three daughters." "I do not see the Miss Mapletons very often, but just as often as I like; we are always very

glad to meet, and I do not wish to wear out our satisfaction."[70]

Edward's health does not seem to have benefited much from
the treatment, as the last letter written on 19th June finds him
with a little feverish indisposition and an occasional particular
glow in the hands and feet. There is no final bulletin on Mrs
Austen.

The whole party returned to Steventon for a few days before
the last stage to Godmersham, and although Jane had appreciated her holiday and the good living that always surrounded
Edward and his family, she was glad to get home.

From now until 25th October 1800, there is a gap in the
correspondence, and it is possible that during this time, Jane
carried out the programme of visits she had mentioned earlier
—to her Leigh cousins at Adelstrop in Gloucestershire and
Harpenden near Henley on Thames, and to her Godfather, the
Rev. Samuel Cooke, husband of her mother's cousin Cassandra,
and his family at Great Bookham in Surrey, where they were
neighbours of Jane's much admired Fanny Burney, now Mme
D'Arblay. Certainly Martha Lloyd would have both visited
Steventon and invited Jane back to Ibthrop.

There is no record of her visiting Henry's wife, Eliza, who
in 1799 spent more than six months not far away at Dorking,
alone with her son, while Henry was apparently having an
agreeable time with his regiment in Ireland. Earlier Eliza had
written happily about her marriage, but now alone in the
country, she missed Henry, she was not in good health, and she
was worried about her son. But there can be little doubt that
causing the greatest concern to the Steventon family in the
autumn of 1799 until the spring of 1800 was the fate of Mrs
Jane Leigh Perrot, Mrs Austen's sister-in-law and Jane's aunt,
who, with her husband, was awaiting her trial in Ilchester
Gaol, charged with grand larceny.

At this time, the Leigh Perrots had been happily married
for thirty-five years, spending their time between their
pleasant home at Scarlets at Hare Hatch near Twyford, and
No 1 The Paragon, Bath, where Jane, Cassandra, and their
mother had stayed with them in 1797. As the years went by
and Mr Leigh Perrot's gout grew steadily worse, they had
gradually grown to spend more and more time in Bath seeking
treatment.

Aunt Jane Leigh Perrot was by no means a family favourite.
Perhaps because she and her husband had no children of their
own and belonged to the older generation, she may have been

critical of young people, and in particular of the attractive niece who knew her own mind, was inclined to be pert, and appeared to be making no proper and determined effort to find herself a husband. Jane's attitude towards her aunt, who seems to have somewhat dominated and overshadowed her husband, emerges quite plainly in the letters: " 'Tis really very kind of my Aunt to ask us to Bath again; a kindness that deserves a better return than to profit by it."[71]

"My aunt has a very bad cough—do not forget to have heard about *that* when you come, and I think she is deafer than ever."[72]

"My Aunt is in a great hurry to pay me for my Cap, but cannot find it in her heart to give me good money."[73]

"In spite of all my mother's long and intimate knowledge of the writer, she was not up to the expectation of such a letter as this; the discontentedness of it shocked and surprised her—but *I* see nothing in it out of nature—though a sad nature."[74]

Yet with all her defects of character, Mrs Leigh Perrot, as Jane was later to recognize, had some redeeming virtues of kindness and affection, and above all, she loved and cared for her husband with a single-minded devotion. That he was equally happy in their relationship is rather touchingly demonstrated by the conclusion of a letter he was to write his "Dearest Jenny" some years later, when he was seventy and his wife in her early sixties: "If I was able to say how much I love you and how much I long to be with you perhaps you would not believe me."[75] Like many childless couples, they lived entirely for each other, which may have given outsiders an impression of selfishness. But from the letters Jane Leigh Perrot wrote and received during her time of trial, it is clear that she was also a woman of sound principles, capable of inspiring respect and admiration, steadfast and courageous in adversity, who always gave first place to the interest and comfort of her husband.

Not long after Jane and her party had returned from Bath to Steventon, on 8th August 1799, Mrs Leigh Perrot had set forth on a modest shopping expedition. She wanted a little card of black lace. She made her purchase in a shop called Smith's (afterwards found to have a dubious background) in Bath Street, and since she paid the £1.19s. due with a £5 note, the shopman went to the back of the shop to get her change and make up her parcel. Mrs Leigh Perrot then hastened away in the hope of catching her husband on his return from drinking the water. Luckily, she soon met up with him and they went on together, going to the post office, paying a bill, and then finding themselves once more in Bath Street, near Smith's shop. To their surprise, the assistant who had served Mrs Leigh Perrot hurried across the street to ask whether there was not also some white lace in the parcel with the black. Unperturbed, because since she left the shop it had not been out of her hand, Mrs Leigh Perrot handed over the parcel for the assistant to inspect, when it was found that as well as the lace she had chosen, it also contained a card of white edging.

Concluding that this was simply a careless mistake, the Leigh Perrots continued on their way, only to be accosted a little later by the shopman who had wrapped the parcel, declaring that he had not included the white edging, and demanding their names and address.

Even now, the full seriousness of what seems to have been a particularly inept and clumsy attempt at extortion did not strike them until several days later on 14th August, when there arrived at No 1 The Paragon, a constable with a warrant calling for Mrs Leigh Perrot's attendance before the Mayor. There they found the assistant and the shopman, who swore on oath, the one that she had seen Mrs Leigh Perrot stealing the white lace, and the other that he had found her in possession of the stolen property. The pair of them, and the proprietress of the shop, Miss Elizabeth Gregory, seem to have been under the influence of a local printer, a character with a record and a sinister reputation named William Gye. There was no other course for the Mayor and the magistrates, reluctant though they were to take it, than to commit the accused for trial at the next assizes to be held at Taunton in the following March. Until then, she must be detained in Ilchester Gaol: ". . . to prison I was sent—my dearest affectionate Husband ill as he was never left me—his tenderness has been beyond description—After above 17 Weeks confinement, with his large Shoe, and unable to move but with two Sticks, has he never seemed to have a thought but for me."[76]

At that time, the theft of any article valued at more than one shilling constituted a grand larceny, the statutory penalty for which was death. Well aware that the law was long over-due for reform, few judges, especially in such a case, would have exacted the ultimate penalty. Even so, had she been found guilty, Mrs Leigh Perrot would have been in grave danger of transportation to Botany Bay for a period as long as fourteen years. For a fastidious, respectable couple in their late middle age, the Leigh Perrots were in a very sad plight, which they bore with admirable fortitude and resignation. Mr Scadding and his wife, their gaolers at Ilchester, provided them with all the comforts at their command:

My dearest Perrot with his sweet composure adds to my Philosophy; to be sure he bids fair to have his patience tried in every way he can. Cleanliness has ever been his greatest delight and yet he sees the greasy toast laid by the dirty Children on his Knees, and he feels the small Beer trickle down his sleeves on its way across the table unmoved. . . . Mrs *Scadding's* knife, *well licked to clean it from fried onions* helps me now and then—you may believe how the Mess I am helped to is disposed of—here are *two dogs and three Cats* always *full as hungry* as myself.[77]

Their friends and relations rallied round, and since her son James was laid up at the time with a broken leg, Mrs Austen offered her sister-in-law the help of Cassandra and Jane. But this, Mrs Leigh Perrot refused: "to have two Young Creatures gazed at in a public Court would cut one to the very heart".[78]

When the time of the trial came on 29th March 1800, there seems to have been very little case to answer, which was just as well, as by now Mrs Leigh Perrot had reached the end of her endurance, and was scarcely able to stammer out the speech she had prepared on her own behalf: "Is it possible that at this time of Life my disposition should so suddenly change and that I should foolishly hazard the well earned reputation of a whole Life by such Conduct, or endanger the Peace of Mind of a Husband for whom I would willingly lay down that Life?"[79]

The jury took seven-and-a-half minutes to reach their verdict of Not Guilty, and amid scenes of great joy and emotion, Mrs Leigh Perrot's long ordeal was over. The costs of this case, turning on the matter of a little card of white lace valued at something over £1, amounted to nearer two than one thousand pounds. "What a comfort," declared the victim, "that we have no Children!"[80]

Over the years Mrs Leigh Perrot must have often discussed this shattering affair, and perhaps Jane picked up from her account of domestic life in Ilchester Gaol some of the details for her description of the slovenly Price household at Portsmouth.

Jane's letters are resumed in October 1800, when Cassandra

was again at Godmersham, having travelled there with Edward who, with his eldest son, had been visiting his parents. Amid a good deal of local gossip, Jane reports the sad news of the failure of Mrs Martin's library after less than two years. Perhaps, after all, she should have confined herself to novels.

Some improvements were carried out to the garden of Steventon Rectory: "the bank along the *elm walk* is sloped down for the reception of thorns and lilacs, and it is settled that the other side of the path is to continue turfed, and be planted with beech, ash, and larch."[81]

Her next letter on 1st November, gives news of Frank and his ship the *Petterel* which was sailing in the Egyptian Squadron to Alexandria. The sisters had been busy sewing shirts for Charles, whose ship the *Endymion* was at home awaiting orders.

On the last Thursday in October, there had been a ball at Basingstoke. In spite of a scarcity of men, Jane danced "nine dances out of ten, five with Stephen Terry, T. Chute and James Digweed and four with Catherine. There was commonly a couple of ladies standing up together, but not often any so amiable as ourselves."[82] She wore Cassandra's favourite gown, "a bit of muslin of the same round my head, border'd with Mrs Cooper's band—and one little Comb."[83]

A week later, Jane writes again, reporting that she had just finished the first volume of Madame de Genlis's novel *Les Veillées du Château*. Evidently she was keeping up with her reading in French. Some new furniture had arrived and was giving great pleasure. She and Mary had dined with Mr Holder, the tenant of Ashe Park. "We had a very quiet evening, I believe Mary found it dull, but I thought it very pleasant. To sit in idleness over a good fire in a well-proportioned room is a luxurious sensation. Sometimes we talked & sometimes we were quite silent; I said two or three amusing things, & Mr Holder made a few infamous puns."[84] From Mr Holder's paper, Jane learned that Frank had seen action on the *Petterel*, and had captured and set fire to a Turkish ship off Cyprus.

One of their father's former pupils, the Rev. Richard Buller, son of the Bishop of Exeter, had recently married and Jane's comment on his letter reveals her own dislike of any exaggerated or sentimental display of affection: "I was afraid he would oppress me by his felicity & his love for his wife, but this is not the case; he calls her simply Anna without any angelic embellishments, for which I respect & wish him happy."[85] Vicar of Colyton, just a few miles from the coast north of Seaton in Devon, the Rev. Buller had extended a pressing invitation to the whole family to visit him, and it seems a holiday in Devon the next year was already being discussed.

Once more, the Harwood family at Deane House had been alarmed by an exploit of Earle, apparently the scapegrace son. Two years before he had fallen in love and made an indiscreet marriage; this time he had shot himself accidently in the thigh. He was recovering in hospital at Gosport, though still in some danger, and the family was reassured that this injury had nothing to do, as they had feared, with a duel.

The weather had been stormy, and the big winds had played havoc with the Steventon trees. Two of Jane's favourite great elms had been blown down.

Unusually Jane's next letter is written to Martha Lloyd and there is a slight but unmistakable change of tone. In a fortnight's time Jane was to stay with this good friend at Ibthrop, and Martha had evidently suggested that to help pass the time, Jane should bring with her a good store of books.

> You distress me cruelly by your request about books; I cannot think of any to bring with me, nor have I any idea of our wanting them. I come to you to be talked to, not to read or hear reading, I can do that at home; and indeed I am now laying in a stock of intelligence to pour out on you as my share of the conversation. I am reading Henry's *History of England*, which I will repeat to you in any manner you may prefer, either in a loose, desultory, unconnected stream, or dividing my recital as the historian divides it himself, into seven parts:— The Civil & Military: Religion: Constitution: Learning and Learned Men: Arts & Sciences: Commerce, Coins, and Shipping: and Manners. So that for every evening in the week there will be a different subject. The Friday's lot—Commerce, Coins, and Shipping—you will find the least entertaining; but the next evening's portion will make amends. With such a provision on my part, if you will do yours by repeating the French Grammar, and Mrs Stent will now and then ejaculate some wonder about the cocks and hens, what can we want?"[86]

It is difficult to believe that, as well as Miss Milles who appears in the letters later, Miss Bates of *Emma* owes nothing to Mrs Stent, who in straitened circumstances and considered somewhat socially inferior, lived with Martha's mother until her death. There are other references to her:

"I have been here ever since a quarter after three on

thursday last, by the Shrewsbury Clock, which I am fortunately enabled absolutely to ascertain, because Mrs. Stent once lived at Shrewsbury, or at least at Tewkesbury."[87]

"Poor Mrs Stent! it has been her lot to be always in the way; but we must be merciful, for perhaps in time we may come to be Mrs Stents ourselves, unequal to anything & unwelcome to everybody."[88]

Charles had confirmed the rumour they had heard that his commander, Sir Thomas Williams was thinking of a second marriage. He was soon, in fact, to marry Miss Emma Wapshire of Salisbury where she had been "for many years a distinguished beauty.—She is now seven or eight & twenty, and tho' still handsome less handsome than she has been. This promises better than the bloom of seventeen"[89]—a description that brings to mind Miss Anne Elliot as she appears in the early pages of *Persuasion*.

Both Jane and Martha had been invited to the ball given at Hurstbourne Park to celebrate the third anniversary of his wedding by the Earl of Portsmouth, another past pupil of Mr Austen's. This was described to Cassandra in some detail the next week. Jane was particularly pleased that Charles had arrived home in time to attend, danced the whole evening without fatigue, and was very relieved at not finding there Miss Terry, a former friend to whom he was now perfectly indifferent. During his last voyage, he had distinguished himself by putting out to sea, with only four others and in a violent gale to board the surrendered *Scipio*. He was now looking forward cheerfully to some prize money.

"There were but fifty people in the room; very few families indeed from our side of the county, & not many more from the other. . . . There were very few beauties, & such as there were were not very handsome. Miss Iremonger did not look well, & Mrs. Blount was the only one much admired. She appeared exactly as she did in September, with the same broad face, diamond bandeau, white shoes, pink husband, & fat neck."[90]

One wonders whether the other dancers had any idea that they were under such close and critical scrutiny, about to be preserved for posterity as vividly as bystanders today may unsuspectingly be captured by a stranger's camera.

A few days later, Jane spent a pleasant day at Ashe: "we sat down 14 to dinner in the study, the dining room being not habitable from the Storm's having blown down it's chimney. Mrs. Bramston talked a good deal of nonsense, which

Mr. Bramston and Mr. Clerk seemed almost equally to enjoy.—
There was a whist & a casino table, & six outsiders. Rice &
Lucy made love. Mat: Robinson fell asleep, James & Mrs.
Augusta alternately read Dr. Jenner's pamphlet on the cow
pox, & I bestowed my company by turns on all."[91]

Work was still going on in the garden, fruit trees were
being planted, and a new plan had been suggested for the
plantation on the right side of the elm walk. There was some
debate as to whether more fruit trees, or larch, mountain ash,
and acacia should be planted.

On 30th November, Jane was writing from Ibthrop to her
sister, who was still at Godmersham.

My Journey was safe & not unpleasant;—I spent an hour in
Andover, of which Messrs Painter & Pridding had the larger
part:—twenty minutes however fell to the lot of Mrs. Poore
& her mother, whom I was glad to see in good looks & spirits.—
The latter asked me more questions than I had very well time
to answer; the former I beleive is very big; but I am by no
means certain;—she is either very big or not at all big,
I forgot to be accurate in my observation at the time, & tho'
my thoughts are now more about me on the subject, the power
of exercising them to any effect is much diminished.[92]

It can only seem strange today that in 1932, such a writer
as E. M. Forster should have seen in this innocent, comic
passage a deplorable lapse of taste in Jane's comments on
expectant motherhood.[93]

There had been heartsearchings about some material which
Cassandra had bought in London for gowns both for herself
and her sister. Jane had liked it, but her mother thought it
very ugly, and Cassandra herself had soon begun to have
doubts: "Your abuse of our gowns amuses but does not dis-
courage me; I shall take mine to be made up next week, and
the more I look at it, the better it pleases me."[94] Jane's faith
was rewarded as Miss Summers, the local dressmaker, made a
good job of it: "I get more and more pleased with it. Charles
does not like it, but my father and Mary do. My mother is
very much resigned to it; and as for James, he gives it the
preference over everything of the kind he ever saw, in proof
of which I am desired to say that if you like to sell yours
Mary will buy it."[95]

Before long, Charles too was converted, and now Martha
had the opportunity of seeing it: "*She* is pleased with my
Gown, & particularly bids me say that if you could see me in

it for five minutes, she is sure you would be eager to make up your own.—I have been obliged to mention this, but have not failed to blush the whole time of my writing it."[96]

The gay and amusing letter written from Ibthrop on 30th November 1800 marks the end of an era in the life of Jane Austen. When she wrote it, she was established and contented in a familiar and happy routine. She had a home she loved, many good friends about her, her own family extending and developing, and the regular round of events which marked each passing year. She had not yet married as was expected of her, but she was only just twenty-five and there was still time. Her mother sometimes irritated her, but she had patience enough, and there was always Cassandra to share a laugh with. She was talented and appreciated, and although she had not yet achieved publication, she had written three novels which she very well knew were far above the usual productions of the day. She had an inner stability; a calm, serene confidence; and it may even have been that she was in love.

When she returned to Steventon, Martha was to go with her, ". . . our plan is to have a nice black frost for walking to Whitechurch, & there throw ourselves into a postchaise, one upon the other, our heads hanging out at one door, & our feet at the opposite."[97] It seems unlikely that they travelled in this manner, but within the next few days, the two young women went back to Steventon together. As always, Jane was delighted to be home, and gazed contentedly about the familiar scene. It was then that the bombshell exploded, and without preamble, her mother announced, "Well girls, it is all settled; we have decided to leave Steventon, and go to Bath."[98] Quite uncharacteristically, Jane fainted away.

Although her father was now nearly seventy, there was no real need for him, with James nearby, to go into retirement, and there was every reason for Jane's surprise, especially in view of the recent work of improving the Rectory garden, which gives the impression of a tenant envisaging a further lengthy residence. She had never really liked Bath, and her attachment to her birthplace, and to the friends she had known for most of her life, was exceedingly strong.

Apart from the reported fainting fit, there is no direct reaction from Jane to this sudden change, simply because no letter exists from her between 30th November and 3rd January of the new year. That letters there were is certain, as Cassandra was away for the whole of this period, which included Christmas. It can only be concluded that in her correspondence at this time, Jane gave expression to thoughts that Cassandra considered it wisest to conceal. By 3rd January, she had regained her equilibrium, and was managing to view the prospect, if not with enthusiasm, with resignation.

As everyone knows, unexpected news of a move can be upsetting. But a faint is an extreme reaction, particularly in such a controlled and well balanced personality as Jane Austen's. She was not given to fainting, and in fact had often made fun of it. In her case, it is no exaggeration to see evidence of severe emotional disturbance, and to wonder whether Jane was about to be snatched away from some still unresolved and unrequited love.

A careful examination of references in her letters to her lists of dancing partners is unrewarding. But in the *Life* written by her great nephew and his son, there is a hint, which is promptly dismissed, and may yet be significant. "So hasty, indeed, did Mr Austen's decision appear to the Perrots that they suspected the reason to be a growing attachment between Jane and one of the three Digweed brothers."[99]

The Digweed brothers with whom the Austens were so friendly were all living at home at the time at Steventon Manor House. Mr Hugh Digweed, their father, had died in 1798; Harry, who was four years older than Jane, and William, who was probably a year or two younger, were tenants in common of the manor, until eight years later, Harry married and went to live at Alton. The Reverend James, who was about to spend some time in Kent, eventually settled near to home at Dummer, and married in 1803. Very recently, Jane had suggested that James must be in love with her sister, since he had expressed the romantic notion that the two great elms had fallen from grief at her absence. There are only passing references to these brothers in Jane's letters, and little that would suggest she had a special interest in any of them. The most likely contender for her affections was probably Harry, and in her letter written on 24th October 1798, when describing the loss of her writing box, she mentions that among other treasures, it contained "my dear Harry's deputation". This was apparently a request to his brother James. Even though Jane was a reticent person, it is little enough to go on, and it is also hard to see what the Austens would have found objectionable in the match, unless they feared that their fortuneless daughter's love could never in this case lead to marriage. But that Jane was distressed at leaving someone she loved, or an un-

(*Above left*) A miniature of the Rev. George Austen, Jane's father, 1801.
(*above right*) Silhouette of Mrs. George Austen, Jane's mother.
(*below left*) The Rev. James Austen, Jane's eldest brother.
(*below right*) Silhouette of Cassandra Austen, Jane's beloved sister

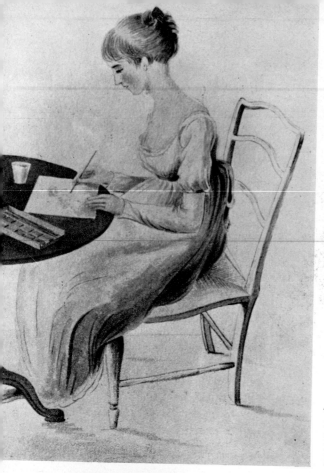

(*left*) Water colour sketch of Jane's favourite niece, Fanny Knight, by Cassandra Austen

(*below left*) Eliza Hancock, Comtesse de Feuillide, later wife of Jane's brother, Henry Austen. (*below right*) Henry Austen, Jane's favourite brother and literary adviser

completed relationship, behind her in Steventon, must remain a possibility.

In any case, there can be no doubt that her parents' sudden decision at the end of 1800 to uproot her from the life she knew and loved, heralded the beginning of what must often have seemed to Jane Austen, no matter how cheerfully she appeared to put up with it, like eight years of wandering in a wilderness.

F

THREE

A Time of Disappointment

Early in the New Year of 1801, Jane Austen had come to terms with the proposed move. She was a sensible woman, there was nothing she could do about it, and she did not long repine. Yet, as it will be seen, for the next few years, there is a shift in key. Company, for example, is no longer so agreeable to her, and the fun she makes of people is tinged with bitterness. One feels she is aware of being gradually but inexorably, pushed to the fringe of the social scene.

Evidently, her mother was enjoying the contemplation of her change of circumstances: "My mother looks forward with as much certainty as you can do to our keeping two maids; my father is the only one not in the secret. We plan having a steady cook, and a young giddy housemaid, with a sedate, middle-aged man, who is to undertake the double office of husband to the former and sweetheart to the latter.—No children, of course, to be allowed on either side."[1]

The discussion, which was to go on for some months, of the pros and cons of various houses and streets in Bath had already begun, and they began to think about what they should take of their lifelong home. Impractically enough, the first items to be considered seem to have been the pictures, most of which it was decided, to leave *in situ* for James. Their beds, particularly the Austens' indispensable matrimonial couch, were to go with them. Most other items, including the library, were to be sold. Mr Austen was doing all he could to start his life in retirement with an adequate income, and "nearly six hundred a year"[2] was the figure mentioned.

"I get more and more reconciled to the idea of our removal", Jane writes. "We have lived long enough in this neighbourhood, the Basingstoke balls are certainly on the decline, there is something interesting in the bustle of going away, and the prospect of spending future summers by the Sea or in Wales is very delightful. . . ."[3]

Martha Lloyd, who was a great help to Jane in getting the books ready to sell, was to return home to Ibthrop with her sister on 13th January for the celebration of James and Mary's wedding anniversary. "I was asked, but declined it.— Eliza has seen Lord Craven at Barton, and probably by this time at Kintbury, where he was expected for one day this week. She found his manners very pleasing indeed. The little flaw of having a mistress now living with him at Ashdown Park seems to be the only unpleasing circumstance about him."[4]

As the days went by, the unsettlement and excitement increased. The house was being decorated for its new inmates, and there were visits to and from the Steventon neighbours. Jane talks of days of dissipation. . . . "Hardly a day passes in which we do not have some visitor or other; yesterday came Mrs. Bramstone, who is very sorry that she is to lose us, and afterwards Mr. Holder, who was shut up for an hour with my father & James in a most awful manner. John Bond *est à lui*. Mr. Holder was perfectly willing to take him on exactly the same terms with my father, and John seems exceedingly well satisfied."[5] Jane would have been happier if her father's faithful bailiff had gone to work for Harry Digweed, who was prepared to offer him the post.

The general air of change and bustle apparently suited Mrs George Austen who had "not been so well for many months as she is now".[6]

After her long stay at Godmersham, before returning to take farewell of her home, Cassandra went up to London to spend a few weeks with Henry and Eliza. Henry had visited Steventon in January, and Jane had found him "as agreeable as ever".[7]

Perhaps because of his wife's ill health and loneliness, Henry had resigned from the Army, and although they had toyed with the idea of also resigning the world and retiring to Wales, they were now living "quite in style", with a French chef and their own carriage in Upper Berkeley Street. Eliza's son, Hastings, now nearly fifteen, was in rapidly failing health, and in October 1801 he died.

Henry had also caused his frail wife a good deal of anxiety. In answer to a letter of condolence from her cousin Philadelphia, Eliza writes:

In addition to my affliction on poor Hastings' account, I have undergone much anxiety concerning Henry, who for five months never enjoyed an hour's health. His complaints were a cough, hectic pain in the side and in short everything which denotes a galloping consumption in which I believe all his acquaintance thought him. At length a prescription of Dr Baillie's (who had already tried a variety of medicines to no purpose) removed some of the above symptoms, & from that time he has mended so fast that he is nearly as well as I had always known him to be previous to this attack.[8]

It appears that since the death of her first husband, Eliza had been hoping one day to recover some of his wealth, and during the brief Peace of Amiens, some time during 1802–3, she and Henry were to travel to France to see what might be done. But the treaty was broken while they were there, and it was only Eliza's perfect mastery of spoken French that enabled them to escape detention and to get safely back home. It had been a fruitless quest, which they were never to attempt again.

After he left the Army, Henry, who was nothing if not versatile, interested himself in finance, and by 1806 he was to become a partner in Austen, Maude, and Tilson, bankers of 10 Henrietta Street; he later extended his activities to a branch at Alton.

While Cassandra was busy in London, no doubt shopping and, as her sister directed, seeing "everything worthy notice, from the Opera House to Henry's office in Cleveland Court;"[9] —Jane and her mother were spending a few days at Manydown. Time was running out when the family was reunited at Steventon, and the next two months must have been busy ones, with farewell visits from Edward and his wife, and with extraordinarily good timing from the sailor brothers.

Before the Austens left Steventon, news began to arrive about Nelson's victory at Copenhagen, when although the opposition was so formidable, putting his telescope to his blind eye, he chose to ignore the signal to withdraw, and went on virtually to destroy the hostile Danish navy. He accomplished this great feat, which has been described as the most testing action of his career, in a ship called the *Elephant*, which Frank himself was later to command and which, with his permission, was to have the additional honour of a mention in his sister's novel *Mansfield Park*.

Jane's feelings, when the time came for the final wrench of departure can perhaps best be imagined from the words she gave to Marianne Dashwood on leaving Norland : high flown and exaggerated, as befits this particularly romantic heroine, and yet expressing some of the genuine emotion and regret that she herself must have felt on leaving her only and much loved home:

Oh! happy house, could you know what I suffer in now viewing you from this spot, from whence perhaps I may view you no more! And you, ye well known trees.—but you will continue the same.—No leaf will decay because we are removed, nor any branch become motionless although we can observe you no longer!—No; you will continue the same; unconscious of the pleasure or the regret you occasion, and insensible of any change in those who walk under your shade! But who will remain to enjoy you?[10]

Leaving Cassandra behind at Ibthrop, and Mr Austen about to set forth on a trip to Kent, the advance party of Mrs Austen and her younger daughter arrived at No 1 The Paragon early in May. They were kindly received both by the Leigh Perrots and their servants, and Jane had the delight of her "own room up two pairs of stairs, with everything very comfortable about me".[11]

For once, Jane had entered Bath in fine weather, but it does not seem to have pleased her any the more for that. "The first view of Bath in fine weather does not answer my expectations; I think I see more distinctly through rain. The sun was got behind everything, and the appearance of the place from the top of Kingsdown was all vapour, shadow, smoke, and confusion."[12] Jane's shortsightedness perhaps had something to do with this blurred Turneresque impression of the town's crisp terraces.

Househunting began immediately, but an attractive house in Green Park Buildings, after a good deal of consideration, had to be rejected because of the damp. As usual, in such cases, the sale of their effects gave rise to some pleasant surprises and some disappointments. "Sixty-one guineas & a half for the three cows gives one some support under the blow of only eleven guineas for the tables. Eight for my pianoforte is about what I really expected to get; I am more anxious to know the amount of my books, especially as they are said to have sold well."[13] In fact, although some good prices were obtained, more than 500 volumes were sold for approximately £70.

On 11th May, Jane attended a disappointing ball.

Think of four couple, surrounded by about an hundred people, dancing in the Upper Rooms at Bath!—After tea we *cheered up*; the breaking up of private parties sent some scores more to the Ball, & tho' it was shockingly & inhumanly thin for this place, there were people enough I suppose to have made five or six very pretty Basingstoke assemblies.—I then got Mr Evelyn to talk to, & Miss Twisleton to look at; and I am proud to say that I have a very good eye at an Adultress, for tho' repeatedly assured that another in the same party was the *She*, I fixed upon the right one from the first.[14]

The object of Miss Twisleton's indiscretion was Mr Evelyn. But this did not prevent the ladies giving him groundsel for his birds, nor Jane from going in his "bewitching phaeton & four" for a very pleasant drive with him.

This affair was followed by a stupid card party. "I cannot anyhow continue to find people agreeable", Jane grumbles, "I respect Mrs. Chamberlayne for doing her hair well, but cannot feel a more tender sentiment. Miss Langley is like any other short girl with a broad nose and wide mouth, fashionable dress, and exposed bosom.—Adm. Stanhope is a gentlemanlike man, but then his legs are too short and his tail too long."[15]

When Jane wrote again to her sister on 21st May, arrangements had been made for Mr Austen to collect his elder daughter from Kintbury, where she was now staying with Eliza and Fulwar Fowle, and for the two of them to travel together to Bath to rejoin the rest of the family on 1st June. Jane gives a lively account of a walk she had enjoyed with Mrs Chamberlayne: "climbing a hill Mrs. Chamberlayne is very capital; I could with difficulty keep pace with her, yet would not flinch for the world. On plain ground I was quite her equal. And so we posted away under a fine hot sun, *she* without any parasol or any shade to her hat, stopping for nothing, and crossing the churchyard at Weston with as much expedition as if we were afraid of being buried alive."[16]

More houses had been viewed, this time in New King Street: "They were smaller than I expected to find them; one in particular out of the two was quite monstrously little; the best of the sitting rooms not so large as the little parlour at Steventon, and the second room in every floor about capacious enough to admit a very small single bed."[17]

The social round continued, this time with a tiny party. "I hate tiny parties, they force one into constant exertion. Miss Edwards & her father, Mrs. Busby & her nephew, Mr. Maitland, and Mrs. Lillingstone are to be the whole; and I am prevented from setting my black cap at Mr. Maitland by his having a wife and ten children."[18] The ten children proved an exaggeration, and Jane later admitted they were only three, but Mr Maitland remained equally unattainable.

There had been a second walking contest with Mrs Chamberlayne, in which this time, Jane seems to have been the winner, ". . . for many, many yards together on a raised narrow footpath I led the way.—The walk was very beautiful as my companion agreed, whenever I made the observation— And so ends our friendship, for the Chamberlaynes leave Bath in a day or two."[19] Possibly one of the disadvantages of Bath as a place of permanent residence was that friends once made were so often moving away.

Unfortunately, Marianne Mapleton, one of the three daughters of the successful Bath physician whom Jane and Cassandra had met on previous visits to Bath, had died a few days earlier. Jane called on her sisters, Jane and Christiana, and "sat with them about ten minutes.—They looked pale & dejected, but were more composed than I had thought probable. —When I mentioned your coming here on Monday, they said they should be very glad to see you."[20]

A tentative friendship was in progress with the widowed sister-in-law of Mr Holder of Ashe Park and her daughter, who had the merit of owning she had no taste for music. "Miss Holder & I adjourned after tea into the inner Drawing room to look over Prints & talk pathetically. . . . She has an idea of your being remarkably lively; therefore get ready the proper selection of adverbs, & due scraps of Italian & French."[21]

A letter had been received from Charles, who had been spending some of his £40 prize money on gold chains and a pair of attractive topaz crosses for his sisters, a generous action commemorated forever in the similar kindness of William Price to his sister Fanny in *Mansfield Park*. Jane pretended to scold him for such extravagance, but "We shall be unbearably fine", she wrote proudly."[22]

As always after a separation, she was beginning to look forward to her sister's return, making plans for engagements, and the dressmaker, Mrs Mussell. "She made my dark gown very well & may therefore be trusted I hope with yours." But Jane reminds us that dressmaking then, as now, was a hazardous business, "she does not always succeed with lighter colours.—My white one I was obliged to alter a good deal."[23]

At this point, once more Jane's letters are interrupted, and there is a silence that lasts for more than three years. It appears that the family was reunited as planned and that before moving into a home together in Bath, they carried out their intention of spending the holiday in Devonshire which they had all anticipated with so much pleasure. The event is confirmed by a letter from Eliza on 29th October 1801: "I conclude that you know of our uncle & aunt Austen & their daughters having spent the summer in Devonshire. They are now returned to Bath where they are superintending the fitting up of their new house."[24]

It seems that the summer of 1801 was spent at Sidmouth, and that of 1802 at Teignmouth. According to family tradition, during one of these holidays, Jane Austen fell deeply in love more or less at first sight, with an extremely charming young clergyman who has never been satisfactorily identified. Although he returned her feelings, and arrangements had been made to the great pleasure of her parents, for them to meet again, before this could take place, Jane received the tragic news that, just like Cassandra's fiancé, the man she loved had suddenly died.

The story has been related in various versions, in the *Memoir* by her nephew; by her niece Caroline; by Mrs Bellas, the daughter of her niece Anna; by Frank's daughter, Mrs Catherine Hubback. The details vary, but the substance remains much the same. In each case, the source of the story must have been Cassandra, who was a woman of utter integrity. It may well have been true, or it may have been Cassandra's way—without revealing any biographical particulars—of emphasising what it is hard to doubt, that her talented sister had herself been in love, that she had been able to draw on experience as well as imagination for her descriptions of the states of falling and being in love. Certainly one strives to find some explanation for Jane's change of tone in the second half of her twenties, and for the long period in which she apparently lost the will or the energy to continue her creative writing at the level she previously and subsequently maintained.

This shadowy lover supplies a convenient key to the mystery, and yet the subtle but quite perceptible change had already taken place in the letters which follow the news of the move from Steventon, and before the holiday in Devon. If only there were some letters existing from this period, the course of Jane Austen's self-contained emotions might have been less difficult to track, but it is September 1804 before we hear from her directly again.

Fortunately, Mrs James Austen passed on to her family the details of a revealing incident which took place in 1802. By this time, the Austens had settled into their own Bath home at 4 Sydney Place, which can still be seen, and is in a dignified four-storied terrace, very conveniently situated, at that time on the edge of town, and opposite the Sydney Gardens. Pulteney Street, a broad level thoroughfare, led to Laura Place, and the attractive shop-lined Pulteney Bridge, the far side of which emerges directly into the busy centre of the city, near the Guildhall, the Abbey, and the Pump Rooms.

By the early summer of 1802, the Austens must have been comfortably settled in their new home, and they set off on their travels once more. This year, they stayed at Dawlish and Teignmouth. Then, while their parents returned to Bath, the two young women went on to their old home at Steventon. It must have seemed a very different place to them already, under the charge of Mrs James, with her stepdaughter Anna, now a bright and sometimes difficult girl of nine, and her own four-year-old son, James Edward.

After a couple of days, they left to spend a month with Edward and his family in Kent, returning again to Steventon on 28th October. No doubt one of the pleasures of this visit was to be seeing old friends, and a stay had been arranged with the Bigg-Wither family at Manydown, to commence on 25th November. Jane and Cassandra duly departed, but to Mary's astonishment, and probably annoyance, by 3rd December, unexpectedly, they were back again. They had travelled in the Bigg-Wither's carriage, accompanied it seems by all three sisters who had been home together at the time to receive their visitors—Elizabeth Heathcote's husband having died in the March of that same year at the age of thirty, after only four years of marriage.

The young women alighted, highly emotional farewells were said, and the carriage quickly drove off again, leaving the Austen sisters in a state of great agitation, with Jane on the verge of tears, to face the bewildered Mrs James. Without explanation, they insisted that their brother must escort them home the next day, which was a Saturday, in spite of the inconvenience this would obviously cause him. Naturally enough James tried to persuade them to wait until after the weekend, so that he could carry out his Sunday duties as usual. But for once, these two young women, whose entire lives had been spent in suiting other people's arrangements and fitting in, were adamant, and James could do no less than take his sisters home as they asked.

It was some while later before the reason was given for this strange behaviour. Young Harris Bigg-Wither had proposed to Jane and she had accepted him.

On the face of it, her acceptance was natural and sensible. She would soon be twenty-seven years of age, and such emotional attachments as she may have had, had failed to result in marriage. Harris was a promising young man of twenty-one, and his father's heir. His sisters were among the best and most affectionate of her friends, and she had known and enjoyed visiting the handsome Manydown house, situated in the part of the country she regarded as home, since her girlhood. For a young woman in Jane Austen's financial position, the opportunity of marriage, motherhood, and eventually becoming the mistress of such an establishment, where one day she might be able to offer her sister a comfortable home, was not an offer to be turned down lightly.

But Harris himself had clearly failed to make any impression on Jane, however much she herself had succeeded in attracting him. There are only a few passing references to him in the letters and he appears as a purely incidental figure, not in the best of health. It cannot be known whether Jane was unprepared for his proposal and accepted out of surprise and embarrassment, or whether she had recognized he was gathering courage to make it and had managed to convince herself that it was in everyone's best interests for her to say yes. No doubt the family were told the happy news, Harris's father and sisters were delighted, and Jane departed to bed amid universal rejoicing, only to ponder with increasing panic on the serious step she had taken.

But it was not yet irrevocable, and as the sleepless night dragged by, in the battleground of Jane's heart and mind, sense was totally defeated by sensibility. She did not love Harris Bigg-Wither and she could not marry him. It was as simple as that.

The certainty that she had now come to the right decision did not make the inevitably distressing scene in the morning any easier. Whether or not he was truly in love with her, Harris's hopes had been dashed from joy to dismay overnight. Miserable and hurt, he may also have felt he had been made to look ridiculous. The rest of the family was sorry for Harris, and surprised and disappointed by Jane's sudden and determined change of mind. No wonder she wanted to depart from the scene with all possible haste. Her momentary weakness and self-betrayal which involved upsetting a family she loved and respected, must have shamed and grieved her. She knew she was acting rightly and in the only way possible for her, but as her niece Caroline was later to remark with justification, "most young women so circumstanced would have gone on trusting to love after marriage".[25]

Harris's name does not occur again in the letters, and two years later he married a girl called Anne Frith and founded a family. To Jane's relief and gratitude, and to their credit, his sisters proved understanding as well as affectionate, and their friendship continued unimpaired to the end.

It was in the spring of 1803, that Jane Austen made her second attempt at publication. The book she offered was her original version of *Northanger Abbey*, at this time entitled *Susan*. She may have chosen it in preference to her two other novels because she was already aware that its topicality was likely to diminish, or because her present residence in Bath had given her the impetus to complete it. On her behalf, a Mr Seymour, an employeee of Henry Austen's, wrote to Messrs Crosby and Co. of London, and Jane must have been pleased and elated when she received an acceptance and a modest payment of £10. It was the first sum of money she had earned in her life, and it encouraged her confident belief that her work deserved publication. Most writers will agree that nothing has such a tonic effect as that first fee. The book was duly advertised as *Susan: a novel in two volumes*, but it never appeared. The strangest thing about this episode is that neither Jane nor her brother took any further steps about it. Having proceeded so far, it was to be expected, at the very least, they would have continued to make enquiries about the book's progress. But curiously, the matter was allowed to remain in abeyance for the next six years. After success and high hopes, there followed only the frustration of silence.

This second disappointment, together with the upheaval of another move, the anxiety of her father's last illness, and the uncertainty following his death, were no doubt among the reasons why Jane abandoned the new work she had in hand, which is known as *The Watsons*. The opening of the novel exists in the form of a heavily corrected first draft of some 16,000 words on paper bearing a watermark of 1803. By the time she began writing creatively again, her interest in the story had waned, and she was already deeply inspired by the characters and themes of her next great work, *Mansfield Park*.

Mrs Q. D. Leavis believes that much of the material from *The Watsons* was reshaped and incorporated into *Emma*.[26] The strongest argument against this theory seems to be the striking difference in the feeling and aim of these two works. As H. W. Garrod has strenuously asserted, it is true that there is a strong similarity in the broad outline of all Jane Austen's plots.[27] But there is a very distinctive difference between what might be described as the essential atmosphere of each of the novels, and this is particularly marked in *The Watsons*. Elizabeth Jenkins has defined it as "painful" and "too near to morbidness";[28] Mary Lascelles speaks of "a peculiar oppression",[29] and there is such a sense of the crowding of uncongenial characters into the small house at Stanton, that we are glad to escape with Emma to the peace and quiet of her widowed father's sickroom upstairs. Nothing resembling this appears in *Emma*.

As in all her works, in *The Watsons*, Jane Austen had something particular to say, and with her habit of working on the same novel over a very long period, had she lived, it is possible that her interest might have sufficiently revived to bring it eventually to a conclusion.

Like that of *Sanditon*, the manuscript of *The Watsons* has the fascination and importance of showing Jane Austen, the writer, at work on her revisions, cropping, for example, "her account of the Edwards' house of its minute particulars". Dr Chapman says, "she knows all the details, and gives us very few of them".[30] It also demonstrates the revisions necessary to produce the right tone of voice for each different character. No writer has been more adept than Jane Austen at revealing her characters by means of their own speech, but the individual effects she produced with such apparent ease were the result of much labour.

The Watsons is also important in being the only known original work of this particular period in the life of the author. The very fact that it was not completed tells a good deal of the unsettled, unsatisfactory state in which she found herself at the time. Without recognition for her gifts and achievements, she was still unmarried, unfulfilled, without her own home, with her life entirely governed by the wishes of her parents. No wonder that at the age of twenty-seven, she began to write a realistic and ironic study of women's place in society.

Getting married—its process and mechanics—is a major

theme in all Jane Austen's novels, but nowhere is it considered with more concentration than in the opening scenes of *The Watsons*. The characters and situations of four unmarried sisters and their suitors, and the attitude of their families are minutely examined, and the device of an assembly ball enables the introduction of a broad cross-section of local society.

Having only recently returned home, Emma, the heroine of the novel, is a stranger to the scenes in which she now finds herself, and acts as an observer in somewhat the same position of the reader. From the first, she is subjected to "society's tendency to place a price, quite blatantly and complacently"[31] on the intimate relationship of marriage. There can be little doubt that the need to describe this prevalent social situation came from pressures in Jane Austen's own life, and Emma is justifiably appalled by the attitudes revealed.

Other aspects of the structure and economics of society are also discussed. For example, the crucial point of the hour at which dinner is taken is observed throughout with such irony that it assumes the importance of a symbol, that the firm principles on which a well-regulated society should be based have become subordinate to the inexorable rule of trivial convention. As B. C. Southam has said, these few pages amount to the "most serious and pessimistic view of society to be found in all Jane Austen's work".[32]

As in the case of the intriguingly unfinished *Edwin Drood*, one or two continuations of this novel have been published. Clearly no-one can be sure through what events and turns of the plot Jane Austen would have proceeded to relate her story. But according to family tradition, in spite of the prevailing pessimism, *The Watsons* was to end in a happy marriage.

After their removal to Bath, neither George Austen nor his wife seems to have enjoyed good health. George Austen became the subject of attacks of "an oppression in the head, with fever, violent tremulousness, and the greatest degree of Feebleness",[33] while Mrs Austen has left some verses to mark the happy conclusion of her own serious illness.

Says Death, "I've been trying these three weeks and more
To seize on old Madam here at Number Four,
Yet I still try in vain, tho' she's turned of three score;
     To what is my ill-success owing?"

"I'll tell you, old Fellow, if you cannot guess,
To what you're indebted for your ill success—

To the prayers of my husband, whose love I possess,
To the care of my daughters, whom Heaven will bless,
To the skill and attention of Bowen."[34]

Happily however, this did not prevent the seaside trips they had planned being made. It seems that in 1803, Jane travelled the considerable distance to Ramsgate, probably taking in Godmersham on her way.

At this time, Frank, who during the Peace of Amiens had been on half pay, was based at Ramsgate employed on raising a corps of "sea-fencibles", a kind of naval home guard drawn from the Kentish fishermen, to help protect the coast against the threatened invasion. With her brother taking a vigorous part, Jane Austen must have been a well informed observer of the preparations for the new national emergency.

Frank himself was glad to be active again, and it was during this spell of duty at Ramsgate that he met and fell in love with Mary Gibson, whom he was to make his wife in July 1806. Although Jane, Cassandra, and their mother were to grow fond of Mary, Frank's romance was a disappointment to them all. For many years, they had hoped that Frank would marry and fully enrol as a member of the family, their best loved friend, the elegant Martha Lloyd. In fact, more than twenty years later, Frank and Martha were to marry, when he was a widower, and Jane had long ago been dead. She would have been glad to know that, after all, Martha was to find happiness and share the honours of his knighthood with her successful brother, who was to end his long career as Queen Victoria's Admiral of the Fleet.

In 1804, Frank was given command of first the *Leopard*, and then the *Canopus*, serving under Nelson in the Mediterranean in the long and crucial period of the blockade of French shipping which ended in Nelson's tragic death at the great victory of Trafalgar and was utterly to destroy Napoleon's plans for the destruction of the navy and the invasion of Britain.

After Jane's visit to Kent, it appears she joined her parents and Cassandra in a late autumn holiday in Lyme Regis. Evidently this was a success, since it was to be repeated the following year in the company of Henry and Eliza.

Dr Chapman approximately dates the 1803 visit from Jane's later reference to a fire which is known to have occurred on 5th November, no doubt the result of an over-enthusiastic Guy Fawkes night. The famous excursion of the party from Uppercross to Lyme Regis, which provides one of the best known passages of *Persuasion* took place in November, and when Jane Austen described it, she was clearly drawing on her own memories of the town at the same season.

They were come too late in the year for any amusement or variety which Lyme, as a public place, might offer; the rooms were shut up, the lodgers almost all gone, scarcely any family but of the residents left—and, as there is nothing to admire in the buildings themselves, the remarkable situation of the town, the principal street almost hurrying into the water, the walk to the Cobb, skirting round the pleasant little bay, which in the season is animated with bathing machines and company, the Cobb itself, its old wonders and new improvements, with the very beautiful line of cliffs stretching out to the east of the town, are what the stranger's eye will seek.[35]

The next year's holiday at Lyme with Henry and Eliza must have been a happy one, as a year later Henry was still talking of "the rambles we took together last Summer with pleasing affection".[36] But by the time Jane writes on 14th September 1804 she was alone with her parents. Henry and Eliza had departed, taking Cassandra with them on her way to Ibthrop, where old Mrs Lloyd was very ill.

The depleted party had evidently changed lodgings, and Jane was in charge of the new situation. "I endeavour as far as I can to supply your place & be useful, & keep things in order. I detect dirt in the water-decanter as fast as I can & give the Cook physic which she throws off her stomach. I forget whether she used to do this under your administration. James is the delight of our lives, he is quite an Uncle Toby's annuity to us. My mother's shoes were never so well blacked before, & our plate never looked so clean."[37]

With her parents, Jane had attended a ball:

Nobody asked me the first two dances; the next two I danced with Mr Crawford, and had I chosen to stay longer might have danced with Mr Granville, Mrs Granville's son, whom my dear friend Miss Armstrong offered to introduce to me, or with a new odd-looking man who had been eyeing me for some time, and at last, without any introduction, asked me if I meant to dance again. I think he must be Irish by his ease, and because I imagine him to belong to the noble Barnwalls, who are the son, and son's wife of an Irish viscount, bold queer-looking people, just fit to be quality at Lyme.[38]

The letter ends with an addition after the signature, which shows Jane was enjoying the bathing, and taking a kindly, educational interest in that efficient servant, James:

The bathing was so delightful this morning & Molly so pressing with me to enjoy myself that I believe I staid in rather too long, as since the middle of the day I have felt unreasonably tired. I shall be more careful another time, & shall not bathe tomorrow as I had before intended. Jenny & James are walked to Charmouth this afternoon. I am glad to have such an amusement for him, as I am very anxious for his being at once quiet and happy. He can read, & I must get him some books.[39]

The low rent at 4 Sydney Place had been dependent on the very short lease, and by the summer of 1804, this had expired. In her letter from Lyme, Jane mentions already the new tenants, the Coles "have got their infamous plate upon our door".[40]

The Austens returned to Bath to a new house in Green Park Buildings—not one of the damp and "putrifying Houses" they had viewed three years before, but to No 27 on the western side of the little park, a handsome house with a balcony, and views of the river and the open country. Unfortunately their sojourn in this pleasant part of the city was to be neither long nor happy.

The first blow fell when they received the news that on Jane's birthday, 16th December 1804, their old and much loved friend, Mrs Lefroy, had been killed by a fall from her horse. There is no record of Jane's feelings at the time, but their depth may judged by the lines she was to write on the anniversary four years later:

The day returns again, my natal day;
What mix'd emotions in my mind arise!
Beloved Friend: four years have passed away
Since thou were snatched for ever from our eyes.[41]

Mrs Lefroy's death was to be followed just over a month later by a severer sorrow.

On the morning of Saturday 19th January 1805, Mr George Austen had a recurrence of one of his feverish attacks. When all was over, Jane described the course of their father's brief fatal illness and the family's reaction to it in a letter to her brother Frank, whose ship the *Leopard* she believed to be at Dungeness:

Heavy as is the blow, we can already feel that a thousand comforts remain to us to soften it. Next to that of the consciousness of his worth & constant preparation for another World, is the remembrance of his having suffered, comparatively speaking, nothing. Being quite insensible of his own state, he was spared all the pain of separation, & he went off almost in his Sleep.—My Mother bears the shock as well as possible; she was quite prepared for it, & feels all the blessing of his being spared a long illness. My Uncle and Aunt have been with us, and show us every imaginable kindness. And tomorrow we shall I dare say have the comfort of James's presence, as an express has been sent to him.[42]

The next day, Jane learned that Frank was already at Portsmouth, and so that he should have the sad news without delay, she sent him a second, similar letter, in which she also speaks of the serenity of her father's expression, still with the "sweet benevolent smile which always distinguished him".[43] By this time, James was with them and the funeral had been arranged at Walcot Church near the Paragon, where forty years before George and Cassandra Austen had been married. The memorial in the crypt of the church records: "Under this stone rest the remains of the Rev. George Austen, Rector of Steventon and Dean in Hampshire—who departed this life the 21st of January, 1805, aged 73 years."

Henry had travelled down from London to attend the ceremony, and the first concern of the two brothers had been the future financial situation of what Henry described as their "dear trio". In a letter to Frank, the banker set out the figures. James had offered fifty pounds a year, and Henry himself was to contribute the same figure "so long as my present precarious income remains",[44] the wealthy Edward was expected, at least, to provide a further hundred. Mrs Austen and Cassandra had small incomes of their own amounting to about an annual £210. Frank came forward with a generous offer, considering his circumstances, of another £100 a year, of which his grateful mother would only agree to accept half. In all, the three women were to be in receipt of a "clear 450 pounds per ann.—She will be very comfortable, & as a smaller establishment will be as agreeable to them, as it cannot but be feasible, I really think that My Mother & sisters will be to the full as rich as ever. They will not only suffer no personal deprivation, but will be able to pay occasional visits of health and pleasure to their friends."[45]

G

Jane would never, of course, have seen this letter, but no doubt Henry held forth to his mother and sisters in much the same vein. If this has an uncomfortably familiar ring to readers of *Sense and Sensibility*, Henry was never to notice.

In fact the boys proved affectionate and generous sons, only Charles not being in a position to help. Nevertheless, it cannot be doubted that Jane, who unlike her sister, had nothing of her own to contribute, was sensitively aware of her dependence.

The Green Park Buildings house was theirs until Lady Day, 25th March, and in the meantime, there was the job of tidying up the rest of Mr Austen's affairs, and disposing of his little personal property. A small compass and sundial in a shagreen case, and a pair of scissors, were set aside for Frank.

For both Jane and Cassandra, their father's death represented a significant change in their lives. Their parents had been a devoted couple who enjoyed each other's company. But now Mrs Austen must rely on her daughters for support and companionship. They were three women living on their own in what was very much a man's world. True, they could always call on the brothers for help which they knew would be answered. But from having been accustomed for so long to a predominantly masculine household, from now on their day-to-day round was largely confined to the society of women.

A beautiful day in April finds Jane writing from their new lodgings in 25 Gay Street, the steep slope of which connects The Circus with Queen Square, where they had stayed with Edward and his family six years before. The houses are small and elegant, and the street runs parallel to the fashionable shopping thoroughfare of Milsom Street, situated conveniently near the Assembly Rooms and The Paragon.

"Here is a day for you! Did Bath or Ibthrop ever see a finer 8th of April? It is March & April together, the glare of the one and the warmth of the other. We do nothing but walk about; as far as your means will admit I hope you profit by such weather too. I dare say you are already the better for change of place."[46]

Together with Mrs James Austen, Cassandra was staying with Martha Lloyd, lending her support and presence in the nursing of their mother, who was by now in the final stages of her last illness. Jane appears worried about Cassandra's own health, and it is likely that during this period of their lives, both sisters were subject to occasional spells of tension and depression.

Jane and her mother had been busy with outings and visits, "what request we are in!", and she writes with reflective irony: "This morning we have been to see Miss Chamberlayne look hot on horseback.—Seven years & four months ago we went to the same Ridinghouse to see Miss Lefroy's performance! What a different set we are now moving in! But seven years I suppose are enough to change every pore of one's skin, & every feeling of one's mind."[47]

Newly arrived visitors to Bath were the Bullers from Colyton. Although not yet thirty, the Rev. Richard Buller was in very bad health, and hoped to find a cure in Bath from the waters and the renowned Doctor Bowen: "tho' he is altogether in a more comfortable state as to Spirits and appetite than when I saw him last, & seems equal to a good deal of quiet walking, his appearance has exactly that of a confirmed De-cline."[48] Jane's diagnosis was right, and Mr Austen's affectionate former pupil was to die towards the close of the following year.

A lady applying to Jane for a character for their former servant, Anne, sparks off a comment on contemporary teachers: "Were I going to send a girl to school I would send her to this person; to be rational in anything is great praise, especially in the ignorant class of school mistresses—& she keeps the School in the Upper Crescent."[49]

An affectionate, kind, and entertaining letter had arrived from Henry, and plans were being made for another holiday together on the sea coast.

Jane's next surviving letter, two weeks later, was written after the death of Mrs Lloyd. Martha was now left alone in the world, and it had been decided that she should make her home with the Austens—"our intended Partnership"—as Jane calls it. The Cooke cousins and Mr Hampson had both been in Bath, so she and her mother were busy with relations as well as friends. Somewhat reluctantly, Jane had arranged a little evening party at home for their mother—"I shall be glad when it is over, & hope to have no necessity for having so many dear friends at once again."[50]

In June, good news arrived from Steventon, Mrs James had given birth to a little girl, Caroline. She was to be the last of James's children, as she grew up, an observant affectionate child, with an especial love for her Aunt Jane, cherishing and later recording many still lively memories of her.

During this summer for once Jane and Cassandra were able to get away together, leaving their mother in the capable and

congenial companionship of Martha Lloyd. They spent some
time at Godmersham together, then each sister in turn, first
Cassandra and then Jane, went off for a few days at Goodnestone Farm with Elizabeth's mother, Lady Bridges, and her
daughters.

Elizabeth was in one of her short and surely blessed intervals between her many pregnancies. Her daughter Louisa had
been born the year before, and she and Edward were now the
parents of a thriving family of nine. Much of Jane's visit was
spent with these children, whose company she evidently
enjoyed.

Yesterday was a very quiet day with us; my noisiest efforts
were writing to Frank, & playing at battledore and shuttlecock
with William . . . In the evening we took a quiet walk round
the farm, with George & Henry to animate us by their races
and merriment. Little Edward is by no means better, and his
papa and mamma have determined to consult Dr Wilmot. Unless he recovers his strength beyond what is now probable, his
brothers will return to school without him, and he will be of
the party to Worthing.—[51]

There is no evidence that the Worthing holiday actually
took place, but although it may have been delayed by a trip
to London, there seems no reason to doubt that it did, and that
once again Henry and Eliza were of the company. Perhaps it
was her memories of Worthing and its surrounding districts
that came later to Jane's mind when she began to write
Sanditon.

During what must have been a busy summer social season
Elizabeth was enjoying the luxury of her own hairdresser, Mr
Hall, from whose presence Jane also benefited. "Towards me
he was as considerate as I had hoped for from my relationship
to you, charging me only 2s 6d for cutting my hair, though
it was as thoroughly dressed after being cut for Eastwell as it
had been for the Ashford Assembly. He certainly respects
either our youth or our poverty."[52] Jane was by no means in
funds, once again worried about tipping, and only able to
afford ten shillings for Sackree, the devoted nursemaid.

When she writes next, Jane has transferred to Goodnestone
Farm, while her sister is back at Godmersham. In this letter
comes a mention of a young man, some three or four years
Jane's junior, who was one of her admirers. This was the
Reverend Brook Edward Bridges, Elizabeth Austen's brother,
who appeared unexpectedly for dinner shortly after her

arrival. "It is impossible to do justice to the hospitality of his attentions towards me; he made a point of ordering toasted cheese for supper entirely on my account."[53]

On a trip to Canterbury, Jane had encountered Miss Sharpe, the governess at Godmersham, with whom, when she moved on, Jane and Cassandra were to keep in contact. It appears she was a pretty, intelligent girl, who had gained the affection of her pupils, and from their elders a good deal of well deserved admiration.

A subject always of interest, she mentions her reading: "I am glad you recommended 'Gisborne', for having begun, I am pleased with it, and I had quite determined not to read it."[54] This was not a novel, but a work by Thomas Gisborne with the rather forbidding title, *An Enquiry into the Duties of the Female Sex*.

When Jane and Cassandra returned to Bath, it was to help their mother to move into what was to be their last home in the city, lodgings in Trim Street. For some reason, although conveniently situated, this was an address regarded with horror by Cassandra. Five years before, when they had been searching for accommodation, Jane had written, "In the meantime she [Mrs Austen] assures you that she will do everything in her power to avoid Trim Street, although you have not expressed the fearful presentiment of it which was rather expected."[55] Their dislike of this last home, may have helped to account for the particular sense of joy and relief which Jane and her sister felt when at last they left Bath for good on 2nd July 1806. They had spent five sad and disappointing years in a city they neither of them cared for, although they had made the best of it, engaged in a busy, useless, social round, measuring out their lives with coffee spoons.

Her pleasure at moving again was so great, that in 1808 Jane was to write: "It will be two years tomorrow since we left Bath for Clifton, with what happy feelings of escape!"[56] When they reached Clifton, Martha Lloyd left them for a trip to Harrogate, and a little later, Mrs Austen and her daughters moved on to Adelstrop Rectory in Gloucestershire, to visit their Leigh cousins.

The family there was in a state of some excitement, as on the very day the Austens left Bath, the death had occurred of the Hon. Mary Leigh, the old lady to whom her late brother, the mentally unsound Lord Leigh had entrusted in her lifetime his great Stoneleigh estates. The provisions of his will following her death were somewhat obscure, since he then devised the estates "unto the first and nearest of my kindred being male and of my name and blood" then living. This meant that the Rev. Thomas Leigh, and Mrs Austen's brother, James Leigh Perrot, took precedence over the heir apparent, James Henry Leigh, the Rev. Thomas Leigh's nephew.

In view of the general uncertainty, the Rev. Thomas Leigh had immediately set forth for Stoneleigh, apparently to secure possession—a hasty step which gave rise to considerable indignation. Eventually, however, after some meetings in London, which caused Mr Leigh Perrot a good deal of annoyance, and a most regretted short separation from his beloved Jenny, the matter was settled amicably according to the terms of the will. This meant that Stoneleigh should go first to the elderly Rev. Thomas Leigh, then upon his death to Mr James Leigh Perrot, descending finally to James Leigh. But clearly, at his time of life, Mr Leigh Perrot had no wish to leave the comfort of his well loved home at Scarlets for the grandeur of Stoneleigh, and without much persuasion, he relinquished his claim on provision of suitable recompense. The terms he received were, in fact, extremely favourable, and it can only be ironically that Jane later refers to the "vile compromise". Twenty thousand pounds was secured to him by a mortgage on the Stoneleigh estates, a personal bond of £4,000 was provided by James Leigh, who in fact was to come into his inheritance on the death of his Uncle Thomas in 1813, and there was an annuity of £2,000 for the rest of Mr Leigh Perrot's life, or his widow's if she survived him. She did, until 1836, so her husband had struck a good bargain. As soon as all this had been decided, the Rev. Thomas Leigh was anxious to take stock of his magnificent new home, and the entire house party, including his sister Elizabeth, Mrs Austen, Jane, and Cassandra, set forth for Stoneleigh Abbey. Mrs Austen has left a vivid account of this visit, and perhaps Stoneleigh furnished some additional details when Jane came to revise *Northanger Abbey* for the last time, and also provided some hints for the descriptions of Sotherton in *Mansfield Park*.

The house is larger than I could have supposed. We can *now* find our way about it, I mean the best part; as to the offices (which were the old Abbey) Mr Leigh almost despairs of ever finding his way about them. I have proposed his setting up *directing posts* at the Angles. . . .

At nine in the morning we meet and say our prayers in a handsome Chapel, the pulpit &c now hung with black. Then follows breakfast consisting of Chocolate Coffee and Tea, Plumb Cake, Pound Cake, Hot Rolls, Cold Rolls, Bread and Butter and *dry toast for me*. . . .

One Man servant is called the Baker, He does nothing but Brew & Bake. The quantity of Casks in the Strong Beer Cellar is beyond imagination: Those in the *small Beer* Cellar bear no proportion, tho' by the bye, the small Beer may be called an Ale without misnomer.

Although Mrs Austen stuck to dry toast at breakfast, it appears she sampled the beer.

I will now give you some idea of the inside of this vast house. . . . On the left hand of the hall is the best drawing room, within that a smaller; these rooms are rather gloomy Brown wainscot and dark Crimson furniture; so we never use them but to walk thro' them to the old picture gallery. Behind the smaller drawing Room is the state Bed Chamber, with a high dark crimson Velvet Bed: an *alarming* apartment just fit for a Heroine. . . .

Our visit has been a most pleasant one. We all seem in a good humour disposed to be pleased, endeavour to be agreeable and I hope succeed. Poor Lady Saye & Sele to be sure is rather tormenting, tho' sometimes amusing, and affords Jane many a good laugh—but she fatigues me sadly on the whole.[57]

This family excitement over, Mrs Austen and her daughters proceeded to what must have been a visit in the nature of an anticlimax to the worthy but dull Rev. Edward Cooper and his growing family, ultimately to number nine, at Hamstall.

The Austen ladies were now virtually homeless, and their next change of address to Southampton was no doubt suggested by Frank. For him, it had been an important year. He had taken part in Sir John Duckworth's cruise to the West Indies, and in action which had ended in victory over the French at San Domingo. The squadron returned home with three prizes, arriving in May to receive the thanks of Parliament. As soon as he could, Frank presented himself to Mary Gibson at Ramsgate, and on 24th July 1806 they were married. Jane had long recovered from her disappointment on Martha's behalf, and the year before had written, "he [Frank] is in a great hurry to be married, and I have encouraged him in it."[58]

For the young bride, making her new home with her mother- and two sisters-in-law, and sometimes an attractive friend who was eventually to become her husband's second wife, hardly seems an ideal arrangement. But it may have enabled Frank to provide her with more spacious accommodation, and he seems to have been genuinely anxious to offer a practical solution to the problem of his mother's residence. Clearly, there must have been occasional difficulties, but on the whole, it worked well, and the tone of Jane's letters from Southampton is more contented than that of those from Bath.

The first of these was written from the lodgings which they occupied from the autumn of 1806 until March 1807, when they moved into a handsome house in Castle Square. Martha was away at Eversley, and Cassandra was once again at Godmersham.

Elizabeth had recently been confined with another little girl, named Cassandra Jane in compliment to her paternal grandmother and aunts. She was making a slow recovery from this tenth birth in sixteen years, and this time, Cassandra's stay was a lengthy one. It might have been hoped that another quickly following pregnancy should have been strenuously avoided, if only, as Jane was to recommend for another luxurious couple, by the "simple regimen of separate rooms".[59] But Edward and his beautiful Elizabeth were still in love, and the following year were once more awaiting a child.

Mrs James Austen and her two children had been visitors already at Southampton, and her husband joined them whenever he could get away. This was not always as agreeable as it should have been. "I am sorry & angry that his Visits should not give one more pleasure; the company of so good & so clever a Man ought to be gratifying in itself; but his chat seems all forced, & his Opinions on many points too much copied from his Wife's & his time here is spent I think in walking about the House & banging the doors, or ringing the bell for a glass of water."[60]

Of the two Marys, although a new member of the family, Frank's wife was a more congenial companion for Jane than Mrs James had ever been, with whom she was able to share her interest in reading. Mrs Frank was already pregnant, and Cassandra was asked for some hints from that expert on the subject of baby-care, Elizabeth: "Mary will be obliged to you to take notice how often Elizabeth nurses her baby in the course of twenty-four hours, how often it is fed, and with what. . . ."[61]

The January weather had been cold, "It is one of the pleasantest frosts I ever knew, so very quiet. I hope it will last some time longer for Frank's sake, who is quite anxious to get some skating; he tried yesterday, but it would not do.''[62]

Jane, who had perhaps hoped for more leisure in their new home complains:

Our acquaintance increase too fast. He [Frank] was recognized lately by Admiral Bertie, and a few days since arrived the Admiral and his daughter Catherine to wait on us. There was nothing to like or dislike in either. To the Berties are to be added the Lances, with whose cards we have been endowed, and whose visit Frank and I returned yesterday. . . .

We found only Mrs Lance at home, and whether she boasts any offspring besides a grand pianoforte did not appear. She was civil and chatty enough, and offered to introduce us to some acquaintance in Southampton, which we gratefully declined.

I suppose they must be acting by the order of Mr Lance of Netherton in this civility as there seems no other reason for their coming near us. They will not come often, I dare say. They live in a handsome style and are rich, and she seemed to like to be rich, and we gave her to understand that we were far from being so; she will soon feel therefore that we are not worth her acquaintance.[63]

In fact, this proved an unjust view. Mr and Mrs Lance had two daughters, Emma and Mary, and the families seem to have kept in contact as long as the Austens remained in Southampton.

At this time, two main preoccupations were the provision of the coming baby's layette, and the putting in order of the handsome house they had taken in Castle Square. Temporarily without a ship, Frank who was a practical man and like so many sailors deft with his hands, was making a fringe for the drawing room curtains. After so many lodgings in Bath without one, Jane was looking forward eagerly to having a garden again, and a garden which she reports was one of the best in town.

Our garden is putting in order by a man who bears a remarkably good character, has a very fine complexion, and asks something less than the first . . . at my own particular desire he procures us some syringas. I could not do without a syringa, for the sake of Cowper's line.—We talk also of a laburnum.[64]

> Then, each in its peculiar honours clad,
> Shall publish, even to the distant eye,
> Its family and tribe. Laburnum, rich
> In streaming gold; syringa, iv'ry pure;
> The scentless and the scented rose.[65]

All her life, Jane Austen was to love the work of William Cowper, that gentle and tragic forerunner of the Romantics.

Once again, a letter disproves the assumption that Jane Austen did not care for children. She had been entertaining a little girl, and after some initial doubts about her lack of shyness, writes: "Our little visitor has just left us, and left us highly pleased with her; she is a nice, natural, open-hearted, affectionate girl, with all the ready civility which one sees in the best children in the present day; so unlike anything that I was myself at her age, that I am often all astonishment and shame. Half her time here was spent at spillikins, which I consider as a very valuable part of our household furniture, and as not the least important benefaction from the family of Knight to that of Austen."[66]

Spillikins, defined by the Oxford dictionary as "a game played with a heap of slips or small rods of wood, bone, or the like, the object being to pull off each by means of a hook without disturbing the rest", and bilbo catch, or cup and ball, which entailed catching a ball joined to a rod either in the cup at one of its ends or the spike at the other, were both games at which Jane Austen excelled, depending on a skilful, steady hand. Writing about this ability, her biographer nephew Edward also comments on her strong clear handwriting, and the way in which she folded and sealed her letters in the days before the use of envelopes. "Some people's letters always looked loose and untidy; but her paper was sure to take the right folds, and her sealing-wax to drop into the right place."[67]

No doubt both Cassandra and Martha returned to Southampton in time for the move to Castle Square on 9th March. Young Edward Austen sometimes stayed in the "commodious old-fashioned" house and naturally enough seems to have been most impressed by the garden "bounded on one side by the old city walls" wide enough to walk on, and by the view from the window of the fairy-tale-like castle built by the second Marquis of Lansdowne, which unfortunately was pulled down in 1809.[68]

Rather in the style of Congreve, Jane also reports that Lord Lansdowne retained a domestic painter, named Mr Husket:

". . . he lives in the castle.—Domestic chaplains have given way to this more necessary office, and I suppose whenever the walls want no touching up he is employed about my lady's face."[69]

Not long after they were installed in their new house, Frank's wife was confined and their daughter, Mary Jane, was born on 27th April 1807. Her birth coincided with her father's appointment to his new ship, the *St Albans*.

This was soon followed by another important event in the family. Since 1805, Charles had been on the North American station, engaged in active service, "enforcing the right of search on the Atlantic seaboard of America". In between spells at sea, he had made the most of several local leaves, and on 1st May, he married Frances Fitzwilliam Palmer, daughter of the Attorney General of Bermuda. But Jane and Cassandra were not to meet the wife of their "particular little brother" for another four years.

In spite of Mrs Austen's bright financial position, having begun 1807 with £99, probably the expenses of the move and their pleasant situation in Southampton meant there were no seaside rambles this year. However, she and her daughters did pay a prophetic visit to Chawton House, Edward Austen's Hampshire residence. It is unlikely that at the time they had any idea of the importance this pleasant part of their home county was soon to have for them, but evidently all three were favourably impressed.

A year now passes silently, until Jane's next letter in June 1808. This time it was her turn to travel, first to London, and then with James and his new family to Godmersham.

There is no letter surviving from Jane's London visit of early June. Clearly she must have written to Cassandra then, since references in subsequent letters are so scanty. For some reason, Jane's description of life with Henry and Eliza, who were now living at No 16 Michael's Place in what was then the village of Brompton, failed to pass the vigilance of her sister's censorship. Apparently, the house was somewhat cramped and damp, and perhaps Eliza found in it cause for complaint. By now, she was forty-seven, probably beginning to show her age and her ten years' seniority to Henry, and not in the best of health. Although she retained much affection for this brilliant little figure from her girlhood, it is likely that Jane found less to admire in her than formerly. Little is known of this visit, except that Jane watched "the ladies go to Court on the 4th", the King's birthday.[70] No doubt she visited the theatre, and

almost certainly, she and Henry discussed her plans for publication and for future work.

Her welcome to Godmersham was as warm as she could
wish, where Edward's eldest daughter, Fanny, was now emerging as a favourite niece. It seems that the morning after her
arrival was spent in arranging Jane's return home at the end of
her visit, which was to be somewhat curtailed so that she
might travel with Edward, who was planning a business trip
to Alton. Elizabeth was six-months pregnant and as tireless
as ever in her attendance on her children. But Jane did not
think she looked well.

Perhaps because she had a cold, she missed Cassandra, and
in spite of her spacious Yellow Room, where she usually
enjoyed two or three hours quietly after breakfast, at the
beginning of her visit, Jane felt "rather languid and solitary".[71]

On 20th June, she writes to describe a trip to Canterbury,
where she called on her old friend Harriet Bridges, now
married to the "gentlemanlike—but by no means winning"[72]
Rev. George Moore, son of the former Archbishop of Canterbury, and a fond but not foolish mother of two little daughters, one plain and one pretty. She also visited her brother's
benefactress, Mrs Knight, receiving later by post an invitation
to spend a day or two with her, and a gift of money, which
Jane describes as "the usual Fee",[73] revealing at once her
gratitude and a certain degree of resentment.

Mrs Knight's invitation was accepted, and Jane enjoyed "a
very agreeable visit" seeing a great number of acquaintances
while she was there, "with such short intervals between any
as to make it a matter of wonder to me that Mrs K. and I
should ever have been ten minutes alone or have had any leisure
for comfortable talk".[74] It seems likely that old Mrs Knight
was not always so busy, and that people were anxious to see
Jane on one of her rare visits.

While her parents and young step-brother and sister were
at Godmersham, Anna had been staying at Castle Square.
Fifteen years of age, lively, and attractive, she had startled
her family by adopting the latest fashion and having her hair
cropped. If it curled like her aunt's, it must have looked pretty,
and in any case as Jane comments: "I am tolerably reconciled
to it by considering that two or three years may restore it
again."[75]

While she was there, her mother's sisters came to see
her and Mrs Maitland made her a present, an event which
seems not to have been too well received by her stepmother,

who was also displeased by Anna's tardiness, soon to be remedied, in answering her letter. "Mary begins to fancy, because she has received no message on the subject, that Anna does not mean to answer her letter, but it must be for the pleasure of fancying it."[76] On the whole, however, the difficult Mary was disposed to be pleased during her visit, "Mary finds the children less troublesome than she expected, and independent of them, there is certainly not much to try the patience or hurt the spirits at Godmersham."[77]

The Edward Austens were a particularly handsome and exuberant family and, of course, there were a lot of them. Little Caroline apparently looked plain among them, and her aunt decided that she would be glad to get home; "her cousins are too much for her".[78] James Edward, however, thoroughly enjoyed the young company, and "His uncle Edward talks nonsense to him delightfully; more than he can always understand".[79]

Generally in the family circle, there was a good deal of excitement about the expected arrival of Frank's ship, the St Albans, which had returned from a year's service in the Peninsular War. "We are all very happy to hear of his health & safety; he wants nothing but a good prize to be a perfect character.—This scheme to the island is an admirable thing for his wife; she will not feel the delay of his return in such variety."[80] Not only Mary, but also Cassandra and Anna enjoyed a "spirited voyage" to the Isle of Wight, entailing an heroic embarkation at 4 a.m. Later there appear to have been some raised eyebrows in the family when Mrs Frank chose to complete her holiday and did not rush home as expected, with the little daughter he had scarcely seen, to greet her husband. "When are calculations ever right? I could have sworn that Mary must have heard of the St Albans return, and would have been wild to come home, or to be doing something. Nobody ever feels or acts, suffers or enjoys, as one expects."[81]

Someone else who acted out of character at this time was a Southampton acquaintance, Mrs Powlett. "This is a sad story about Mrs Powlett. I should not have suspected her of such a thing.—She staid the Sacrament I remember, the last time that you & I did.—A hint of it, with Initials, was in yesterday's Courier; and Mr Moore guessed it to be Ld Sackville, believing there was no other Viscount S. in the peerage, & so it proved—Ld Viscount Seymour not being there."[82]

Although the arrangements for her return home had been settled so early, an opportunity arose later for her to extend her visit, as Henry offered to accompany his sister home in September. On the strength of this, she was pressed to stay. But she was now particularly anxious to be back in Southampton in time for the proposed visit from the Bigg sisters, and was not to be persuaded. "I have felt myself obliged to give Edward and Elizabeth one private reason for my wishing to be at home in July. They feel the strength of it and say no more, and one can rely on their secrecy. After this I hope we shall not be disappointed of our friend's visit;—my honour, as well as my affection will be concerned in it."[83]

The need for such secrecy is somewhat mysterious, and one can only conclude that Edward and Elizabeth had not known previously of Harris Bigg-Wither's rejected proposal. In view of her gauche behaviour on that occasion, no doubt, Jane was always to remain particularly anxious to show every amending courtesy and affection to his sisters.

It is very possible that at some time during this visit to Godmersham, Jane received a proposal from Elizabeth's brother, Edward Bridges. If so, this time she seems to have been prepared, and no doubt guided by her earlier experience and a greater poise and maturity, dealt with it firmly but gracefully. Like Harris, Edward was a few years Jane's junior, but there must have been every advantageous reason for accepting this agreeable and suitable young man, except that once again she did not love him.

Jane travelled back to Southampton early in July, as originally planned, except that the rigorous Dr Goddard, headmaster at Winchester, in spite of his pupil's favourable prediction, refused to allow young Edward Austen leave to be of the party. Life at Godmersham was well regulated and luxurious, but as always, Jane was pleased to be going home. "The orange wine will want our care soon.—But in the meantime for elegance and ease and luxury, the Hattons & Milles' dine here today, and I shall eat ice and drink French wine, and be above vulgar economy. Luckily the pleasures of friendship, of unreserved conversation, of similarity of taste and opinions, will make good amends for orange wine."[84]

By the time Jane writes again on 1st October, the roles are once more reversed. She is at home in Castle Square and Cassandra has repaired to Godmersham where Elizabeth has just been delivered of another little boy, Brook John. Cassandra reported that everything had gone well, and Jane sent her best wishes to mother and baby son. Like her sister, Cassandra was delighted with Fanny.

There was news of the wedding in a fortnight's time of Catherine Bigg, two years Jane's senior, to the Rev. Herbert Hill of Streatham. The husband was some twenty-four years older than his bride, and later Jane was to comment on the "melancholy disproportion between the Papa and the little Children".[85] There had been a great deal of company, not all of whom went uncriticized: "The Miss Ballards are said to be remarkably well-informed; their manners are unaffected and pleasing, but they do not talk quite freely enough to be agreeable, nor can I discover any right they had by taste or feeling to go on their late tour."[86]

By this time, there was already some discussion of the Southampton household's breaking up. Frank and his family were at the moment in comfortable lodgings in Yarmouth, and Mrs Austen was contemplating a move to Alton, where Henry was now running a branch of his bank.

Jane was reading aloud by candlelight the letters of *Espriella* by Southey, who was to be connected by marriage with Catherine Bigg when she became Catherine Hill. The Rev. Herbert Hill was the brother of Southey's mother, and in later years, Catherine's son Herbert married Southey's daughter, "dark eyed Bertha, timid as a dove".

The next letter of 7th October, suggested that Elizabeth was fast recovering, and there seemed no reason for any further fears. Martha had returned, to Jane's evident pleasure, and with several good things for their well stocked larder. On her way, she had stopped off at Winchester to see the schoolboys, including her own nephew, Fulwar William Fowle.

In this letter, occurs the oblique reference to Edward Bridge's proposal; "I wish you may be able to accept Lady Bridge's invitation, though *I* could not her son Edward's".[87]

Curiously, in this letter Jane refers twice to a mourning gown that her mother was making from an old pelisse for the expected death of the late Mr Knight's still surviving sister Elizabeth, who was in fact to die in March 1809.

But the mourning was to be needed earlier, for in the letter dated 13th October, Jane records the tragic news of the death of Edward's wife, Elizabeth, at the age of thirty-five. Her last baby, himself thriving healthily and destined to reach his own allotted span of seventy years, had proved too much for her. Since she had seemed well on the way to recovery, and the crisis came suddenly and unexpectedly, her death was all the more distressing. "We have felt—we do feel—for you all as you will not need to be told: for you, for Fanny, for Henry, for Lady Bridges, and for dearest Edward, whose loss and whose sufferings seem to make those of every other person nothing."[88]

All the Austen brothers were to lose their first wives, but Edward, the most eligible, left with eleven children, a vigorous man of forty still only half way through his long life, was the only one who did not re-marry.

Luckily, he had a great support in his sister Cassandra, and his eldest daughter, Fanny, and "God be praised" Jane wrote, "that he has a religious mind to bear him up, and a disposition that will gradually lead him to comfort".[89]

Mourning clothes were a preoccupation, both for themselves and the two Winchester schoolboys, who had been taken to Steventon. Jane had written to her cousin Edward Cooper at Hamstall and hoped, "he will not send one of his letters of cruel comfort to my poor brother";[90] a fear which arouses a suspicion that something of Edward Cooper went to the making of Mr Collins.

Having so recently spent a happy visit at Godmersham herself, Jane was only too easily able to share with their grief in her imagination. "I see your mournful party in my mind's eye under every varying circumstance of the day; and in the evening especially figure to myself its sad gloom: the efforts to talk, the frequent summons to melancholy orders and cares, and poor Edward, restless in misery, going from one room to the other, and perhaps not seldom upstairs, to see all that remains of his Elizabeth."[91] Everyone who has suffered a bereavement must recognize the truth of this picture, and had Jane Austen cared to dwell on misery, she would have been well equipped to do so. Of the children, she mentions particularly her mother's namesake, Lizzie—"one's heart aches for a dejected mind of eight years old".[92]

When Jane next writes on 24th October, Edward and George had arrived from Steventon for a few days' stay with their grandmother and aunt before returning to school. Naturally, the boys were upset and cried over the letter sent them by their father, but Jane worked hard to divert them with bilbocatch, spillikins, paper ships, conundrums, and cards.

On Sunday she took them to church, and for a blow on the quay. The water as usual, proving a fascination for the boys. Jane arranged excursions to Northam and Netley. "I had not proposed doing more than cross the Itchen yesterday, but it proved so pleasant, and so much to the satisfaction of all, that when we reached the middle of the stream we agreed to be rowed up the river; both the boys rowed great part of the way, and their questions and remarks, as well as their enjoyment, were very amusing; George's enquiries were end-less, and his eagerness in everything reminds me very often *of his Uncle Henry.*"[93]

Jane had found the best of all recipes for amusing the boys —to let it be seen how much she was enjoying herself too. The visit was clearly an unqualified success which, under the circumstances, was a triumph of kindness and tact.

In this letter comes the first news of Edward's proposal for their next home. He offered his mother and sisters a choice of two cottages, one at Godmersham, the other on his estate at Chawton. After some discussion, the ladies settled happily on Chawton. First Frank, just sailed from Yarmouth on the *St Albans*, must be told, the two little boys had been let into the secret, and then the rest of the family were to be informed. There was no need to act in a hurry as the cottage was tenanted until mid-summer, for after which time the move could be planned.

Cassandra's sojourn at Godmersham during this sad time was to be a long one, until well into the new year of 1809. By 21st November, Jane had learned the news of Edward Bridge's engagement. Apparently his family was doubtful about his choice of Harriet Foote, a younger sister of his brother's late wife, and there was some discussion of her "pros and cons". Jane's feelings appear to have been of cheerful relief at his having, this time, committed himself successfully, and of optimism, later seen to be somewhat unjustified, about his bride. "I wish him happy with all my heart, and hope his choice may turn out according to his own expectations, and beyond those of his family; and I dare say it will. Marriage is a great improver.—"[94]

The affairs at Stoneleigh Abbey were now concluded, and over the next four years there hovers a somewhat frail hope that Mr and Mrs Leigh Perrot might do something substantial for Mrs Austen. According to Jane, Mrs Leigh Perrot was in one of her prevailing grumbling moods, when nothing pleased her. But she had recently written to James announcing that she and her husband were to make him an annual allowance of £100. A sum which Jane and her mother ascertained brought James's yearly income up to "eleven hundred pounds, curate paid, which makes us very happy—the ascertainment as well as the income".[95] The Leigh Perrots had been im-pressed by their nephew's conscientious refusal of a plurality

H

in the form of the living of Hampstead Marshall, which Lord Craven had asked him to hold until the protégé to whom he wished to present it eventually, grew old enough to take it.

Although she appreciated the affectionate tone of her aunt's letter and her brother's good fortune, Jane comments regretfully, "My expectations for my mother do not rise with this event".[96]

The new house at Chawton was much in their minds. It contained six bedrooms and garrets for storeplaces, one of which might be suitable for a manservant. Certainly in an all female establishment in those pre-labour saving days, a sturdy manservant could well be considered indispensable, difficult though he might be to control and retain. Choles, a recent holder of this office, had to be turned away—"he grew so very drunken and negligent, and we have a man in his place called Thomas".[97]

No doubt with the move in view, Mrs Austen had been doing some dealing in silver. "My mother has lately been adding to her possessions in plate—a whole tablespoon and a whole dessertspoon, and six whole teaspoons—which makes our sideboard border on the magnificent."[98] They had decided to have a pianoforte, "as good a one as can be got for thirty guineas, and I will practise country dances, that we may have some amusement for our nephews and nieces, when we have the pleasure of their company".[99] One of these nephews, ten-years-old William, who had taken up cross stitch during a period of convalescence, was working a footstool for his Grandmamma's new home. Mrs Austen herself was particularly interested in the garden.

Old neighbours from Steventon were now once more to be neighbours again, Mr and Mrs Harry Digweed. The asperity with which Jane speaks of his wife lends a little weight to the tentative suggestion that she might once have been inclined towards Harry herself. "Mrs. H. Digweed looks forward with great satisfaction to our being her neighbours. I would have her enjoy the idea to the utmost, as I suspect there will not be much in the reality."[100] Mrs Knight had pointed out that an eligible suitor would not be lacking, as the Rector of Chawton, the Rev. John Papillon, was still unmarried, "I *will* marry Mr. Papillon", Jane answers, "whatever may be his reluctance or my own. I owe her much more than such a trifling sacrifice."[101]

Although her thoughts were now fixed on the future, Jane was determined to enjoy the last pleasures of Southampton.

Mary and Frank were away, and she and her mother were looking after little Mary Jane. But James was expected, and, "we mean to take the opportunity of his help to go one night to the play".[102]

"A larger circle of acquaintance, and an increase of amusement, is quite in character with our approaching removal. Yes, I mean to go to as many balls as possible, that I may have a good bargain."[103]

Of the first ball she attended after this decision, Jane writes in a spirit of cheerful reconcilement.

It was the same room in which we danced fifteen years ago. I thought it all over, and in spite of the shame of being so much older, felt with thankfulness that I was quite as happy now as then . . . You will not expect to hear that *I* was asked to dance—but I was—by the gentleman whom we met *that Sunday* with Captain D'Auvergne. We have always kept up a bowing acquaintance since, and being pleased with his black eyes, I spoke to him at the ball, which brought on me this civility; but I do not know his name, and he seems so little at home in the English language, that I believe his black eyes may be the best of him.[104]

Seeing friends at home was not always so entertaining. "Our evening party on Thursday produced nothing more remarkable than Miss Murden's coming too, though she had declined it absolutely in the morning, and sitting very ungracious and very silent with us from seven o'clock till half after eleven, for so late was it, owing to the chairmen, before we got rid of them."[105]

Later, with Martha's aid having found a suitable board and lodging, Miss Murden cheered up, and Jane writes remorsefully, "I was truly glad to see her comfortable in mind and spirits; at her age, perhaps, one may be friendless oneself, and in similar circumstances quite as captious."[106]

Another little insight into the lives of the not so fortunate was given by a visit to friends at the boarding house kept by Mrs Kelly in the High Street: "our curiosity was gratified by the sight of their fellow inmates, Mrs. Drew and Miss Hook, Mr. Wynne and Mr. Fitzhugh; the latter is brother to Mrs. Lance, and very much the gentleman. He has lived in that house more than twenty years, and, poor man! is so totally deaf that they say he could not hear a cannon, were it fired close to him; having no cannon at hand to make the experiment, I took it for granted, and talked a little with my fingers, which was funny enough. I recommended him to read Corinna."[107] It has been suggested that George Austen, the unfortunate invalid brother, may also have been deaf, which would account for his sister's ability to talk with her hands.

At Southampton, it was a quiet Christmas, but Jane was glad to know that Henry was to help cheer up the party at Godmersham, especially as the 27th, the anniversary of Elizabeth and Edward's wedding, was bound to be a day of sad remembrance. He and Eliza were well, Cassandra reported later, and Henry's bank was prospering.

In their thirties though they now were, neither Jane, Cassandra, nor Martha were free from being teased about suitors.

The widowed Sir Brook Bridges had evidently wasted an opportunity of a private conversation with Cassandra immersed in his newspaper, and Jane wrote, "Do not imagine that your picture of your *tête-à-tête* with Sir B. makes any change in our expectations here; he could not really be reading, though he held the newspaper in his hand; he was making his mind up to the deed, and the manner of it. I think you will have a letter from him soon."[108] But although Sir Brook was soon to remarry, his bride was not to be Cassandra.

In Martha's case, the jokes were occasioned by the attention paid her by Dr Mant, a married man, Rector of All Saints Church, Southampton. "Martha and Dr. Mant are as bad as ever; he runs after her in the street to apologise for having spoken to a gentleman while *she* was near him the day before. Poor Mrs. Mant can stand it no longer; she is retired to one of her married daughters'."[109] But in view of Martha's kindness to Cassandra and herself, Jane declared herself willing to overlook "a venial fault, and as Dr. M. is a clergyman, their attachment, however immoral, has a decorous air".[110]

A Kentish acquaintance, the widowed Lady Sondes, had remarried: "I consider everybody as having a right to marry *once* in their lives for love, if they can, and provided she will now leave off having bad headaches and being pathetic, I can allow her, I can *wish* her, to be happy."[111]

Jane's note of irritation here, reminds us that she still has her own hypochondriac at home to humour. "For a day or two last week, my mother was very poorly, with a return of *one* of her old complaints, but it did not last long, and seems to have left nothing bad behind it. She began to talk of a serious illness, her two last having been preceded by the same symptoms; but—thank Heaven! she is now quite as well as one can expect her to be in weather which deprives her of exercise."[112]

The bad weather had revived the problem of the store-room in which Jane had long battled against the intrusion of the elements: "the contest between us and the closet has now ended in our defeat. I have been obliged to move almost everything out of it, and leave it to splash itself as it likes."[113] A little later, this inconvenience was cured simply by cleaning a blocked gutter.

In the new year of 1809, good news came from Charles, still based in Bermuda, where his wife had given birth to their first child, a little girl christened Cassandra. On his ship *The Indian*, Charles had captured a small French privateer.

Frank's ship, the *St Albans*, was expecting to be sent off to help with the evacuation of the troops from Corunna. In this connection, Jane Austen has been criticized for one of her rare comments on public affairs and religion.

Sir John Moore, who had replaced Sir Arthur Wellesley in this area of operations, having risked an advance into Spain, found himself pursued by an overwhelming force under Marshal Soult and was forced to retreat to Corunna. "It was a retreat of horrifying hardship, through barren and desolate country, in the depths of winter, with little food and less shelter."[114]

Not until three days after the remnants of the army had limped into Corunna did the transport ships arrive, and just as the men were about to embark, the French attacked. In a decisive British victory, the enemy was beaten back, the bulk of the army was sucessfully evacuated, but Sir John himself was fatally wounded.

Jane's reference to this in her letter to Cassandra of 30th January, runs as follows: "I am sorry to find that Sir J. Moore has a mother living, but tho' a very heroic son he might not be a very necessary one to her happiness . . . I wish Sir John had united something of the Christian with the hero in his death. Thank Heaven! we have had no one to care for particularly among the troops—no one in fact nearer to us than Sir John himself."[115]

"Thank Heaven! we have had no one to care for particularly among the troops", and a very similar statement in a later letter, are exclamations by no means as callous as they have been represented, implying an utter lack of concern for the many who suffered. On the contrary, they were surely the heartfelt cries echoed by everyone who has lived through a war and been lucky enough to have no near and dear friend or relation at risk. This might suggest a lack of universal imagination, and that "nerve o'er which do creep the else unfelt oppressions of this earth",[116] but it is perfectly honest.

Exactly what Jane meant by the rest of the paragraph it is difficult to say, although no doubt Cassandra fully comprehended her meaning. But on his deathbed, which was widely reported, Sir John had been sufficiently lucid to justify his actions and send messages to friends, and yet had made no reference to his own faith as a Christian. However little she writes overtly about her convictions, Jane Austen was a deeply committed Christian and would certainly have believed that at such a juncture, a man's thoughts should not be bound to the life he was leaving, but turning towards the better world ahead.

A less controversial passage in the letter of 10th January, shows that Jane Austen kept in touch with political news. "The 'Regency' seems to have been heard of only here; my most political correspondents make no mention of it. Unlucky that I should have wasted so much reflection on the subject."[117] Jane must have heard an anticipatory rumour about the King's health, as his son's appointment as Prince Regent did not take place until the next year. If the letters to and from these "most political correspondents" were extant, they might well provide a very different picture of Jane Austen's range of interests.

In those days of self-provided entertainment, a principal source of amusement in the Austen family, as well as in the families Jane drew in her novels, was a game of cards. Jane had introduced her young nephews to Speculation when they were staying in Southampton, and she was sorry to learn from Cassandra that Edward still maintained a preference for Brag.

In their letters, Jane and Cassandra had been mentioning their current reading. The Gothic tale was still by no means dead, and Jane had been reading aloud *Margiana* or *Widdrington Tower* by Mrs S. Sykes. They liked it "very well indeed. We are just going to set off for Northumberland to be shut up in Widdrington Tower, where there must be two or three sets of victims already immured under a very fine villain."[118]

In reply to Cassandra, Jane remarks somewhat dismissively "To set against your new novel of which nobody ever heard before and perhaps never may again, we have got *Ida of Athens* by Miss Owenson; which must be very clever, because it was written as the authoress says, in three months. We have only read the preface yet; but her Irish girl does not make me expect much.—If the warmth of her language could affect the body it might be worth reading in this weather.—"[119]

Cassandra's next choice of book fared little better. This was Hannah More's *Coelebs in Search of a Wife*. "You have by no means raised my curiosity about Caleb. My disinclination for it before was affected, but now it is real. I do not like the evangelicals. Of course I shall be delighted when I read it, like other people, but till I do I dislike it."[120]

Another which not surprisingly failed to arouse her enthusiasm was the third volume of sermons published by their cousin, the Rev. Edward Cooper of Hamstall, *Practical and Familiar Sermons: Designed for Parochial & Domestic Instruction*. Jane was fond of a good sermon, with a preference for those of the eighteenth-century preacher Sherlock, but Edward's were too full of "Regeneration and Conversion".[121] No doubt they were also exceedingly boring.

It seems characteristic that Jane Austen should have preferred the calm, well balanced tradition of the Anglican Church in which she had been brought up, to the reforming zeal, the passionate fervour, and the more simplified concepts of the Methodists, the nonconformists, and those who were trying to introduce a measure of this enthusiasm into the established church. Although later, perhaps under the influence of her brother Henry, she was somewhat to modify her view of the evangelicals.

Since her ill-fated initiative in 1803 for the publication of *Susan*, and her abandonment of *The Watsons* shortly after, there is no evidence that Jane was now engaged in any creative writing, although throughout the ensuing five years she may have been at work as the opportunity offered on the revision of her other two full length novels, originally entitled *Elinor and Marianne* and *First Impressions*. The first suggestion that she was still writing seriously comes in her letter to Cassandra of 24th January 1809.

You rejoice me by what you say of Fanny. . . . While she gives happiness to those about her she is pretty sure of her own share. I am gratified by her having pleasure in what I write but wish the knowledge of my being exposed to her discerning criticism may not hurt my style, by inducing too great a solicitude. I begin already to weigh my words and sentences more than I did, and am looking about for a sentiment, an illustra-

tion, or a metaphor in every corner of the room. Could my
ideas flow as fast as the rain in the store-closet it would be
charming.[122]

Fanny's pleasure might, of course, have been simply in the
letters, yet it suggests that perhaps this favourite niece had
been admitted to the select little band who had read Jane's
novels, or passages from them. It certainly indicates her continuing concern with the practical craft of writing, and is one
of several factors that tend to confirm Mrs Q. D. Leavis's
assumption that an early form of *Mansfield Park*, probably
epistolary, was conceived and drafted in 1808–9, and that the
dating usually given for this work, from February 1811 to
June 1813 refers to a substantial revision and final rewriting.
This can be considered independently of the theory that just as
The Watsons was finally transformed into *Emma*, so *Lady
Susan* provided the basis for *Mansfield Park*.

The principal piece of evidence for this dating of *Mansfield
Park*, which in the view of some critics was the most profound,
complex, and disturbing work Jane Austen was to write, is
that the chronology is based on the calendars of 1808 and
1809. This is reinforced by a number of correspondences between points of interest in the novel and Jane's life at this
time.

It can hardly be doubted from all we know of them that
certain aspects of the characters of Mary and Henry Crawford
were influenced by their author's observation of her cousin
Eliza and her husband, Jane's brother Henry. On her recent
visit, she had had opportunities for noticing their present
relationship and condition, and perhaps in contrast was sharply
reminded of the history of their love affair. The magnificent
scenes of the rehearsal of the Mansfield Park presentation of
the play *Lovers' Vows*, owe much to her memories of the
theatricals in which Eliza had shone, and by means of which
she may have both masked and furthered her flirtations with
the two Austen brothers.

Mary Crawford was no admirer of the clergy, deeply against
the idea of having a parson for a husband, and shocked to
know that the attractive and eligible Edmund was so near
ordination. Eliza had written, and no doubt expressed the
same sentiment more widely, that Henry had "now given up
all thoughts of the Church, and he is right for he certainly is
not so fit for a parson as a soldier".[123] That Henry was influenced by Eliza in this decision is supported by the fact that

when he was later forced again to change career, he entered the Ministry with every sign of a vocation.

In Mr Collins and Mr Elton, Jane portrayed with humour and irony two career clergymen. But in *Mansfield Park*, her clergyman elect, Edmund Bertram, is clearly designed to be a parson of a more dedicated kind, and in this work, there occur some serious passages about the duties involved. The clergy—their role in the church and in society—are likely to have been in the forefront of Jane's mind at this particular time, when she herself had probably made a decision not to become a clergyman's wife, and when her brother James had taken a conscientious stand on the question of accepting a plurality.

Once again the affairs of Stoneleigh Abbey had been under discussion, no doubt vividly recalling to Jane her visit there, and suggesting details for the great house at Sotherton. She herself had been staying during the summer of 1808 in the luxurious, secure, well regulated harmony of Godmersham, which may have provided the pattern for Mansfield Park.

Apart from her name, young Fanny appears to have little in common with Fanny Price. But in 1808, she was a girl just beginning to become a woman, and her aunt had observed her with a good deal of tenderness and understanding. After the death of her mother, thrust before she was ready into a role of greater responsibility, Fanny must have felt lost and bewildered for a while, just as Fanny Price was to feel, though for such different reasons. The letters show warmly that her Aunt Jane had a keen admiration for this particular niece, and as an author she certainly displays a similar admiration for Fanny's high principled, constant, and faithful young namesake who, though not every reader's favourite, is the heroine of *Mansfield Park*.

Towards the end of 1808, Mrs Leigh Perrot appears once again as a leading character in some of her niece's letters. Whether justly or not, Jane found a good deal more to criticize than to admire in this formidable aunt, and it seems very likely that some of the qualities she most disliked found their way into one of the most detestable and brilliantly drawn of all her characters, Mrs Norris.

As has been seen, the game of Speculation had been played and discussed by Jane at this time. It was this game of chance that she selected as a device to illuminate the group of characters that play it in a crucial scene in the novel.

Finally, the story of the runaway Mrs Powlett, which she

reported to her sister in June, recalls sharply the elopement of Maria Rushworth with Henry Crawford. "A hint of it, with initials, was in yesterday's Courier",[124] Jane wrote of the real event; and of the fictional one, "it was with infinite concern the newspaper had to announce to the world, a matrimonial *fracas* in the family of Mr. R. of Wimpole Street; the beautiful Mrs R. whose name had not long been enrolled in the lists of hymen, and who had promised to become so brilliant a leader in the fashionable world, having quitted her husband's roof in company with the well known and captivating Mr C. the intimate friend and associate of Mr R. . . ."[125]

Taken together, all these small clues prove a reasonable case for work having been begun on *Mansfield Park* at some time in the second half of 1808 or the beginning of 1809. Another important consideration is that during much of this time, Frank and his family were away, Cassandra was at Godmersham, she had more spare time on her hands, and luxury of luxuries, an unshared bedroom of her own in which to write.

Further proof of an active resumption of her literary career is furnished by the letter she wrote on 5th April 1809, under the delightful assumed name of Mrs Ashton Dennis to Crosby and Company, the publishers who had purchased and failed to publish *Susan*. "Six years have since passed, & this work of which I am myself the Authoress, has never to the best of my knowledge, appeared in print, tho' an early publication was stipulated for at the time of sale. I can only account for such extraordinary circumstance by supposing the MS. by some carelessness to have been lost: & if that was the case, am willing to supply you with another copy if you are disposed to avail yourself of it, & will engage for no farther delay when it comes into your hands."[126]

Richard Crosby's reply was prompt and decisive. The author might buy back the manuscript for the same sum of £10 which had been paid for its purchase, but should publication be attempted elsewhere, proceedings would be taken to stop the sale.

Disappointed, most probably without an available £10 to spare, once again Jane failed to pursue the correspondence, and *Susan* was neglected for another seven years. But on this occasion, Jane Austen was not discouraged. She had two other full-length works that she knew were worthy of publication, her mind was simmering with ideas, and for the first time since her departure from Steventon, she was about to enjoy the peace and serenity of a settled home.

FOUR

The Years of Fulfilment

Mrs Austen and her daughters left Southampton in April 1809, and after visits to the Cookes at Bookham, to Edward at Godmersham, and other friends in Kent, they moved on to Chawton. Very likely they stayed in the big house there while their own cottage was being cleaned and decorated. In celebration of the birth of Frank's second child, Francis William, Jane wrote a few lines:

> My dearest Frank, I wish you joy
> Of Mary's safety with a Boy,
> Whose birth has given little pain
> Compared with that of Mary Jane.—
>
> Our Chawton home, how much we find
> Already in it, to our mind;
> And how convinced, that when complete
> It will all other Houses beat
> That ever have been made or mended,
> With rooms concise, or rooms distended.[1]

Although known then as Chawton Cottage, as visitors can see today, the new home was in fact a fair sized house, which in former days had been an inn. James's daughter, Caroline, was a frequent visitor, and recorded some impressions of it as it was when Jane Austen lived there.

> Everything indoors and out was well kept—the house was well furnished, and it was altogether a comfortable and lady-like establishment, tho' I beleive the means which supported it, were but small—
> The house was quite as good as the generality of Parsonage houses then—and much in the same old style—the ceilings low and roughly finished—*some* bedrooms very small—*none* very large but in number sufficient to accommodate the inmates, and several guests.[2]

The family group now settling into this snug and comfortable home was very different from that which had left Steventon for Bath almost a decade before. Then they had been a mother and father with two attractive daughters in their twenties. Now they were a widowed mother and two unmarried women getting on in their thirties, with their chances of finding a suitable match retreating faster every year. Yet, paradoxically, Cassandra and Jane were both much happier now. No longer did Cassandra mourn her fiancé with such intensity, she was reconciled to a single life, and at Godmersham, particularly after the tragic death of Elizabeth, she had found a niche where she was often vitally needed. With her sister, she shared a remarkably close, frank, and communicative relationship.

If the figure of Cassandra remains somewhat shadowy, it is largely because she features in the correspondence as the participant in a dialogue who never replies. Had her letters survived, a crisper portrait would have emerged. Yet, the candid, comical letters that Jane had no hesitation in writing to her elder sister, certainly suggest a vigorous, responsive, humorous character, with more toughness and spirit than the gentle Jane Bennet, with whom she has often been identified.

As for Jane, she was happy at last in her determination, cost what it might, to embark on her literary career. No doubt this had been discussed exhaustively with Henry, and after her previous disappointments, she had decided that her next attempt at publication must be at her own risk.

At this time, Jane Austen was thirty-four years of age, and although still attractive, with no pretensions to appear any younger. Just as she had always been, she was keenly observant, highly critical, and extremely intelligent. She was more mature. Her wit sprang to mind as readily as ever, but she had learned to restrain its immediate expression in speech. Always unsentimental, she had gained greater tolerance and serenity.

Although she had not found married happiness with a man she loved, and for Jane Austen there was no other way, she had developed close and intimate friendships with Cassandra and with Martha Lloyd, and she was deeply aware of the value of loving and harmonious personal relationships in enabling individuals to adjust to the demands of society and an often hostile world. It was this perception which, in spite of her concurrent and ruthless examination of its defects, gave such symbolic force to her use of marriage (loving and happy, sensible and suitable marriage) as the ultimate goal for the heroines of all her works. As far as she herself was concerned, emotionally she well under control. It also seems likely that sexually her physical responses were naturally cool.

With children and young people, and although occasionally irritated by them, with the elderly, she was understanding and sympathetic. Following the custom of her Steventon girlhood, she continued to spend time and money on well-merited charity, making and distributing garments, and generally assisting the needy of the parish in a practical way. She still read continually and widely, often aloud in her clear, expressive voice. She played and practised regularly on her new piano, usually first thing in the morning. When her eyes were not tired, she enjoyed fine sewing. Although she still liked to dance, she was not so fond of company as formerly.

As was natural in a girl brought up in a family of boys, she was at ease with men, and she appreciated masculine conversation and company. It must be confessed that, like many women, she enjoyed a good gossip. She was always interested in details of dress and domestic affairs.

Her household tasks were performed with efficiency and despatch, and when Cassandra was at home, her particular duties included looking after the stocks of tea (she preferred hers without milk), sugar, and wine. When staying with Edward, and no doubt Henry, she enjoyed the opportunity of drinking French wine. At home, the drinks were more modest, and she not only supervised the stocks, but also helped to make the available alcoholic refreshments, which included beer, various home-made wines, such as orange and currant, and mead. When Cassandra was away, she cheerfully managed all the duties of the household. She enjoyed her food, mentioning with relish such pleasures as toasted cheese, asparagus and lobster, goose, dumplings, and apple pies.

She liked walking in all kinds of weather, she was fond of the garden, and she particularly loved trees. Always delighted by travel, especially to places of interest and beauty near the sea, she was never able to go abroad, principally because throughout most of her adult life the country was at war; and also because, even had this not been the case, it is unlikely she would have been able to afford it. But for a country parson's daughter, she moved about a good deal.

Her letters reveal that her greatest interest was quite simply people. She must have thoroughly agreed with Pope that the proper study of mankind is man. All her life, people fascinated her. She studied their outward appearances, their inner natures, their relations with one another, their conscious and unconscious motives, their consistencies and incongruities, their manners and their morals. Sometimes one feels that, like Keats, she suffered from the pressure of other people's identities. But all this contributed to what was probably her greatest strength as a novelist, her ability to create recognizable, living, truthful, and memorable characters.

Although she is recorded to have said, "I am too proud of my gentlemen to admit that they were only Mr A or Colonel B",[3] that she was assisted in this by her observation of life is undeniable. She did not copy, but she certainly used qualities and eccentricities she had seen and remembered.

Virginia Woolf supposes that her constant critical awareness and ironic vigilance must have made Jane Austen an uncomfortable companion, "for my own part, I would rather not find myself alone in the room with her. A sense of meaning withheld, a smile at something unseen, an atmosphere of perfect control and courtesy mixed with something finely satirical, which, were it not directed against things in general rather than against individuals, would be almost malicious, would, so I feel, make it alarming to find her at home."[4]

There may be an element of truth in this assertion, but the evidence is against it. Throughout her life, Jane Austen enjoyed many happy friendships with a wide variety of people; she aroused the affection and admiration of children; she had considerable powers of charm and attraction; and her daily life, even at its bleakest and most frustrating, was coloured and enlivened by her gift for humour and laughter. So many things, as her letters prove and as Mrs Austen once remarked, afforded Jane "many a good laugh", that for the most part life in her company must have been entertaining. If she talked as she wrote, and there is every reason to believe that she did, her conversation must have been a constant source of delight and gaiety to all who shared it.

The Austen ladies were most probably settled in Chawton Cottage by September 1809. Little is known of their activities from then until Jane's letter from London of 18th April 1811. But it is clear that during these intervening months, she had been hard at work, and she had come to an important and no doubt carefully considered decision. Under its new title, *Sense and Sensibility*, she was preparing *Elinor and Marianne* for the press in its revised, no longer epistolary form, and it had been accepted by Thomas Egerton of the Military Library, Whitehall. Egerton undertook the cost of publication, but any loss involved was to be borne by the author, a contingency for which Jane prudently set aside a little fund, and she knew that if the worst came to the worst, Henry, who had conducted the negotiations, would help her. It seems likely, even so, that she had faith in the saleability of the work.

It may be wondered why she now chose to make her debut with *Sense and Sensibility*, which is considered by some critics to be her least successful work. But as has been seen, she had arrived at an impasse in her dealings with Crosby, so that *Susan* was not available to her; *First Impressions* had already, although long ago now, suffered a rebuff; and she may have felt it might be a case of third book lucky. She may also have been drawn to the work again by the coincidence that her life had now caught up with her fiction; and that although so much older, she, Cassandra, Martha, and Mrs Austen were living in much the same style as the widowed Mrs Dashwood and her three girls. Most important, her highly developed critical sense must have told her that a revision of *First Impressions* would result in a far more brilliant book. To follow this with *Sense and Sensibility* was likely to be in the nature of an anti-climax; while by succeeding her first by a more engaging work would have the effect of augmenting any reputation she might have made.

From this first London letter there is a feeling of buoyancy, confidence, and excitement that until her illness was to last throughout the short, successful span of the life of Jane Austen, the published writer. At last she was doing what she had always known she must, and without the slightest craving for a fashionable triumph or entry into the London literary scene, she radiates the contentment of one who is beginning to fulfil her destiny.

The most important and exciting object of her visit to Henry and Eliza was that Egerton was beginning to run off the proof sheets for her to correct. At this time, the Henry Austens had moved to their last home at 64 Sloane Street. Henry had reached the crest of his banking career, Eliza was now installed in a spacious and beautiful home that provided an ideal setting for the gracious entertainments which she delighted to arrange, and a grand musical party had been planned for Jane's visit.

As usual when she was in London, Jane was busy shopping. She bought checked and coloured muslin for herself and

Cassandra, and after waiting half an hour at a thronged counter before being attended to, she came away from Grafton House well pleased with "Bugle Trimming at 2/4d and 3 pr silk stockgs for a little less than 12./s a pr".[5] Bugles were tubular glass beads, usually black, fashionable for trimming. She had also to match some Wedgwood ware at the showroom in York Street, St James's Square.

Her social programme was a busy one, with people to call on, others calling, and she found all the little parties that Eliza had arranged for her "very pleasant".

Evidently Cassandra had enquired about the progress of *Sense and Sensibility*, for on 25th April Jane replied: "I can no more forget it than a mother can forget her sucking child. . . . I have scarcely a hope of its being out in June. Henry does not neglect it; he has hurried the printer, and says he will see him again today."[6] In fact, publication was delayed until November.

Eliza's party had been a success, and Jane had been described by Mr Wyndham Knatchbull as, " 'A pleasing-looking young woman',—that must do; one cannot pretend to anything better now, thankful to have it continued a few years longer!"[7]

Although she had visited the theatre as she always liked to do when in London, and was well entertained by a play based on Molière's *Tartuffe*, she was disappointed at having no chance of seeing Mrs Siddons. "I should particularly have liked seeing her in 'Constance', and could swear at her with little effort for disappointing me."[8]

On their way to visit some of Eliza's French acquaintances, the horses had gibbed at the fresh gravel on the hill approaching Hyde Park Gate, Eliza was frightened, the party alighted for a few minutes in the evening air, and the delicate Eliza caught a bad cold on her chest.

The end of the visit was quieter, as Henry had ridden off to Oxford on business, and Jane and Eliza "were quite alone all day; and, after having been out a good deal, the change was very pleasant".[9]

At the beginning of May, her proof reading for the moment at an end, Jane went to Streatham to stay for a week with her old friend, Catherine Hill, and it was arranged that James would call on her there to take her home to Chawton.

Jane's next letters to Cassandra at the end of May describe the Chawton garden, in which up to the time of her death old Mrs Austen spent many happy hours working in a green

The Rev. George Austen presenting his son Edward to Mr and Mrs Knight

(*left*) A miniature of Francis Austen, later Admiral Sir Francis Austen, showing a singular likeness to Cassandra's sketch of Jane.
(*right*) Charles Austen as a Commander in 1807

(*left*) Thomas Lefroy, one young man whom Jane considered as a possible husband. (*right*) Mrs Leigh Perrot, Jane Austen's aunt

The topaz crosses given to his sisters by their brother Charles bought with some hard-won prize money—a kindness echoed in a famous passage in *Mansfield Park*

round smock frock, like a labourer's; "Our young piony at the foot of the fir-tree has just blown and looks very handsome, and the whole of the shrubbery border will soon be very gay with pinks and sweet-williams, in addition to the columbines already in bloom."[10]

She enquires if her sister has remembered pieces for the patchwork quilt they were making—now at a standstill—which can be seen at Chawton House today.

The goods had arrived from Wedgwood: "It all came very safely, and upon the whole is a good match, though I think they might have allowed us rather larger leaves, especially in such a year of fine foliage as this. One is apt to suppose that the woods about Birmingham must be blighted."[11]

There was a rather premature shopping expedition to provide mourning against the King's death; Mrs Austen taking the frugal view that it would be cheaper "than when the poor King was actually dead".[12] An event she anticipated by some nine years. Instead of a new reign, there began the period of the Regency.

It was a very busy summer, and a great deal of ingenuity was required to fit all the guests into both space and time. Martha and young Anna both spent some time at Chawton, and they were expecting their governess friend, Miss Sharpe. Frank, whose recent voyagings had taken him to China and the enemy coast of France, came with his wife, Mary, and their family of three from Cowes where they had been reunited. Henry had arrived for twenty-four hours with a young Mr Tilson, son of his banking partner, and they enjoyed a neck of mutton. Later Henry brought his wife, who stayed for a fortnight and seemed to be in unusually good health. While Eliza was still there, and most exciting of all, came the return of Charles with his wife and two pretty little girls after almost seven years so far from home.

Then, at last, in November came the event to which Jane must have been looking forward throughout all the happy confusion of the summer, her first appearance in print. *Sense and Sensibility* was published in three volumes, at fifteen shillings in boards, its authorship modestly announced in a line of capitals, "BY A LADY".

Jane was anxious that the secret of her identity should be kept, and for a while it was. Cassandra had written to Fanny at Godmersham to "beg we would not mention that Aunt Jane wrote *Sense and Sensibility*".[13] Anna was so far from sharing the secret that she rejected the work at the Alton circulating library on the grounds that it must be rubbish with such a title.

The book was advertised several times in the *Morning Chronicle*, but it was not until February that it received its first unsigned notice in the *Critical Review*, followed by another in May in the *British Critic*. Both were encouraging and appreciative. Dr Chapman estimates this first edition at between 750 to 1,000 copies,[14] from the first the book achieved a steady sale, and there was no need for Jane to dip into her pocket. On the contrary, she was to write happily in July 1813, when the first edition had been exhausted, that *Sense and Sensibility* had earned the welcome sum of £140.[15] A figure which should be multiplied at least by ten to give a present day equivalent.

The novels of Jane Austen, like the symphonies of Mozart, can be enjoyed on two levels. There is the simple story, or the melody to follow, there are the more serious undertones to listen for, or the two can be appreciated together in a subtle counterpoint. The more attentive reader, like the more attentive listener, reaps the richer reward.

Because they are quiet novels of everyday life, it took a reader of the calibre of Walter Scott to realize that they, in fact, represented a totally new beginning, and that in the class she had chosen, Jane Austen stood almost alone. Now we should say she stood quite alone. Looking back on the slow growth of her general popularity, it can only be concluded that she was far in advance of her time. Today, she is one of the most enduring and widely read of our classical novelists and her modernity, or the timelessness of her appeal, is striking. As more intense and searching critical attention is turned upon her work, so more and more complexity emerges.

Her novels have been described as social comedies. Yet though there is much that is amusing in *Sense and Sensibility*, *Mansfield Park* and *Persuasion*, in the final analysis they are far from purely comic. Perhaps one of the best definitions of her works comes from Malcolm Bradbury, who sees them as "moral assault courses . . . in which the candidates give their qualifications, undergo a succession of tests, and are finally rewarded by the one prize that is possible and appropriate in their social context—marriage. . . ."[16]

The progression from innocence to experience in each of the novels is basically the same; and yet within each work, the particular path and atmosphere is totally different. It is this that makes the consideration of Jane Austen's works as a canon both fascinating and necessary. In fact, she did not repeat herself.

Although less so than *Northanger Abbey*, *Sense and Sensibility* derives from Jane Austen's early literary burlesques. In those juvenile works, excessive sensibility provided her with a more frequent target than the Gothic novel. By the time she arrived at the final version of *Sense and Sensibility*, her satiric purpose had mellowed, and although the work is emotionally uneven, in Marianne Dashwood, one of the most lovable and certainly the most passionate of her heroines, she gives a sympathetic study of the difficulties of an artistic, imaginative, romantic, sometimes selfish and thoughtless girl, in conforming to what she can only see as the artificial standards and compromises of society.

In the character of Marianne, she poses one of the most significant questions she was ever to ask; a question on which she must have pondered in her own life, and which remains a basic and far-reaching human predicament—to what extent should individual behaviour be regulated by the demands of society?

This story of two sisters, Marianne and Elinor, and their contrasted and very different responses to love and society, can also be seen as representing the inward struggle of the author. Jane Austen recognized the virtues and defects of both responses to life—the fundamental conflict of reason and romance, and the difficulty of striking a just balance.

The central passages of the book reach almost the level of tragedy, when Marianne's loss of control and her emotional suffering bring her near the point of mental illness. Perhaps in Marianne Dashwood, whose character Jane Austen never attempted to repeat, she had created too persuasive a protagonist, like Milton's Satan. After all, the conclusions must have been very different had her Willoughby, not impossibly, proved all that he first seemed and a worthy lover.

Economics provide a framework for the emotional content of the story, and it is evident that in her own life, as in the novels, Jane Austen must often have been worried about money.

After so many years of writing and revising, it was to be expected that by the time she first went before her public, Jane Austen had already forged the great instrument of her style. Although this proved capable of further development, from the first, she spoke with authority. Critics vary very considerably in their estimates of this style, but it is her clear, economical, functional prose; the liveliness of her dialogue; her narrative skill; and her great gifts of irony, wit, and humour that are largely responsible for the fact that her novels continue to be so readable.

One of the characteristics of her style is its comparative absence of visual imagery, metaphor, and simile, and it is only recently that critics have begun to examine her use of symbolism. In his preface to *Sense and Sensibility*, Tony Tanner has drawn attention to Elinor's skill at screen painting, which is symbolic of her role of 'screening' in life, as she tries to give "the raw social realities a veneer of art".[17] When Edward is about to propose to Elinor, he takes up a pair of scissors ". . . spoiling them both and their sheath by cutting the latter to pieces as he spoke . . . There are times when the scissors will destroy the sheath just as there are times when the sheath will contain the scissors. Edward's feelings can break from the sheath at this point to some purpose because he is directing them towards marriage."[18] Throughout her own life, Jane Austen's feelings invariably remained sheathed, but there must have been many times when she yearned to use the scissors.

In *Sense and Sensibility*, traces remain of the original epistolary form, and yet one important question raised in the *Life* by the Austen-Leighs has never been satisfied. Between whom were the letters written? For it could not have been Elinor and Marianne, who unlike Jane and Cassandra, were never apart.

From 6th June 1811 until 29th November 1812, none of Jane's letters have survived. But a letter from Cassandra to their cousin Phila, now Mrs Whitaker, on 20th March 1812, reports a quiet Christmas, and visits from Edward, Henry, and Charles and his wife, who went on to take up residence on H.M.S. *Namur* at Sheerness, largely it seems for reasons of economy.[19] Edward was to return in April for a longer stay at Chawton House with his daughter Fanny. In June, Jane and her mother spent a fortnight at Steventon. Mrs Austen felt the time had come for her last trip away from home, and after her nostalgic farewell to Steventon, for the rest of her long life she was never again to sleep a night away from Chawton Cottage.

In her letter, Cassandra mentions the long illness of Edward's lifelong benefactress, Mrs Catherine Knight, who finally died on 14th October 1812. Edward now inherited the remainder of her estate, and from this time, he and his family adopted the name of Knight. Jane commented, "I must learn to make a better K.".[20]

Unusually, her correspondence recommences with a letter to Martha Lloyd, and the exciting news it contains reveals her main occupation during the intervening time. She had completed and sold *Pride and Prejudice*. "Egerton gives £110 for it. —I would rather have had £150, but we could not both be pleased, & I am not at all surprised that he should not chuse to hazard so much."[21]

Early in the New Year, Jane is writing again to Cassandra, who by this time was staying with James and Mary at Steventon. By now thoroughly at home in Chawton, she seems to have landed among a society of enthusiastic readers—with the exception of Mrs Harry Digweed, and the Clements who, she notes, "are reduced to read"![22] She reports they are "quite run over with books", and was herself enjoying with some surprise, *Essay on the Military Police and Institutions of the British Empire* by Captain Pasley of the Engineers; another favourite was *Rejected Addresses* by James and Horatio Smith, a collection of witty parodies in the manner of various authors on the subject of the opening of the newly rebuilt Drury Lane theatre, which naturally greatly appealed to her.

Far from marrying the eligible Mr Papillon, she now sets him down as anxious, fidgety, and lacking in conversation. During the evening of a party at his house, she is glad to use her mother as an excuse to leave early, "As soon as a whist party was formed, & a round table threatened. . . ." There is a nice little picture of her running home with their man-servant—"my own dear Thomas at night in great luxury".[23]

This letter indicates that concurrently with the extensive revisions which changed *First Impressions* into *Pride and Prejudice*, Jane had been at work on her next novel, which as has been suggested probably already existed in some form of draft, *Mansfield Park*. She had been checking up on the government establishment at Gibraltar, and she talks of leaving just as many for the round table at the Papillons, as there were at her Mrs Grant's—"I wish they might be as agreeable a set".[24] It seems unlikely.

On 29th January, she is excited by the arrival of the first copy of *Pride and Prejudice*:

I want to tell you that I have got my own darling child from London. . . . The Advertisement is in our paper today for the first time 18s . . . Miss Benn dined with us on the very day of the books coming & in the evening we set fairly at it, and read half the first vol. to her, prefacing that, having intelligence from Henry that such a work would soon appear, we had desired him to send it whenever it came out, and I believe it passed with her unsuspected. She was amused, poor soul! *That* she could not help, you know, with two such people to lead the way, but she really does seem to admire Elizabeth. I must confess that I think her as delightful a creature as ever appeared in print, and how I shall be able to tolerate those who do not like *her* at least I do not know. There are a few typical errors; and a 'said he', or a 'said she', would sometimes make the dialogue more immediately clear; but

> I do not write for such dull elves
> As have not a great deal of ingenuity themselves.

The second volume is shorter than I could wish, but the difference is not so much in reality as in look, there being a larger proportion of narrative in that part. I have lop't and crop't so successfully, however, that I imagine it must be rather shorter than S. & S. altogether.[25]

It is, in fact, just a little longer.

The excitement of publication had not, however, driven *Mansfield Park* from her mind. Since she was already well advanced with the work, rather curiously, she remarks, "Now I will try to write of something else, & it shall be a complete change of subject—ordination—I am glad to find your enquiries have ended so well. If you could discover whether Northamptonshire is a country of Hedgerows I should be glad again."[26]

When she next wrote on 4th February, Jane had received a welcome budget of praise from Steventon. By this time, she had suffered something of a reaction, or as she phrased it, "some fits of disgust".

Upon the whole, however, I am quite vain enough and well satisfied enough. The work is rather too light, and bright, and sparkling; it wants shade; it wants to be stretched out here and there with a long chapter of sense, if it could be had; if not, of solemn specious nonsense, about something unconnected with the story; an essay on writing, a critique on Walter Scott, or the history of Buonaparté, or anything that would form a contrast, and bring the reader with increased delight to the playfulness and epigrammatism of the general style.[27]

Clearly this was not meant to be taken too seriously, yet the feeling that this brilliant work, to a great extent the production of her youth, "wants shade", was probably the genuine response of the mature writer at present absorbed in the more sombre and complex *Mansfield Park*.

By 9th February, Jane had received a gratifying letter from her niece Fanny, "Her liking Darcy & Elizabeth is enough, she might hate all the others if she would",[28] and she decided that the time had come to let Anna into the authorship secret.

Later that month, Jane wrote again to Martha, who had also been making enquiries into the landscape of Northamptonshire. Jane now told her not to pursue them, as Henry, who had some business in the area, would be able to provide the answers. The letter is interesting in that it contains another of her infrequent comments on public affairs.

After their brief, stormy marriage, and long years of inimical separation, relations between the Prince Regent and Caroline of Brunswick were reaching the point of crisis which was soon to result in her setting forth on her disastrous and scandalous foreign travels. But at this time, public sympathy was firmly on her side, and Jane was expressing the majority opinion when she wrote: "Poor woman, I shall support her as long as I can, because she *is* a Woman, & because I hate her Husband. . . . but if I must give up the Princess, I am resolved at least always to think that she would have been respectable, if the Prince had behaved only tolerably by her at first.—"[29]

This time, the *British Critic* was the first to publish its notice of *Pride and Prejudice*, while a longer review with extensive quotations and a detailed account of the plot appeared the next month in the *Critical Review*.[30] That the critic was aware of the level of Jane Austen's achievement in this work was best shown by his apt comparison of her Elizabeth with Shakespeare's Beatrice. Certainly a star danced when Elizabeth Bennet was born.

Every lover of the novels of Jane Austen cherishes an individual preference, and the consensus of opinion is that *Emma* is the masterpiece, the distillation of all that is unique in her art. But there can be little doubt that the universal favourite among her works—and one of the best loved of all classic novels in English is *Pride and Prejudice*.

The affection that this work arouses can be attributed to that very light, bright, and sparkling, champagne atmosphere that Jane Austen—not very strenuously—raises as an objection; to its quality of youthfulness; to the firm dramatic symmetry of its basic Cinderella story; and above all, to the character of its heroine.

Virginia Woolf considered that, great writer though she was, it was difficult to catch Jane Austen in the act of greatness.[31] Yet careful readers of the first chapter of *Pride and Prejudice* might justifiably consider themselves to have done so. Boldly beginning with an aphorism, "It is a truth universally acknowledged, that a single man in possession of a good fortune must be in want of a wife",[32] in rather less than two and a half pages of witty dialogue an astonishing amount of information, intention, and tone, is conveyed; interest in the narrative immediately aroused; and the novel is launched on its course with a skill, economy, and assurance, the more remarkable for being totally unobtrusive.

When Jane Austen decided to rename *First Impressions*, she took a quotation from her much admired Fanny Burney's *Cecilia* for her new title. At the conclusion of this long work, when after many trials and harrowing circumstances, the lovers are at last to be united, it is pronounced that "the whole of this unfortunate business has been the result of PRIDE and PREJUDICE", and in Jane Austen's novel, much of the pride and prejudice is due to a reliance on first impressions.

To a certain extent, *Sense and Sensibility* is a duet between two devoted and contrasted sisters; while *Pride and Prejudice* can be seen as a duel between the hero and the heroine. Close and affectionately drawn though the relationship is between Jane and Elizabeth Bennet, Jane has only a passive role to play. It is between the spirited, courageous, witty, high-principled heroine, and the proud, intelligent, reserved, and wealthy hero that the dramatic action takes place. Both Elizabeth and Darcy are engaged on this particular "moral assault course", and just as both Elinor and Marianne share the qualities of sense and sensibility though in very different proportions, so Elizabeth's prejudice is mixed with pride, and Darcy's pride supported by his prejudice.

The events of the story force both heroine and hero to admit their faults; Elizabeth recognizes the intellectual vanity which led to her prejudice, and Darcy the blindly accepted social assumptions that led to his appearance of pride. Both emotionally and socially, the novel is harmoniously resolved by their marriage.

Much has been written about Jane Austen's social attitudes, and it is frequently maintained that she was a snob. But her position throughout *Pride and Prejudice*, and indeed all her novels makes it clear that this was far from the case. The snobbery of Lady Catherine who "likes to have the distinction of rank preserved",[33] the initial pride of Mr Darcy, and the sycophancy of Mr Collins are all ridiculed and disapproved. Moreover, the rigid social barriers of the time are set aside by Darcy's friendship with Mr Bingley, whose family wealth stemmed from trade; by his acceptance of Elizabeth's aunt and uncle, the unassuming Gardiners; and by his marriage to Elizabeth. Jane endured snobbery rather than practised it.

During the course of the work, a great deal is said on the subject of marriage, and to a certain extent the structure of the novel is founded on the intelligent but indolent Mr Bennet's unsuitable marriage. Many moments of high comedy flow from the exchanges between Mr Bennet and his foolish wife. Yet both father and mother share the burden of responsibility for their failure in the upbringing up their three youngest daughters. It may be wondered how it was that Jane and Elizabeth turned out so well. Hints of Mr Bennet's utter failure to take his role as a father seriously occur throughout the work, culminating in his refusal to prevent the fifteen-year-old Lydia's ill-fated trip to Brighton. The tragic aspect of his marriage is revealed only at the end of the novel in the moving scene between Elizabeth and her father, when he is still unsure of her motives for accepting Darcy, "My child, let me not have the grief of seeing *you* unable to respect your partner in life. You know not what you are about."[34] Mrs Bennet views marriage in tinsel terms of youthful attraction, pretty clothes, a handsome establishment, a good table, and the best possible income with which to maintain a position.

Unique in the novels is the careful study of Charlotte Lucas, a sympathetic, sensible, plain girl, who, with her eyes wide open, chooses marriage with the intolerable Mr Collins; she does so for a position in life and an establishment, but however objectively she views him, she must be a wife to her husband and bear his children. This was the compromise forced on them by economics and accepted by the majority of middle-class young women at the time, but clearly unacceptable to Jane Austen.

A hint of her resentment at the enhanced social status automatically bestowed by marriage can be inferred from Lydia's first entry into the dining parlour on her return to Longbourn, "Ah! Jane, I take your place now, and you must go lower, because I am a married woman."[35]

This second published novel firmly established Jane Austen's genius for characterization. Her people seem to live and move beyond the confines of the pages that describe them. She herself clearly felt this when she writes of looking for portraits of Mrs Bingley and Mrs Darcy at London exhibitions, and for her family's benefit continued the story to include Kitty Bennet's marriage to a clergyman near Pemberley, and Mary's to one of her Uncle Philip's Meryton clerks.

Elizabeth is among the most attractive heroines of all fiction, and it is tempting to believe she must have greatly resembled her youthful creator. These words, for example, might be spoken with as much justice by Jane Austen as by her Elizabeth: "I hope I never ridicule what is wise or good. Follies and nonsense, whims and inconsistencies *do* divert me, I own, and I laugh at them whenever I can."[36]

One of the most attractive pictures of Elizabeth is on her arrival at Netherfield after a three-mile walk in dirty weather to visit her sick sister, "crossing field after field at a quick pace, jumping over stiles and springing over puddles with impatient activity, and finding herself at last within view of the house, with weary ancles, dirty stockings, and a face glowing with the warmth of exercise".[37]

It is not surprising that the self-controlled Mr Darcy should be attracted by this vibrant figure, to which it is particularly hard to reconcile Charlotte Brontë's criticism of *Pride and Prejudice* as "an accurate daguerreotyped portrait of a common-place face; a carefully fenced, highly cultivated garden, with neat borders and delicate flowers; but no glance of a bright vivid physiognomy, no open country, no fresh air. . . ."[38]

As for Darcy himself, the criticism has often with justice been levelled that the transformation in his character is too sudden and too great. But of all Jane Austen's heroes, Darcy is the most purely romantic; he alone has the dramatic physical presence, the air of mystery, the quality of aloof remoteness, that admits him to the small and fascinating band of such eternally magnetic figures as Heathcliff, Mr Rochester, and the characters created in his own image by Lord Byron. The future Lady Byron, it is interesting to note, was particularly taken by Mr Darcy.

A sad event this year, was the death of Henry's wife, Eliza. It was a long while since she had been the sparkling, gay, flirtatious figure of Jane's girlhood, and after a long and hopeless illness, she died at the age of fifty-one on 25th April 1813.

Jane's next surviving letter was written on 20th May from

Henry's home in Sloane Street. Henry had been visiting Chawton and his sister had travelled home with him for a short
trip to town. It was not the melancholy occasion that it might
have been, for as Jane was able to write to Frank just two
months later: "Upon the whole his Spirits are very much
recovered.—If I may so express myself, his Mind is not a
Mind for affliction. He is too Busy, too active, too sanguine.—
Sincerely as he was attached to poor Eliza moreover, &
excellently as he behaved to her, he was always so used to be
away from her at times, that her Loss is not felt as that of
many a beloved wife might be. . . . He very long knew that
she must die, & it was indeed a release at last."[39]

As she told Cassandra, Jane was pleased to be "very snug
with the front drawing-room all to myself, & would not say
'Thank you' for any companion but you. The quietness of it
does me good".[40] One may conjecture that this quietness was
also of value to *Mansfield Park*.

She had visited Martha's young cousin, Charlotte Craven,
who was at a school in London. "She looks very well, and her
hair is done up with an elegance to do credit to any education.
Her manners are as unaffected and pleasing as ever. . . . I was
shewn upstairs into a drawing-room, where she came to me,
and the appearance of the room, so totally unschoolike, amused
me very much; it was full of all the modern elegances—& if it
had not been for some naked Cupids over the Mantelpiece,
which must be a fine study for Girls, one should never have
smelt instruction."[41]

As usual, there was a good deal of shopping to be done, and
several exhibitions of paintings to be seen, including that of
the Society of Painters in Oil and Water Colours in Spring
Gardens, where Jane spotted Mrs Bingley, but could see no-
one she could identify with Mrs Darcy. Nor did she have any
better luck at an exhibition of 130 works of Sir Joshua
Reynolds. "I can only imagine that Mr. D. prizes any picture
of her too much to like it should be exposed to the public
eye. I can imagine he would have that sort of feeling—that
mixture of love, pride, and delicacy. Setting aside this disappointment, I had great amusement among the pictures;
and the driving about, the carriage being open, was very
pleasant. I liked my solitary elegance very much, and was
ready to laugh all the time at my being where I was. I could
not but feel that I had naturally small right to be parading
about London in a barouche."[42]

Despite this feeling of modesty, Henry's partner and his

wife, Mr and Mrs Tilson, had invited them to meet Miss Burdett, the sister of Sir Francis Burdett, the reforming politician. Jane's secret was beginning to leak out. "I should like to see Miss Burdett very well, but that I am rather frightened by hearing that she wishes to be introduced to *me*.—If I *am* a wild beast, I cannot help it. It is not my own fault."[43] Since brother and sister were both in mourning for Eliza, on this visit, there were no trips to the theatre.

This summer, while Godmersham was being painted, Edward and his family were at the big house at Chawton, and both Jane and Cassandra were glad of the opportunity of seeing more of the children, particularly their eldest niece, Fanny, now a pretty girl of twenty.

As well as for Eliza, the family was now in mourning for Mr Thomas Leigh of Stoneleigh Abbey, and Jane suggests that Mrs Leigh Perrot may have regretted her husband's decision about his inheritance: "Poor Mrs L. P.—who would now have been Mistress of Stoneleigh had there been none of that vile compromise, which in good truth has never been allowed to be of much use to them."[44]

From Deputy, Henry had now been appointed Receiver-General for Oxfordshire, for which Uncle Leigh Perrot and his brother Edward stood surety for him to a considerable extent.

Frank's ship, the *Elephant* was on convoy duty in the Baltic, the Southern shores of which, after Napoleon's retreat from Moscow, were included in the "great arena of the battles" which preceded his downfall.[45] Jane was pleased to tell her brother about the financial success of her writing and her current work:

> You will be glad to hear that every Copy of S. & S. is sold & that it has brought me £140 besides the Copyright, if that shd ever be of any value.—I have now therefore written myself into £250—which only makes me long for more.—I have something in hand—which I hope on the credit of P. & P. will sell well, tho' not half so entertaining. And bye the bye—shall you object to my mentioning the Elephant in it, & two or three other of your old Ships? I *have* done it, but it shall not stay, to make you angry.—They are only just mentioned.

She concludes, "God bless you.—I hope you continue beautiful and brush your hair, but not all off.—We join in an infinity of Love."[46] She would have been glad to know that a photograph of Frank taken at the age of ninety shows a bald patch on top, but a bushy abundance of white hair at either side.

In September, Jane accompanied Edward and three of his daughters, Fanny, Lizzie, and Marianne, to London, where they stayed with Henry in the newly fitted apartment in Henrietta Street. "Mde Bigeon was below dressing us a most comfortable dinner of soup, fish, bouillée, partridges, and an apple tart, which we sat down to soon after five, after cleaning and dressing ourselves and feeling that we were most commodiously disposed of. The little adjoining dressing-room to our apartment makes Fanny and myself very well off indeed, and as we have poor Eliza's bed our space is ample every way."[47]

During the summer, Henry had taken a holiday tour in the south of Scotland with Edward's eldest son, Edward. Proud of his sister's achievement, and no doubt pleased with his own share in it, Henry had not been able to keep her authorship a secret. "Lady Robert [Kerr] is delighted with P. & P., and really *was* so, as I understand, before she knew who wrote it, for, of course, she knows now. He told her with as much satisfaction as it were my wish. He did not tell *me* this, but he told Fanny. And Mr. Hastings! I am quite delighted with what such a man writes about it."[48]

Henry was out of mourning now, so there were visits to the theatre, first the Lyceum, where they saw "three musical things. 'Five Hours at Brighton', in three acts—of which one was over before we arrived, none the worse—and the 'Beehive', rather less flat and trumpery".[49] The final item was *Don Juan*, which delighted the girls.

For their visit to Covent Garden, where they were to see *The Clandestine Marriage* and *Midas*, Jane's often neglected hair was dressed at home by Mr Hall, who "curled me out at a great rate. I thought it looked hideous, and longed for a snug cap instead, but my companions silenced me by their admiration."[50]

At Covent Garden, Jane was disappointed with the quality of the acting although, not so critical, "The girls were very much delighted, but still prefer 'Don Juan'; and I must say that I have seen nobody on the stage who has been a more interesting character than that compound of cruelty and lust."[51]

But apart from such diversions, the London visit can hardly have been a treat for the girls who had been taken there largely for the benefit of their teeth. Mr Spence, their dentist, failed to meet with their aunt's approval. "The poor girls and their teeth! . . . Lizzy's were filed and lamented over again,

and poor Marianne had two taken out after all, the two just
beyond the eye teeth, to make room for those in front.—
When her doom was fixed, Fanny, Lizzy, and I walked into
the next room, where we heard each of the two sharp hasty
screams. The little girls' teeth I can suppose in a critical state,
but I think he must be a lover of teeth and money and mis-
chief, to parade about Fanny's. I would not have had him look
at mine for a shilling a tooth and double it."[52]

Jane's purchases included a pretty white satin and lace cap
with a peak in front "and a little white flower perking out of
the left ear, like Harriot Byron's feather", and a gown
"trimmed everywhere with white ribbon plaited on somehow
or other. She says it will look well. I am not sanguine. They
trim with white very much."[53] At Wedgwood's, Edward and
Fanny chose the dinner service, edged with a pattern of small
purple lozenges between narrow gold lines, some of which is
still to be seen at Chawton House today.

Jane provided her sister with a delightful sketch of the
family party, "We are now all four of us young ladies sitting
round the circular table in the inner room writing our letters,
while the two brothers are having a comfortable coze in the
room adjoining. It is to be a quiet evening, much to the satisfaction of four of the six. My eyes are quite tired of dust and
lamps."[54] No doubt Jane was pleased when they left Henry
and travelled on to the peace and quiet of Godmersham, which
she had not visited for the past four years. This stay of nearly
three months was to prove her last visit to Edward's beautiful
Kentish home.

On 23rd September, she was replying to a letter from
Cassandra "rich in striking intelligence". Her aunt had to
report that now she was home, Fanny was disappointed with
her London purchases: "I consider it as a thing of course at her
time of life—one of the sweet taxes of youth to chuse in a
hurry and make bad bargains."[55]

Mr Wadham Knatchbull, nineteen years of age, arrived for
a visit, and put the ladies in something of a flap. "I wish you
had seen Fanny and me running backwards and forwards with
his breeches from the little chintz to the white room before
we went to bed, in the greatest of frights lest he should come
upon us before we had done it all. There had been a mistake
in the housemaid's preparations and *they* were gone to bed."[56]

Jane's bulletin on the state of the pains in her face makes
it clear that she had been suffering from these for some time,
and they had been aggravated by her catching a cold in the

coach. In spite of her suspicions, possibly she too might have benefited from a consultation with the fearsome Mr Spence.

A family expedition was arranged to Goodnestone Farm so that the older girls might enjoy the local annual fair. Jane was very glad to decline her invitation, and looking forward to dining quietly with the current governess, Miss Clewes.

Mrs Cooke had written from Brighton that the Rev. Dr Edmund Isham, Warden of All Souls, admired *Pride and Prejudice*, and was sure he would not "like Madame D'arblay's new novel half so well".[57] Since this was *The Wanderer*, a serious work with an interesting theme but tedious in execution, we may be sure he did not.

On 25th September, Jane wrote to Frank, and her opening sentence is a reminder that in those days it was the recipient who paid for the postage, "I assure you I thought it very well worth its 2s/3d." Frank had reported on the economic conditions of the countries he had visited, and Jane responds with current prices at home, "But I have no occasion to think of the price of Bread or of Meat where I am now; let me shake off vulgar cares & conform to the happy Indifference of East Kent Wealth . . . I have not been here these 4 years, so I am sure the event deserves to be talked of before & behind as well as in the middle."[58] There is something of a sting in this sentence that raises the question of why it was that Jane had not visited Godmersham for so long. Probably the secret was hidden in a discreet silence, or one of the letters Cassandra tactfully destroyed.

Since she was in Kent, she knew that Frank would be hoping she would visit his wife. "I shall be sorry to be in Kent so long without seeing Mary, but am afraid it must be so." Later to Cassandra, she wrote, "I should like to have Mrs F. A. and her children here for a week but not a syllable of that nature is ever breathed. I wish her last visit had not been so long a one."[59] Evidently on that former occasion, Mrs F. A. had outstayed her welcome.

At Godmersham, there was always "a constant succession of small events, somebody is always going or coming". Edward Bridges, Jane's one-time suitor, had popped in unexpectedly to breakfast. His wife, at Ramsgate for her health, had turned out to be "a poor Honey—the sort of woman who gives me the idea of being determined never to be well—& who likes her spasms & nervousness & the consequence they give her, better than anything else.—This is an ill-natured sentiment to send all over the Baltic"[60]

Frank had now replied to his sister's request to use the names of his ships in *Mansfield Park*, that he would be happy for her to do so, but that it might endanger her anonymity. But by this time, Henry's lively tongue had done its work, and Jane was resigned to her identity's becoming known. "I beleive whenever the 3rd appears, I shall not even attempt to tell lies about it.—I shall rather try to make all the Money than all the Mystery I can of it." But she was still grateful for what she described as "the *superior* kindness" he and Mary had shown in doing what she wished, and guarding her secret."[61] Two important items mentioned in this letter are the engagement of James's daughter, Anna, to Ben Lefroy, the youngest son of Jane's dear friend; and the second edition of *Sense and Sensibility*.

Jane's letter to Cassandra of 11th October mentions that Mrs and Miss Milles had been to dinner, and later she was to call on them at Canterbury. Like Mrs Stent, the Milles mother and daughter made a lively contribution to the creation of Mrs and Miss Bates. "I like the mother, . . . because she is cheerful & grateful for what she is at the age of ninety and upwards."[69] . . . "Miss Milles was queer as usual, and provided us with plenty to laugh at. She undertook in *three words* to give us the history of Mrs. Scudamore's reconciliation, and then talked on about it for half-an-hour, using such odd expressions, and so foolishly minute, that I could hardly keep my countenance."[63]

Another visitor, Mrs Britton, seems to have had much in common with Mrs Elton of *Emma*, and it is likely that during this visit to Godmersham, nearing the end of one novel, Jane Austen was already planning the next. "She is a large, ungenteel woman, with self-satisfied and would-be elegant manners."[64]

Edward's older boys were getting to an age when their behaviour alternately provoked their aunt's censure and praise. There was a suspicion, voiced by Sackree, their devoted old nursemaid, that George and Henry had shown "signs of going after" a Chawton girl called Mary Doe. "As I wrote of my nephews with a little bitterness in my last, I think it particularly incumbent on me to do them justice now, and I have great pleasure in saying that they were both at the Sacrament yesterday. After having much praised or much blamed anybody, one is generally sensible of something just the reverse soon afterwards."[65]

In November, Edward and George went up to Oxford. "They got there very safely—Edwd two hours behind the coach,

Pulteney Bridge, Bath, which leads from Jane Austen's home in
Sydney Place to the city centre

Jane Austen's Chawton home as it is today

The famous Cobb, o
jetty, at Lyme Regis
as it is today

The house in College
Street, Winchester,
where Jane Austen
died

having lost his way in leaving London. George writes cheer-fully and quietly . . . and concludes with saying, 'I'm afraid I shall be poor'. I am glad he thinks about it so soon."[66]

There are signs in these comments, and in Jane's discussion of her niece Anna's engagement and marriage, that she and Cassandra were indeed becoming the family "formid-ables".

In this series of letters from Godmersham, Cassandra is given several brisk portraits of the young men who turned up to partake of Edward's generous hospitality, illustrating what has been described as Jane's "deeply-ingrained habit of sitting in judgment on character"[67] in the letters, just as much as in her early works and her novels.

"On Saturday, soon after breakfast, Mr. J. P. left us for Norton Court. I like him very much. He gives me the idea of a very amiable young man, only too diffident to be so agreeable as he might be."[68]

"Mr. W. is about five or six-and-twenty, not ill-looking and not agreeable. He is certainly no addition. A sort of cool, gentlemanlike manner, but very silent. . . ."[69]

"We have got rid of Mr. R. Mascall however. I did not like *him* either. He talks too much and is conceited, besides having a vulgarly shaped mouth."[70]

"Mr. Lushington goes tomorrow.—Now I must speak of *him*, and I like him very much. I am sure he is clever and a man of taste. He got a volume of Milton last night and spoke of it with warmth. He is quite an M.P.—very smiling, with an exceeding good address and readiness of language.—I am rather in love with him. I dare say he is ambitious and insincere."[71]

Reading is mentioned. Not much progress was being made in the worthy endeavour of reading *Modern Europe* with Fanny, beyond the first twenty-five pages. *Self Control*, a novel by Mrs Brunton, Jane decided was "an excellently-meant, elegantly-written work, without anything of nature or proba-bility in it. I declare I do not know whether Laura's passage down the American river, is not the most natural, possible, everyday thing she ever does.—"[72]

In the letter of 14th October occurs one of those remarks in which Jane's sense of reality can be interpreted as heart-lessness: "Only think of Mrs. Holder's being dead! Poor woman, she has done the only thing in the world she could possibly do, to make one cease to abuse her."[73]

But the next day, she is full of affection and excitement at

K

the arrival of her brother Charles and his family: ". . . here they are, safe and well, just like their own nice selves, Fanny looking as neat and white this morning as possible, and dear Charles all affectionate, placid, quiet, cheerful good humour. They are both looking very well, but poor little Cassy is grown extremely thin, and looks poorly. I hope a week's country air & exercise may do her good. I am sorry to say it can be but a week."[74]

Her life on the *Namur* did not suit little Cassy, who suffered from sea-sickness, and yet she was too attached to her parents to wish to be parted from them, or they from her. It is sad to reflect that after so many discussions about Cassy's future welfare, her mother was to die in childbirth within the next year. The new baby did not survive, and Charles was left with three little daughters to rear.

Like her cousin Caroline before her, Cassy was overwhelmed by the Godmersham family: "She agrees pretty well with her cousins, but is not quite happy among them; they are too many and too boisterous for her."[75]

On 21st October, Jane's letter to Cassandra begins with a long message from Lizzie. It appears that Jane continued her visits of charity when she was in Kent, for her niece writes: "I must now tell you something about our poor people. I believe you know old Mary Croucher, she gets *maderer* and *maderer* every day. Aunt Jane has been to see her, but it was on one of her rational days."[76]

When Jane wrote next on 26th October, Cassandra was staying in Henrietta Street with Henry, who had been unwell, "I trust you are seeing improvement in him every day". Once again, Harriot Moore's husband was under discussion, "Owing to a difference of clocks the coachman did not bring the carriage so soon as he ought by half-an-hour; anything like a breach of punctuality was a great offence, and Mr Moore was very angry, which I was rather glad of. I wanted to see him angry; and, though he spoke to his servant in a very loud voice and with a good deal of heat, I was happy to perceive that he did not scold Harriot at all."[77]

If Harriot's marriage had turned out better than expected, it appears that the family fears about her brother's had been justified: "We have had another of Edward Bridges' Sunday visits. I think the pleasantest part of his married life must be the dinners, and breakfasts, and luncheons, and billiards that he gets in this way at Gm."[78]

Early in November, Jane was making her future plans,

which included travelling to town with Edward, and breaking her journey at Henry's, "I wish you would tell him with my best love that I shall be most happy to spend ten days or a fortnight in Henrietta St., if he will accept me. I do not offer more than a fortnight, because I shall then have been some time from home; but it will be a great pleasure to be with him, as it always is."[79]

She describes a visit to Canterbury with Edward, "He went to inspect the gaol, as a visiting magistrate, and took me with him. I was gratified, and went through all the feelings which people must go through, I think, in visiting such a building. We paid no other visits, only walked about snugly together and shopped."[80]

The next day they were to attend a dinner at Chilham Castle, to be followed by a concert. One of the guests was to be Mrs Harrison, the sister of Jane's old friend Mrs Lefroy, and the aunt of Ben, Anna's fiancé. From the point of view of their relations, however it may have seemed to the young couple, the romance was causing some anxiety. Anna exhibited a certain instability which in view of her childhood was not surprising, and Ben was a serious, conscientious, somewhat intractable young man. Jane had reported to Frank: "I beleive he is sensible, certainly very religious, well connected & with some independence.—There is an unfortunate dissimularity of Taste between them in one respect which gives us some apprehensions, he hates company & she is very fond of it;—this, with some queerness of Temper on his side & much unsteadiness on hers, is untoward."[81] In a later letter to Cassandra, her view is even less sanguine, "He has declined a curacy (apparently highly eligible), which he might have secured against his taking orders; and, upon its being made rather a serious question, says he has not made up his mind as to taking orders so early, and that, if her father makes a point of it, he must give Anna up rather than do what he does not approve. He must be maddish."[82]

Jokingly, Jane tells her sister what she proposes to say when they meet to Ben's aunt, " 'My dear Mrs. Harrison,' I shall say, 'I am afraid the young man has some of your family madness, and though there often appears to be something of madness in Anna too, I think she inherits more of it from her mother's family than from ours.' That is what I shall say, and I think she will find it difficult to answer me."[83]

In the event, "Mrs. Harrison and I found each other out & had a very comfortable little complimentary friendly chat.

She is a sweet woman, still quite a sweet woman in herself, &
so like her sister! I could almost have thought I was speaking
to Mrs. Lefroy. . . . By-the-bye, as I must leave off being young,
I find many *douceurs* in being a sort of *chaperon*, for I am put
on the sofa near the fire, and can drink as much wine as I like."[84]

She had heard that Henry's servant, William, was leaving
him for a job in the country: "He has more of Cowper than of
Johnson in him—fonder of tame hares & blank verse than of
the full tide of human existence at Charing Cross."[85]

A letter from Miss Sharpe was full of "sweet flattery", and
"I am read and admired in Ireland, too. There is a Mrs
Fletcher, the wife of a judge, an old lady and very good and
very clever, who is all curiosity to know about me—what I
am like and so forth . . . I do not despair of having my picture
in the Exhibition at last—all white and red, with my head on
one side; or perhaps I may marry young Mr D'Arblay"[86]—an
unlikely conjecture, as Fanny Burney D'Arblay's only son was
nineteen years Jane's junior. Her last long letter from comfortable Godmersham was written on 6th November 1813,
"Having half an hour before breakfast—(very snug, in my own
room, lovely morning, excellent fire, fancy me!)."[87]

Like so many writers, Jane found that people were less
inclined to buy her works than to borrow them, and the
readership must have been far in excess of the small editions
originally printed. "Since I wrote last, my 2nd Edit. has stared
me in the face. Mary tells me that Eliza means to buy it. I
wish she may . . . I cannot help hoping that *many* will feel
themselves obliged to buy it. I shall not mind imagining it a
disagreeable duty to them, so as they do it."[88]

As well as *Sense and Sensibility*, *Pride and Prejudice* had now
gone into a 2nd edition, but this was of no profit to the author,
who had sold the work to Egerton outright.

Before Jane finally left Kent, there was to be a ball, for
which she had kept her "China Crape". "There is some chance
of a good ball next week, as far as females go. Lady Bridges
may perhaps be there with some Knatchbulls. Mrs. Harrison
perhaps with Miss Oxenden and the Miss Papillons—and if
Mrs. Harrison, then Lady Fagg will come."[89]

We do not know whether the ball came up to expectations
for, rather surprisingly, there is no letter surviving to Cassandra from Jane's homeward bound visit to Henrietta Street, and
afterwards it must be presumed she settled down to a busy
winter at Chawton. *Mansfield Park* was practically completed,
and by January she had made a start on *Emma*.

In February 1814, Henry visited Chawton and when he returned to town, Jane travelled up with him. He spent the journey reading the finished manuscript of *Mansfield Park* which on this visit was to go to the printer. "Henry's approbation hitherto is even equal to my wishes. He says it is very different from the other two, but does not appear to think it at all inferior."[90]

When they arrived at Henrietta Street, they were welcomed by one of Henry's bank employees. "Nice smiling Mr Barlowe met us at the door, and, in reply to enquiries after news, said that peace was generally expected."[91] Paris capitulated to the allies on 31st March, Napoleon was allowed to retire to Elba, and in May, Louis XVIII and the royal family entered the capital in triumph. It seemed the interminable war was over.

While her brother continued reading her own new novel, Jane was enjoying *The Heroine* by E. S. Barrett. "It is a delightful burlesque, particularly on the Radcliffe style. Henry is going on with 'Mansfield Park'. He admires H. Crawford: I mean properly, as a clever, pleasant man."[92]

While Jane was away, little Cassandra was visiting Chawton, sleeping in her aunt's bed. "I hope she found my bed comfortable last night and has not filled it with fleas."[93] The subject is mentioned again later, and it sounds strange to hear the fastidious Jane Austen speaking of fleas. Unless it was due to her shipboard sojourn, there seems no reason why little Cassy should have been so suspected, although in those days such unpleasant bedfellows were all too common.

Jane begins her next letter of 5th March, with an apology for writing so soon. "Do not be angry with me for beginning another letter to you. I have read the 'Corsair', mended my petticoat, and have nothing else to do."[94] Edward, who was having legal troubles about his inheritance, had arrived in town with Fanny, "Getting out is impossible. It is a nasty day for everybody. Edward's spirits will be wanting sunshine, and here is nothing but thickness & sleet; and though these two rooms are delightfully warm, I fancy it is very cold abroad."[95]

Young Mr Wyndham Knatchbull had accepted an invitation to dinner on Sunday. "He is such a nice, gentlemanlike, unaffected sort of young man, that I think he may do for Fanny;—has a sensible, quiet look which one likes."[96] But although much later Fanny was to marry a Knatchbull, it was not to be young Wyndham, but his elder widowed brother, afterwards Sir Edward, the Ninth Baronet, in worldly terms at least, a better match. As it happened, young Wyndham did not, in fact, attend the dinner, but sent "a long & very civil note of excuse". They had been to the theatre and enjoyed seeing Edmund Kean, then at the beginning of the most brilliant phase of his career, playing Shylock which was considered one of his greatest roles.

To her pleasure, her brother was enthusiastic about *Mansfield Park*. "Henry has this moment said that he likes my M.P. better & better; he is in the third volume. I believe *now* he has changed his mind as to foreseeing the end; he said yesterday, at least, that he defied anybody to say whether H. C. would be reformed, or would forget Fanny in a fortnight."[97]

Jane did not forget her household duties at Chawton while she was away: "I am sorry to hear that there has been a rise in tea. I do not mean to pay Twining till later in the day, when we may order a fresh supply. I long to know something of the Mead, and how you are off for a cook. . . ."[98]

Mr Wyndham Knatchbull's place as a suitable escort for Fanny was taken by another young man. "Mr. J. Plumtre joined in the latter part of the evening, walked home with us, ate some soup, and is very earnest for our going to Covent Garden again tonight to see Miss Stephens in the 'Farmer's Wife'. He is to try for a box. I do not particularly wish him to succeed."[99]

He did succeed, but Jane did not think a great deal of the entertainment, "The 'Farmer's Wife' is a musical thing in three acts, and as Edward was steady in not staying for anything more, we were at home before ten—Fanny and Mr. J. P. are delighted with Miss S., & her merit in singing is I dare say very great; that she gave *me* no pleasure is no reflection upon her, nor, I hope, upon myself, being what Nature made me on that article. All I am sensible of in Miss S. is a pleasing person and no skill in acting."[100]

Jane was looking forward to being joined in London by her sister, after which she was going on to spend some days with Mrs Catherine Hill at Streatham. "A great many pretty caps in the windows of Cranbourn Alley! I hope when you come, we shall both be tempted.[101]. . . Prepare for a play the very first evening, I rather think Covent Garden, to see Young in Richard."[102] Most important of all: "Henry has finished 'Mansfield Park', and his approbation has not lessened. He found the last half of the volume *extremely interesting*."[103]

Mansfield Park, "by the author of 'Sense and Sensibility' and 'Pride and Prejudice'", was published in three volumes, price 18s, by Thomas Egerton in May 1814. Perhaps dubious of the success of a novel so different from its predecessors, Egerton had offered and Jane had agreed to accept publication on the same terms as *Sense and Sensibility*. Neither need have worried, as the edition of 1,500 copies was sold out by November.

For some reason, *Mansfield Park* received no notices, which was strange in view of the interest already taken in the work of this new novelist by the *British Critic* and the *Critical Review*. Instead, and no doubt disappointed, Jane made her own collection of *Opinions*,[104] a practice she also followed after the publication of *Emma*. Without any comments of her own, she recorded the views of her family and friends, which differed then just as strikingly as do those of readers and critics today. Probably none of Jane Austen's works has provoked such controversial reactions as this third published novel.

Anna could not bear her aunt's latest heroine, Fanny Price; nephew Edward admired her, while George disliked her. Edward thought Henry Crawford's elopement with Maria Rushworth, at a time when he was so much in love with Fanny, was unnatural; on the other hand, Mrs James Austen thought Henry Crawford's going off with Mrs Rushworth very natural. Most of the readers were impressed by Mrs Norris, and the Portsmouth scenes were generally praised. Mr and Mrs Cooke were pleased with the way the clergy were treated. Most people remained loyal to *Pride and Prejudice*, but the Fowles at Kintbury preferred it to either of the others. Fanny Cage found "nothing interesting in the Characters—Language poor", while Lady Robert Kerr "read every line with the greatest interest & am more delighted with it than my humble pen can express . . .". Doubtless most irritating of all, "Mrs. Lefroy liked it, but thought it a mere Novel".

After so many sharply opposed contemporary opinions, Jane Austen would not be surprised to find her modern critics in strongest disagreement about this particular work. To take just a few recent 'opinions': for Kingsley Amis, "the character of Fanny lacks self knowledge, generosity and humility," she is "a monster of complacency and pride who, under a cloak of cringing self-abasement, dominates and gives meaning to the novel. . .". Dr E. G. Selwyn finds Fanny "a beautiful character. Shy, diffident, humble, and infinitely unselfish, she has firm Christian principles to which she adheres with rock-like consistency; and she also has fire". Elizabeth Bowen delights in her "delicate wind-flower fascination", while Marvin Mudrick finds her "alarmingly dim . . . a frozen block of timidity". Kingsley Amis considers that *Mansfield Park* is the witness of the corruption of Jane Austen's "judgment and her moral sense", yet Tony Tanner describes it as "a Stoic book in that it speaks for stillness rather than movement, firmness rather than fluidity, arrest rather than change, endurance rather than adventure"; he believes it to be not only Jane Austen's most profound novel, but "one of the most profound novels of the nineteenth century".[105]

Undoubtedly, *Mansfield Park* confirmed that Jane Austen was not just a successful writer of brilliant social comedy, but a very great novelist. In no other work does she so extend her range of characters and emotions, and none other of her novels can compare with it for strength, melancholy, realism, biting irony, and moral comment. Though it fails to attain the perfection of *Emma*, it is a remarkable attempt at a greater achievement. Occupying as it does, a central position among them, *Mansfield Park* compels a more serious and thoughtful assessment both of the earlier and the later novels.

Throughout the work, Mansfield Park itself embodies the peace, order, and stability which has been imposed by the severe and dignified presence of the head of the family, Sir Thomas Bertram. When he goes away, every member of the household becomes vulnerable to change and danger. This is largely because of the arrival of two disturbing newcomers, Henry and Mary Crawford, a charming and witty brother and sister, used to life in London, and accepting social standards very different from those which rule at Mansfield Park. But the Crawfords not only present a direct threat in themselves, they also reveal and enlarge the cracks and flaws that already exist in the structure of Mansfield, created by the shallow busy activity of Aunt Norris, the selfish indolence of Lady Bertram, and the failure of Sir Thomas to instil "principle, active principle"[106] in three of his children. He has succeeded only with his younger son Edmund, and his adopted niece, Fanny Price, but they too are put in peril by the sophistry of the Crawfords. The period through which Jane Austen lived was one of conflict between conservation and change. Her awareness of the tension this created, which was certainly felt in her own family, is clearly mirrored in the novel.

Jane Austen described this work as being on the subject of ordination, and to a certain extent it is. Had Edmund not been so determined to enter the church, he would soon have proposed and Mary Crawford would have accepted him. But among the main themes of the novel are Edmund's refusal to compromise, and Mary's worldly disdain for his chosen career. In the characters of Mr Collins and Mr Elton, Jane Austen, a daughter of a clerical family, makes fun of a pair of social climbing churchmen. But in answer to Mary's scathing disapproval, even ridicule, Edmund upholds the claims of his vocation with sincerity and dignity.

Apart from this conflict of character and career, the plot of the novel allows for the development of several other significant themes: the influence on the characters of their principles, or lack of them; the part played throughout by selfishness, of which all too often Fanny is the victim; the deleterious effects of vanity, insincerity, and the corrosive misery of jealousy.

The impressive narration of the novel is highlighted by several of the most brilliant scenes Jane Austen was ever to write. The visit to the home of Maria's fiancé, Mr Rushworth, at Sotherton, for instance, which foreshadows all that will happen at the end of the novel when Maria makes her ill-fated escape from the prison of her marriage by eloping with Henry, is a striking example of her subtle use of symbolism. As in most of her novels, it is important to bear in mind that the work was conceived in three volumes, and in none of them does any volume end with a scene of greater dramatic effect than Sir Thomas's unexpected return during the first full rehearsal of the play *Lovers' Vows*.

For many readers of *Mansfield Park*, the moral stand made not only by her hero and heroine, but also by the author herself, against this ostensibly innocent amusement, presents a difficulty in the appreciation of the novel. Especially when it is known that the Austen family had been keen exponents of amateur drama, and Jane Austen herself was a discerning theatregoer. But like the handkerchief in *Othello*, to a great extent the play acting is a device by means of which the author advances the plot and reveals her characters.

Jane Austen's own objections to family play-acting, bearing in mind the history of her brothers, James and Henry, and Eliza, are probably best summed up by Edmund, who agrees he would go any distance to see "real acting, good hardened real acting; but I would hardly walk from this room to the next to look at the raw efforts of those who have not been bred to the trade,—a set of gentlemen and ladies, who have all the disadvantages of education and decorum to struggle through".[107]

Fanny is dismayed by the acting because she knows, as

they all do, that Sir Thomas would never have agreed to it had he been present, and because she realizes that the play eventually chosen, *Lovers' Vows*, an adaptation by Mrs Inchbald from the German of Kotzebue, will provide, as indeed it does, too many opportunities to obscure real motives under a veil of make-believe and pretence. Finding a popular play so perfectly suited to the novel was a stroke of genius.

Henry's courtship of Fanny is cleverly forwarded by the scene of the dinner at the Grants when, while Sir Thomas, Mrs Norris, Dr and Mrs Grant play whist at "the table of prime intellectual state and dignity",[108] a great deal is revealed about the rest of the characters engaged in the simple round game of Speculation. A favourite, it will be remembered of the Austens.

The episode of the ball which Sir Thomas arranged for Fanny and her brother, William, is preceded by Fanny's agitation about how she shall wear the very pretty amber cross which William has brought her from Sicily, and for which she has only a piece of ribbon. Eventually she has two gold chains on which to hang it; one presented by Mary—in fact by Henry, and the other by Edmund. Symbolically, when Fanny dresses for the ball, she finds Mary's chain will not go through the ring of the cross. She wears both necklaces, but it is Edmund's gift that carries William's precious cross, which gracefully recalls Charles Austen's gifts to his sisters of topaz crosses.

The Portsmouth scenes of *Mansfield Park* stand alone in the novels of Jane Austen in the depiction of life at a lower social level with Dickensian realism. Two characteristics of Fanny Price that clearly belong to her author are a love of order and an abhorrence of noise. On both these scores, she is to be severely tried during her sojourn in her parents' home.

The doors were in constant banging, the stairs were never at rest, nothing was done without a clatter, nobody sat still, and nobody could command attention when they spoke.[109] . . . She sat in a blaze of oppressive heat, in a cloud of moving dust; and her eyes could only wander from the walls marked by her father's head, to the table cut and knotched by her brothers, where stood the tea-board never thoroughly cleaned, the cups and saucers wiped in streaks, the milk a mixture of motes floating in thin blue, and the bread and butter growing every minute more greasy than even Rebecca's hands had first produced it.[110]

Although Jane Austen does her best to give some conviction to the culmination of her plot, the elopement of Henry Crawford and Maria Rushworth, for most readers, she fails. It is largely this failure which prevents *Mansfield Park* from reaching the greatest heights of romantic literature. The only motive for this reckless act—or as Jane Austen considered it, sin of adultery—would have been overwhelming passion on both sides. To some extent, this may be discerned in Maria, but not in Henry who, as he has been presented, would surely have found some means of slithering gracefully out of the entanglement. It is untrue, as it is sometimes claimed, that Jane Austen has no understanding of the passions. Examples of heartfelt and passionate declarations in her work, which seem to have the ring of personal experience, are the disillusionment and rejection of Marianne Dashwood; Fanny Price's determined rejection of Henry Crawford in the face of Sir Thomas's equally determined disapproval, and Anne Elliot's long acquaintance with a hopeless love. But it may still be believed that she did not experience, or if she did, she was unable to convey the experience of physical passion. It would have been impossible for her to suggest the inescapable trap of Rosamond Vincy's attraction for Dr Lydgate in George Eliot's *Middlemarch*, or the sexual daydreaming that is the inspiration of Charlotte Brontë's *Villette*. With no suggestion of some such irresistible pressure, the elopement of Henry and Maria seems contrived, and the conclusion of the great novel unsatisfactory, in spite of the happy resolution of the union of Fanny and Edmund.

In her own life, her deepest and most intimate relationship was with her sister, and Jane Austen's novels provide many varied studies of families of sisters. These range from congenial sisters, like Elinor and Marianne Dashwood, and Jane and Elizabeth Bennet, to such incongruous sisters as Anne, Elizabeth and Mary Elliot, and Emma and Isabella Woodhouse. But perhaps never did she display keener realism, irony, and brilliance than in her description of the three Ward sisters: Mrs Price, who muddles through life in her "kind of slow bustle"; Lady Bertram, amusing but dangerously slothful, selfish and shrewd; and Mrs Norris, who perhaps because of her childlessness, seems to have inherited all the Ward family's stock of energy, and is one of the most savagely funny, complete and baleful characters Jane Austen was ever to draw. So consistent is her treatment throughout the novel, it is difficult to escape the impression that in Mrs Norris, her author was working out a long history of resentment, possibly unjustly, with Mrs Leigh Perrot at the core. And yet, even Mrs Norris, whose flattery and spoiling have directly inspired Maria's tragedy, is given her due: Mrs Price "might have made just as good a woman of consequence as Lady Bertram, but Mrs Norris would have been a more respectable mother of nine children, on a small income."[111]

As many critics have commented, in comparison with the responsive shine and sparkle of Mary and Henry Crawford, Fanny and Edmund appear an insipid pair. Vice appears more attractive than virtue. Yet, self-righteous though he sometimes seems, Edmund is not only a man of principle, kind and good, he also has presence and sufficient charm to captivate Mary. As for the constant, industrious, enduring, sensitive, and very pretty Fanny, she is also one of the most poetic of Jane Austen's characters. She is Marianne Dashwood without her fire and recklessness, and she has flashes of humour. On a close second reading, Edmund and Fanny prove by no means dull, while the meretricious sparkle of the Crawfords begins to look tawdry.

In the majority of Jane Austen's novels, the heroine emerges chastened and wiser from her experiences. Curiously, in *Mansfield Park*, the character who gains in self knowledge from the events which have taken place is not Fanny Price, who essentially has always been right, but the middle-aged man of substance and dignity, Sir Thomas Bertram. It is he who is forced to realize that his severe paternalism has cost him the confidence of his children, that his delegation of responsibility for the upbringing of his daughters to Mrs Norris has had an unfavourable effect on their characters, and has become "Sick of ambitious and mercenary connections, prizing more and more the sterling good of principle and temper, and chiefly anxious to bind by the strongest securities all that remained to him of domestic felicity.[112] . . .

Soon after the publication of *Mansfield Park*, Jane began a correspondence with her niece Anna, about her budding literary aspirations, which resulted in some rare and valuable pronouncements about her own views of novel writing. In his *Memoir*, Edward, Anna's half-brother, says she was "at that time amusing herself by attempting a novel, probably never finished, certainly never published, and of which I know nothing but what these extracts tell".[113] Unfortunately, as Mrs Bellas, Anna's daughter, later related, the manuscript was burned. "In later years when I expressed my sorrow that she had destroyed it, she said she could never have borne to finish it, but incomplete as it was Jane Austen's criticisms would have made it valuable."[114]

Possibly the novel had some intrinsic value, and it was not merely kindly encouragement that made Aunt Jane write, "I read it aloud to your G.M.—& At C.—and we were all very much pleased.— The Spirit does not droop at all." There is a sensible but modest criticism, "I do not like a Lover's speaking in the 3d person; it is too much like the formal part of Lord Orville, & I think it is not natural. If *you* think differently however, you need not mind me."[115]

Later, Jane was required to make more detailed comments. She approved of the revised title *Which is the heroine?*, though retaining a preference for the briefer original *Enthusiasm*. "I have scratched out Sir Tho: from walking with the other Men to the Stables &c. the very day after his breaking his arm— for though I find your Papa *did* walk out immediately after *his* arm was set, I think it can be so little usual as to appear unnatural in a book—& it does not seem to be material that Sir Tho: should go with them."[116]

Throughout, it is clear how much Jane Austen valued the accuracy of small details in giving total credibility to a work: ". . . we think you had better not leave England. Let the Portmans go to Ireland, but as you know nothing of the Manners there, you had better not go with them".[117] A month later, Jane writes, "You are now collecting your people delightfully, getting them exactly into such a spot as is the delight of my life. Three or four families in a country village is the very thing to work on—"[118] At this time, she herself was writing *Emma*, and inventing the village of Highbury.

An interesting sidelight on Jane Austen's habits of revision is given in the following, which shows how well she knew the courage needed to delete carefully written and well loved passages: "I hope when you have written a great deal more, you will be equal to scratching out some of the past. The scene with Mrs. Mellish, I should condemn; it is prosy and nothing to the purpose. . . ."[119]

Evidently, sensible Anna did not resent her Aunt's remarks, for three weeks later, Jane is writing, presumably of the next volume, "I have read it to your Aunt Cassandra, however, in our own room at night, while we undressed, and with a great deal of pleasure . . . You have been perfectly right in telling Ben of your work, and I am very glad to hear how much he likes it. His encouragement and approbation must be quite 'beyond everything'. I do not at all wonder at his not expecting to like anybody so well as Cecilia at first, but shall be surprised if he does not become a Susanite in time."[120] A foreshadowing here of the Kipling inspired following she herself was later to gather under the enthusiastic term of the 'Jane-ites'.

"Devereux Forester's being ruined by his vanity is extremely good, but I wish you would not let him plunge into a 'vortex of dissipation'. I do not object to the thing, but I cannot bear the expression;—it is such thorough novel slang—and so old, that I daresay Adam met with it in the first novel he opened."[121]

This was the year of the publication of *Waverley*, when it seems that all England, with the exception of Miss Jane Austen, was in the dark about its author's identity. She was familiar with *The Lay of the Last Minstrel*, *Marmion*, and *The Lady of the Lake*, and apparently had no difficulty in discerning the poet in the novelist. "Walter Scott has no business to write novels, especially good ones. It is not fair. He has fame and profit enough as a poet, and should not be taking the bread out of other people's mouths.—I do not like him, and do not mean to like 'Waverley' if I can help it, but fear I must . . . I have made up my mind to like no novels really, but Miss Edgeworth's, yours and my own.—"[122]

On 8th November 1814, Anna was married to Ben Lefroy, and she went away to her first home at Hendon. She did not give up her novel immediately, for in December Jane is still being asked for her suggestions. Once more she enthuses about the name Anna had invented of Newton-Priors, which she says "one could live upon . . . for a twelvemonth".[123] Previously, she had remarked that "Milton would have given his eyes to have thought of it",[124] revealing her perception of Milton's delight in the sounds of beautiful names.

"Indeed, I *do* think you get on very fast. I wish other people of my acquaintance could compose as rapidly . . . St Julian's History was quite a surprise to me . . . & his having been in love with the Aunt, gives Cecilia an additional interest with him. I like the Idea:—a very proper compliment to an Aunt! —I rather imagine indeed that Neices are seldom chosen but in compliment to some Aunt or other. I daresay Ben was in love with me once, & wd never have thought of *you* if he had not supposed me dead of a scarlet fever."[125]

Evidently, soon after this, Anna's ability to concentrate gave way naturally enough to the new duties of her married life, and soon after the birth of her first baby in October 1815, Jane wrote affectionately: "As I wish very much to see *your* Jemima, I am sure you will like to see *my* Emma, & have therefore great pleasure in sending it for your perusal. Keep it as long as you chuse, it has been read by all here.—"[126] Poor Anna's promising burst of literary activity was at an end, just as her aunt's might have been had she herself married.

During the summer of 1814, Cassandra visited Henry in Henrietta Street, while Jane stayed at Chawton with her mother and enjoyed the company of Edward who was at Chawton Great House. She was glad of the opportunity of carrying out her promise to visit Mrs Cooke at Bookham: "In addition to their standing claims on me they admire 'Mansfield Park' exceedingly. Mr. Cooke says 'it is the most sensible novel he ever read', and the manner in which I treat the clergy delights them very much". She did not want to go, however, until Edward left, "that he may feel he has a somebody to give memorandums to, to the last".[127]

It is pleasant to imagine Jane Austen being driven in strawberry time around the pretty Surrey countryside surrounding Bookham, enjoying the view from Box Hill, which was to be the setting for the most famous picnic in English literature and where three years later young John Keats was to finish his *Endymion*, picking up hints and details for her Highbury from the similar small towns of Dorking and Leatherhead. "Near Leatherhead is a house called 'Randalls'; and in 1761 the vestry of the parish paid their thanks 'in the most respectful manner to Mr Knightley', who had remodelled the pulpit and reading desk of the church."[128] The visit had come at an ideal time for *Emma*, and since the Cookes were sympathetic, no doubt she found some time most days to write. Jane advised her sister: "Take care of yourself, and do not be trampled to death in running after the Emperor."[129] For London was *en fête* for Czar Alexander of Russia, King Frederick of Prussia, and his popular old General Blücher, state visits which, one way and another, proved trying affairs for the Prince Regent.

A letter had arrived from their governess friend, Miss Sharpe, now in what must have been considered a promising situation: "She is at Sir W. P.'s in Yorkshire, with the children, and there is no appearance of her quitting them. Of course we lose the pleasure of seeing her here. She writes highly of Sir Wm. I do so want him to marry her . . . Oh, Sir Wm.! Sir Wm.! how I will love you if you will love Miss Sharpe!"[130]

Some time during that eventful summer, Henry, no doubt tired of living over the shop, had moved to 23 Hans Place. When Jane arrived on her visit during August, it was to this new home that she went. "It is a delightful place—more than answers my expectation . . . I find more space and comfort in the rooms than I had supposed, and the garden is quite a Love. I am in the front attic, which is the bedchamber to be preferred."[131]

Jane confided to Cassandra her suspicions that her brother was beginning to think of marrying again. Clearly, a solitary life was not for him. "Henry wants me to see more of his Hanwell favourite, and has written to invite her to spend a day or two here with me."[132] She enjoyed her peaceful visit: "I shall have spent my 12 days here very pleasantly, but with not much to tell of them; two or three *very* little Dinner-parties at home, some delightful Drives in the Curricle, and quiet Tea-drinkings with the Tilsons, has been the sum of my doings."[133]

To Martha, at present in Bath, she gives a run down on the latest London fashions: "the coloured petticoats with braces over the white Spencers and enormous Bonnets upon the full stretch, are quite entertaining. It seems to me a more marked *change* than one has lately seen.—Long sleeves appear universal, even as *Dress*, the Waists short, and as far as I have been able to judge, the Bosom covered."

She was enthusiastic about West's painting of Christ's rejection by the Elders—it "is the first representation of our Saviour which ever at all contented me".

She concludes her letter to Martha with cheerful news: "We have just learned that Mrs C. Austen is safe in bed with a Girl. It happened on board, a fortnight before it was expected."[134] But sadly, within a week both Fanny and her baby daughter were dead. Their youngest brother Charles was now left a widower at the age of thirty-six, with three little girls to be reared. Fortunately, his wife's sister, Harriet, proved a devoted friend to her unhappy nieces, and later in 1820, she and Charles were married.

Jane's next group of letters, written in November and December 1814 show her exclusively in her role as an aunt. Earlier in the year, when she had been in London with Fanny Knight, now an attractive young woman of twenty-one, she thought she had seen the beginning of a romance between her niece and the diffident Mr John Plumtre. In the interval, other confidences had been given which left Jane in little doubt that the love affair was progressing satisfactorily. But in November, when Fanny was staying with her grandmother, Lady Bridges, at Goodnestone Farm, concealed in a parcel of music, she sent an urgent secret appeal to her aunt, who at this time she must have felt stood much in the place of her own lost mother, expressing her emerging reservations and fears, and asking for advice.

It was not easy for Jane to reply satisfactorily—and this was a rare instance where not even Cassandra was admitted to the secret—as it was a busy time for the Austen family. Frank and his wife were now living in Chawton House, and Edward was staying with them, a guest in his own home. Charles's bereaved father-in-law had been visiting them, to collect his granddaughter Cassy. Martha Lloyd was expected. *Emma* was being written. But in the midst of so many pre-occupations, Jane took time and trouble to write her niece a long, wise letter.

Looking back on it now, it is hard not to wish that Jane had preferred lovable, impulsive, warm-hearted, gifted Anna, who was to remain so attached and loyal to her memory. Yet it was Fanny, who could write, "Aunt Jane for various circumstances was not so *refined* as she ought to have been for her talent", [135] who was her favourite, and we must be forgiven for wondering whether perhaps Mr J. P. had a lucky escape.

But the more devoted he became, the more doubtful Fanny grew. In some way, he managed to demean himself in the eyes of his beloved at the races; he was too modest, he was too religious; when Fanny tried to rouse her flagging feelings by a secret visit to her lover's room, she was downcast by the sight of his dirty shaving rag; he did not sparkle by the side of her witty and handsome brothers.

Poor dear Mr J. P. ! [Jane laments,] Oh! Dear Fanny, your mistake has been one that thousands of women fall into. He was the *first* young Man who attached himself to you. That was the charm, & most powerful it is . . . Do not be frightened from the connection by your Brothers having most wit. Wisdom is better than Wit, & in the long run will certainly have the laugh on her side. . . .

There *are* such beings in the World perhaps, one in a Thousand, as the Creature You and I should think perfection, Where Grace & Spirit are united to Worth, where the Manners are equal to the Heart & Understanding, but such a person may

not come in your way, or if he does, he may not be the eldest
son of a Man of Fortune, the Brother of your particular friend,
& belonging to your own County.

All this is sound reasoning and good advice, but next comes
the wisdom: "Anything is to be preferred or endured rather
than marrying without Affection; and if his deficiencies of
Manner &c. &c. strike you more than all his good qualities, if
you continue to think more strongly of them, give him up at
once . . . I have no doubt of his suffering a good deal for a
time, a great deal when he feels that he must give you up;—
but it is no creed of mine, as you must be well aware, that
such sort of Disappointments kill anybody."[136]

At the end of the month, Jane was staying with Henry at
Hans Place, having travelled up to town with Edward who
was on his way to Godmersham, where Fanny herself had
now returned. They had broken their journey at Hendon to
see the newly married Anna in her first home. Previously, Jane
had written approvingly, "Her Letters have been very sensible
& satisfactory, with no *parade* of happiness, which I liked
them the better for.—I have often known young married
Women write in a way I did not like, in that respect."[137] But
now she comments with an asperity which might have masked
some slight element of jealousy and disturbing memories of
Tom Lefroy.

"I was rather sorry to hear that she *is* to have an instrument; it seems throwing money away. They will wish the
twenty-four guineas in the shape of sheets and towels six
months hence; and as to her playing, it can never be anything.—Her purple Pelisse rather surprised me. I thought we
had known all paraphernalia of that sort."[138]

However, to Anna herself she wrote more kindly:

We all came away very much pleased with our visit I assure
You. We talked of you for about a mile & a half with great
satisfaction, & I have just been sending a very good account of
you to Miss Beckford, with a description of your dress for Susan
and Maria. Your Uncle & Edwd left us this morning. The hopes
of the Former in his Cause, do not lessen. We were all at the
Play last night, to see Miss O'neal in Isabella. I do not think
she was quite equal to my expectation. I fancy I want something
more than can be. Acting seldom satisfies me. I took two
Pocket handkerchiefs, but had very little occasion for either.
She is an elegant creature however & hugs Mr Younge delightfully.—[139]

Fanny was still perturbed and undecided about her love affair, particularly since it seems that his wealthy father's eldest son though he was, Mr John Plumtre was far from being immediately independent. "When I consider how few young men you have yet seen much of, how capable you are (yes, I do still think you *very* capable) of being really in love; and how full of temptation the next six or seven years of your life will probably be—(it is the very period of life for the *strongest* attachments to be formed),—I cannot wish you with your present very cool feelings to devote yourself in honour to him . . . Years may pass, before he is independent; you like him well enough to marry, but not well enough to wait.—"[140]

Fanny did not wait, she decided to give up John Plumtre, though nearly three years later she was still entertaining troublesome regrets. Evidently, the religious aspect worried her too, for Jane concludes, "I cannot suppose we differ in our ideas of the Christian Religion. You have given an excellent description of it. We only affix a different meaning to the Word *Evangelical*."[141]

Miss Eliza Moore, Henry's Hanwell favourite, was coming on a visit, and Jane rather dreaded it, "at my time of life after a day's acquaintance, it is uphill work to be talking to those whom one knows so little."[142] A visit to Charles's little girls in Keppel Street had taken place, young Cassy once more proving somewhat disappointing, "That puss Cassy, did not show more pleasure in seeing me than her Sisters, but I expected no better;—she does not shine in the tender feelings. She will never be a Miss O'neal;—more in the Mrs Siddons line."[143]

Jane and Henry were negotiating for a second edition of *Mansfield Park*, "We are to see Egerton today, when it will probably be determined. People are more ready to borrow and praise than to buy; which I cannot wonder at; but though I like praise as well as anybody, I like what Edward calls *'Pewter'*, too.—"[144] But no agreement was reached, and Jane had come to a parting of the ways with her first publisher.

Cassandra's note about the dates of her sister's novels records that *Emma* was finished on 29th March 1815. Unfortunately, this year there is a gap in the letters until 29th September, and no account of the negotiations that finally led in the autumn to the novel's acceptance by Jane's famous new publisher, very much in the public eye at the time as the publisher of the by now romantically notorious Lord Byron— John Murray.

A little earlier in the month, an event had occurred which electrified Europe. The papers reported on 10th March, " 'Most Important News. Landing of Bonaparte in France', and ten days later, 'Widespread Desertion of Troops to Bonaparte', followed on 23rd March by 'Departure of Louis XVIII from Paris. Arrival of Bonaparte'."[145]

For the next few months, peace-making was forgotten, and it seemed the tragedies of the last twenty years were beginning all over again. Napoleon "announced that he had given up the Grand Empire, but was alarmingly ambiguous as to the scope he envisaged for the French Empire to which he now promised to limit himself. No promises could have disarmed the enmity of the other Great Powers. They declared Napoleon outside the pale of civilized society and had 700,000–800,000 men under arms to back up their ban."[146]

In fact, the tension lasted only until June, with Napoleon's invasion of Belgium, and his total and final defeat at Waterloo. By July, he was on HMS *Bellerophon* on his last journey to exile and death at St Helena.

With two brothers in the Navy, the Austen family must have shared deeply in the general anxiety of the country during these three uncertain months. Although Frank was at Chawton, he was liable to be recalled, and until 1816 Charles was in the Mediterranean. On 6th May 1815, he was able to report from Palermo to his sister that her fame had travelled. "Books became the subject of conversation, and I praised 'Waverley' highly, when a young man present observed that nothing had come out for years to be compared with 'Pride and Prejudice', 'Sense and Sensibility', &c. As I am sure you must be anxious to know the name of the person of so much taste, I shall tell you it is Fox, a nephew of the late Charles James Fox." Then, with true brotherly discretion, he goes on, "That you may not be too much elated at this morsel of praise, I shall add that he did not appear to like 'Mansfield Park', so well as the two first, in which, however, I believe he is singular."[147]

Whether or not Mrs Leavis is right, and *Mansfield Park* and *Emma* were based on earlier works, both these long novels were written, in view of the circumstances under which Jane Austen always had to write, remarkably quickly. After this achievement, she must have needed a period of rest, and it is not surprising that she did not begin another novel until August. This was *Persuasion*, destined to be her last completed work. She must have been absorbed in the opening chapters when she wrote to Anna on 29th September. By this time, Anna and her husband had left Hendon and returned to Hampshire. They had rented part of the farmhouse known as Wyards, a red brick house "of medieval foundations with Tudor additions", which was within walking distance of Chawton.[148]

Once more, "that puss Cassy" was staying with her grandmother and aunts, and on being given "her choice of the Fair or Wyards, it must be confessed that she has preferred the former, which we trust will not greatly affront you;—if it does, you may hope that some little Anna hereafter may revenge the insult by a similar preference of an Alton Fair to her Cousin Cassy."[149]

By 17th October, Jane is writing to her sister from Hans Place, where she had travelled with Henry to finalize the details for the publication of *Emma*. She had already received two letters from Cassandra, and was relieved to know that the new cook was making good apple pies, "a considerable part of our domestic happiness". Her own affairs were proceeding with a letter from Mr John Murray. "He is a rogue of course, but a civil one. He offers £450 but wants to have the copyright of M.P. & S.&S. included. It will end in my publishing for myself I daresay. He sends more praise however than I expected. It is an amusing letter. You shall see it."[150]

Unfortunately, Henry was not well, "a bilious attack with fever. He came back early from H[enrietta] St yesterday & went to bed—the comical consequence of which was that Mr Seymour & I dined tête-à-tête."[151] Dr Chapman records the belief that Mr Seymour, Henry's man of business, had at some time made an unsuccessful proposal of marriage to his employer's sister.

Like his Mother, Henry had "a turn for being ill", but this time, he was seriously unwell, and was soon in the hands of the apothecary from the corner of Sloane Street, the young Mr Charles Thomas Haden. It was a wonder he survived the treatment. "Mr. H. calls it a general inflammation. He took twenty ounces of blood from Henry last night, & nearly as much more this morning, & expects to have to bleed him again tomorrow—"[152]

While she was nursing Henry, Jane generally sat with him in the back-room upstairs, "working or writing". In a day or two, Henry was able to dictate a reply to Murray expressing pleasure at his praise for Emma: "I assure you the quantum of your commendation rather exceeds than falls short of the author's expectation and my own."[153]

Murray's letter was based on the report of his reader, William Gifford, editor of the *Quarterly Review* who had written, "Of *Emma* I have nothing but good to say. I was sure of the writer before you mentioned her." But Henry was considerably disappointed by the terms offered which for the copyrights of *Sense and Sensibility*, *Mansfield Park*, and *Emma* were less than had been cleared by the first edition of *Mansfield Park*.

Before anything further could be settled, Henry's illness grew so alarming that Jane sent expresses to James, Edward, and Cassandra, summoning them to their brother's bedside. It was some days before Henry rallied, and he was pronounced out of danger. Undoubtedly this was a time of great shock, fatigue, and strain for Jane, particularly perhaps as she had never before taken Henry's indispositions too seriously, and there is some reason to think that her own health never recovered from it.

Characteristically, her first letter after the crisis was a kind little note to James's young daughter, Caroline. In the absence of Cassandra, Mrs James and her daughter had gone to look after Mrs Austen at Chawton, and like her half-sister, Anna, Caroline had sent her authoress aunt a manuscript. Naturally enough, Jane had not yet felt equal to reading it, "but think I shall soon, & I hope my detaining it so long will be no inconvenience". Jane congratulated her young niece on the birth of Anna's daughter, "Now that you are become an Aunt, you are a person of some consequence & must excite great Interest whatever you do. I have always maintained the importance of Aunts as much as possible, & I am sure of your doing the same now."[154]

By 3rd November, Henry was well enough for Jane to devote some thought to *Emma*. She wrote asking Murray to call on her believing, "A short conversation may perhaps do more than much writing".[155] Perhaps at this meeting it was settled that Murray would publish at Jane's expense, taking ten per-cent of the profits. He was asked to press ahead with the printing with all possible speed.

Henry's illness had an unexpected result. At its height, Mr Haden had wisely taken the precaution of calling in a more experienced colleague, who also happened to be one of the Prince Regent's physicians. The Regent, with all his faults a patron of the arts of cultivated taste, was a great admirer of the novels of Jane Austen, he read them often, and kept a set in each of his residences. Finding that his patient's devoted sister was also the talented, if little known authoress the physician informed the Prince of her presence in town. In consequence, the Prince had asked Mr Clarke, his librarian, to call on Jane with an invitation to show her the library and other apartments at Carlton House and to pay her every attention.

The visit took place on Monday 13th November, and it is a great pity that Cassandra's presence in London at the time has robbed posterity of Jane's description of this occasion, Mr Clarke himself, and the fantastic, rich, and colourful establishment created over the years at enormous cost at Carlton House by the Prince of Pleasure.

During their conversation, Mr Clarke had apparently mentioned a dedication. Jane must have been torn between delight and horror. Obviously the sale of her new work might be helped by such a mark of royal approval. On the other hand, she held and had expressed strong views about the Prince, and disliked any possible suggestion of sycophancy. But first, she wanted to be quite sure of her ground, and she wrote, "as I am very anxious to be quite certain of what was intended, I entreat you to have the goodness to inform me how such a permission is to be understood, and whether it is incumbent on me to show my sense of the honour, by inscribing the work now in the press, to His Royal Highness—I shd be equally concerned to appear either presumptuous or ungrateful.—"[156]

Mr Clarke replied by return, "It is certainly not *incumbent* on you to dedicate your work now in the press to His Royal Highness; but if you wish to do the Regent that honour either now or at any future period I am happy to send you that permission which need not require any more trouble or solicitation on your part." Then, after some fulsome words of praise, he came up with an embarrassing suggestion: "And I also, dear Madam, wished to be allowed to ask you to delineate in some future work the habits of life and character and enthusiasm of a clergyman—who should pass his time between the metropolis and the country—"[157] Luckily, he was on the point of going away for three weeks, and Jane was able to delay her reply. But after this fairly clear directive, obviously the dedication would have to be made.

Anxious now, after so long an absence, to go home, Jane was fretting at the slow speed of the printing of *Emma*, which may seem somewhat unreasonable in view of the fact that from start to finish the production of this lengthy three volume work in the days of hand-setting of type seems to have taken less than three months. However, she resolved to try the effect of the honour she had been accorded, "Is it likely that the printers will be influenced to greater dispatch and punctuality by knowing that the work is to be dedicated, by permission, to the Prince Regent? If you can make that circumstance operate, I shall be very glad."[158]

Both Murray and Roworth, the printer, reacted favourably, blaming the paper supply for the delay, and Jane wrote cheerfully to Cassandra who had now returned to Chawton, "I am soothed and complimented into tolerable comfort".[159] She was also happier because Henry was getting stronger, and Fanny Knight had joined her.

From mere apothecary, Mr Haden had turned into a favourite visitor and friend. He was a clever young man, later to be highly regarded in his profession. He was a keen amateur musician, a subject on which Jane enjoyed arguing with him, and he seems to have made a conquest of both the older and the younger lady. "Tomorrow Mr. Haden is to dine with us. There's happiness! We really grow so fond of Mr. Haden that I do not know what to expect."[160] Mrs Frank Austen had made Jane an aunt once again, and had been safely delivered of her sixth child, a little boy, Herbert Grey, on 8th November. In her next letter to Cassandra on 26th November, Jane reports contentedly: "The printers continue to supply me very well. I am advanced in Vol. III. to my *arra*-root, upon which peculiar style of spelling there is a modest query in the margin."[161]

Mr Haden was still a frequent dinner guest. He was "reading 'Mansfield Park' for the first time and prefers it to P. and P."[162] He had still not pronounced Henry perfectly well, "but he has no headake, no sickness, no pains, no Indigestions!—Perhaps when Fanny is gone he will be allowed to recover faster."[163]

By 2nd December, Jane was able to report that her brother had convalesced sufficiently to enjoy a visit to Hanwell. "To make his return a complete gala, Mr. Haden was secured for dinner.—I need not say that our evening was agreeable."[164]

Apparently Mrs Austen had been under the weather: "I am sorry my mother has been suffering, and am afraid this exquisite weather is too good to agree with her. *I* enjoy it all over me, from top to toe, from right to left, longtitudinally, perpendicularly, diagonally; and I cannot but selfishly hope

we are to have it last till Christmas; nice, unwholesome, un-
seasonable, relaxing, close, muggy weather!'"[165]

On 6th December, a short note was despatched to her fellow
author, Caroline, "I wish I could finish Stories as fast as you
can.—I am much obliged to you for the sight of Olivia, &
think you have done for her very well; but the good-for-
nothing Father, who was the real author of all her Faults and
Sufferings, should not escape unpunished. I hope he *hung*
himself, or took the sur-name of Bone, or underwent some
direful penance or other."[166]

By the 11th, Jane was busy making final arrangements about
the publication of *Emma*. Murray had put her right about the
proper placing of the dedication, which was finally to read,
"To His Royal Highness The Prince Regent This Work is, by
His Royal Highness's Permission, Most Respectfully Dedicated,
by His Royal Highness's Dutiful and Obedient Humble Servant,
The Author". It had been arranged that a special copy,
splendidly bound in scarlet leather, with the Prince of Wales's
feathers embossed on the spine, should be sent under cover of
the Rev. James Stanier Clarke two or three days in advance of
general publication. The three volumes are today among the
treasures of the Royal Library at Windsor.

The time had now come to answer Mr Clarke's awkward
letter. Of *Emma*, her author wrote:

> I am strongly haunted with the idea that to those readers
> who have preferred 'Pride and Prejudice' it will appear inferior
> in wit, and to those who have preferred 'Mansfield Park' inferior
> in good sense . . . I am quite honoured by your thinking me
> capable of drawing such a clergyman as you gave the sketch of
> in your note of Nov. 16th. But I assure you I am *not*. The
> comic part of the character I might be equal to, but not the
> good, the enthusiastic, the literary. . . . A classical education, or
> at any rate a very extensive acquaintance with English litera-
> ture, ancient and modern, appears to me quite indispensable for
> the person who would do any justice to your clergyman; and I
> think I may boast myself to be, with all possible vanity, the
> most unlearned and uninformed female who ever dared to be
> an authoress.[167]

But Mr Clarke persisted in his request for a novel with a
Clergyman hero, "shew dear Madam what good would be done
if Tythes were taken away entirely, and describe him burying
his own mother—as I did—because the High Priest of the
Parish in which she died—did not pay her remains the respect

he ought to do. I have never recovered the Shock. Carry your Clergyman to Sea as the Friend of some distinguished Naval Character about a Court—. . . ." Then, as if he had not sufficiently indicated that he had himself in mind for this hero, he added: "I have desired Mr Murray to procure, if he can, two little Works I ventured to publish from being at Sea— Sermons which I wrote & preached on the Ocean—& the Edition which I published of Falconers Shipwreck."

But besides being somewhat ridiculous, Mr Clarke was genuinely kind, "Pray, dear Madam, remember, that besides My Cell at Carlton House, I have another which Dr Barne procured for me at No: 37 Golden Square—where I often hide myself. There is a small Library there much at your Service—and if you can make the Cell render you any service as a sort of Half-way House, when you come to Town—I shall be most happy."[168]

On Saturday, 16th December, the day of the advertized publication of *Emma*, Jane was on her way home to Chawton. As in the case of *Mansfield Park*, she collected her friends' opinions of *Emma*, but this new work was reviewed favourably if perfunctorily in the *Literary Panorama*, the *Monthly Review*, the *British Critic*, and the *Gentleman's Magazine*. More important, was the extended criticism in the issue dated October 1815 but appearing in March 1816 of John Murray's influential *Quarterly Review*, in which a vicious article some two years later was to do so much damage to the contemporary reputation of John Keats. Jane Austen was luckier in being the subject of a specially written article by Walter Scott.

Although unsigned, the well considered and highly favourable review of more than four thousand words produced by the popular and successful Walter Scott, whose style many would probably recognize, was an important step forward in the founding of her reputation. Understandably, Jane was disappointed that there was no reference to *Mansfield Park*, which she was probably always to regard as her most serious work. This was perhaps only due to the fact that the title page of *Emma* did not refer to it. Memorably, Scott suggested: "The author's knowledge of the world, and the peculiar tact with which she presents characters that the reader cannot fail to recognize, reminds us something of the merits of the Flemish school of painting."[169]

As he re-read them over the years, Scott gained even greater appreciation of Jane Austen's novels, and on 14th March 1826, he recorded in his Journal, "That young lady had a talent for describing the involvement and feelings and characters of ordinary life which is to me the most wonderful I ever met with. The Big Bow-wow strain I can do myself like any now going, but the exquisite touch which renders ordinary commonplace things and characters interesting from the truth of the description and the sentiment is denied to me. What a pity such a gifted creature died so early!"

Her brother Frank led off Jane's collection of opinions with a decided preference for *Emma*. Perhaps significantly, Cassandra continued to prefer *Mansfield Park*. Fanny Knight could not bear Emma, whom perhaps she somewhat resembled, but found Mr Knightley delightful. Jane's mother "thought it more entertaining than M.P.—but not so interesting as P. & P.—No characters in it equal to Ly Catherine & Mr Collins.—" On the whole, the majority of the readers continued to prefer *Pride and Prejudice*. A double-edged comment came from a Mrs Guiton who "thought it too natural to be interesting". Mrs Digweed, continuing their note of antagonism, "did not like it so well as the others, in fact if she had not known the Author, could hardly have got through it.—" The incomparable Mr Haden was "*quite* delighted with it. Admired the Character of Emma.—" Miss Isabella Herries "did not like it—objected to my exposing the sex in the character of the Heroine—convinced that I had meant Mrs and Miss Bates for some acquaintance of theirs—People whom I never heard of before.—" A Mr Cockerelle "liked it so little, that Fanny wd not send me his opinion". A Mrs Wroughton complained that the authoress was wrong "in such times as these, to draw such Clergymen as Mr Collins & Mr Elton". Near the end came the gratifying intelligence that Mr Jeffery of the formidable *Edinburgh Review* "was kept up by it three nights".[170]

Probably their comments told the author more about her friends than about the book. On the whole, she had good reason to be pleased with its reception, especially as she had begun it with the idea that "I am going to take a heroine whom no one but myself will much like".[171]

In fact, most people do like Emma, as Mr Knightley does, as much for her faults as despite them. Certainly no succeeding heroine could have been in greater contrast to Fanny Price. Fanny is frail, diffident, dependent, and always right. Emma is radiantly healthy, supremely self-confident, utterly independent, and nearly always wrong. With every advantage of beauty, intelligence, wit, and wealth, and very real virtues of frankness, kindness, and generosity, the hidden evils of her situation are "the power of having rather too much her own way, and a disposition to think a little too well of herself".[172] The obstacles in Emma's moral assault course are mistakes and misconceptions arising through her high opinion of her own intelligence, her general self-esteem, misuse of her imagination, and her desire to manipulate the lives of those around her.

The comedy of Emma's errors, although the general atmosphere of the novel is light and witty, allows for the ironic discussion of many of Jane Austen's major themes: marriage, the social life of Highbury and the snobbery of Emma and Mrs Elton; the self-centred hypochondria of that amiable domestic tyrant, Mr Woodhouse, and his older daughter; the position of the single woman in society, as exemplified by the wealthy Emma, the successful ex-governess Mrs Weston, Harriet, the parlour-boarder with the shadowy background, the reluctant accomplished prospective governess, Jane Fairfax, and the needy elderly spinster, Miss Bates. The discovery of the clearly laid trail of clues hinting at the hidden relationship of Frank Churchill and Jane Fairfax is one of the joys of a second reading, and suggests that had she lived today, Jane Austen might have written a very distinguished detective novel.

The flaw in Emma's character that produces the climax and turning point of the novel is her inability to control her witty tongue. From her letters, it is clear that Jane Austen must have often been under similar provocation in the many dull stretches of her social life. The impression is gathered that as she grew older, she was better able to restrain the sharp rejoinders that sprang to mind so readily, and her laughter. When Emma finally reacts ungraciously and in public to the tangle of woolly-minded discourse inflicted on her friends by that compulsive talker, Miss Bates, is justly chastised by Mr Knightley, and with generosity and courage, admits her fault, it is easy to believe that through Emma, Jane Austen was also blaming and absolving herself.

Perhaps in no other novel does she succeed so securely with the whole range of her characters, which among many others include witty wayward Emma, garrulous and good Miss Bates, the insufferable Eltons, the sardonic and strangely likeable John Knightley, sweet silly Harriet Smith, and the sensible yeoman, Robert Martin.

Frank Churchill is not a villain, or even an anti-hero, but he is a charmer, which in Jane Austen's view amounts to practically the same thing. It is interesting to speculate just who it was that had made her so deeply suspicious of masculine charm. Frank Churchill is cast in a similar mould to Willoughby, Wickham, and Henry Crawford. But he is less complex than they, and his fault consists in the deceit and its adroit exploitation of concealing his engagement in his wish to keep both his fortune and his lady. The absence of a more sensational, less convincing sexual secret in the background is one of *Emma's* strengths.

For the majority of readers, Mr Knightley is one of the most attractive and admirable of heroes who fall into that well known romantic category of the older man. He has great presence, intelligence, and kindliness; he is firm, righteous, yet not without humour, and he has the human failing of being jealous. Vigorous, out in all weathers, he is a hard-working manager of his estates. Although Frank Churchill's adoption by his rich relations cannot fail to bring to mind the similar good fortune of Jane's brother, it is probably the character of Mr Knightley which owed more to Edward, whose critical contribution was pointing out his sister's uncharacteristic seasonal error of having an orchard in blossom in July.

Emma is a technical masterpiece, a brilliantly witty entertainment, and it is very funny. But as E. F. Shannon has summarized so effectively, it is also a work of great moral strength and importance:

> Far from having nothing worthwhile to say to modern men and women, through the discrepancy between appearance and reality she reminds us of human fallibility and the need for modesty, unselfishness, and compassion. She requires charity and forbearance towards the less gifted and fortunate than we. She shows the advisability of openness and sincerity, the evil of slander and of hastening to derogatory conclusions, the cruelty of inflicting mental pain, the falseness of snobbery. She demonstrates that we cannot escape the consequence of our acts, that love is not an emotion to be tampered with, and that marriage is not a game. Such truths she inculcates objectively through Emma's progress from self-deception and vanity to perception and humility.[173]

Emma was her last work to be published in Jane Austen's lifetime. The first edition was of 2,000 copies and by the end of 1816, 1,200 had been sold, and Jane's profit amounted to £221. 6s. 4d. Unfortunately, this modest gain was offset by the disappointment about *Mansfield Park*. Egerton had been prudent to hesitate about a second printing of the novel, for Murray's 2nd edition of 1,750 copies printed in 1816 involved Jane in an initial loss of £182, which was still some £60 short of being retrieved by 1821 when the balance of the copies was remaindered. This was at a time when Maria Edgeworth's now practically unread novels were earning her sums of between £1,500 and £2,000. In her lifetime, Jane Austen was by no means a best seller.

It would be pleasant to be able to think that the publication of a masterpiece of comedy like *Emma* ushered in a period of great happiness in Jane's life. But it was not to be. Not only did her health begin to fail, but the year 1816 was clouded for the whole family by Henry Austen's financial collapse. Due to the failure of the Alton Bank, which it had backed, the banking house of Austen, Maude, & Tilson in Henrietta Street was forced to close, and on 23rd March 1816, Henry Austen was declared bankrupt. Henry's enterprise was one of the many which suffered from the economic chaos following the end of the Napoleonic wars, and the dramatic fall in the price of wheat, which caused a fifty-per-cent reduction in the value of farming stock. The Alton branch was largely a farmer's bank.

Apart from Henry himself, the principal losses in the family were sustained by Edward and Uncle James Leigh Perrot, who had stood surety for Henry when he was appointed Receiver General of Taxes for Oxfordshire, to the very considerable tune of £20,000 and £10,000 respectively. Jane was lucky, and lost only £13, part of her profits on the first edition of *Mansfield Park*. It says a good deal for the Austen family spirit that they stood loyally beside Henry in this crisis. But there may have been more internal stresses than were recorded. Mrs Leigh Perrot certainly brooded over the affair, writing to James nearly three years later, "nor would I have Henry's feelings (if he does feel) for more than he has occasioned us to lose by his imprudence".[174] But perhaps, as Jane had hinted on the death of Eliza, Henry did not feel so very much, for he seems to have forgotten the past fairly easily and turned his eager gaze on the future. With no Eliza to hold him back now, he finally decided on ordination, began an enthusiastic study of the New Testament in Greek, and eventually became "an earnest preacher of the Evangelical School".[175]

On 27th March, Jane received Mr Clarke's formal note of thanks on behalf of the Prince Regent for the presentation copy of *Emma*, and a hint for another royal dedication and a future novel. The Regent's only daughter and heir-presumptive to the throne, Princess Charlotte, was to marry Prince Leopold of Saxe-Coburg in May, and Mr Clarke suggested: "Perhaps when you again appear in print you may chuse to dedicate your volumes to Prince Leopold: any historical romance, illustrative of the history of the august House of Coburg, would just now be very interesting".[176]

Like the suggestion about the clergyman, this proposition had to be firmly scotched:

> I am fully sensible that an historical romance, founded on the House of Saxe Coburg, might be much more to the purpose of profit or popularity than such pictures of domestic life in country villages as I deal in. But I could no more write a romance than an epic poem. I could not sit seriously down to write a serious romance under any other motive than to save my life; and if it were indispensable for me to keep it up and never relax into laughing at myself or other people, I am sure I should be hung before I had finished the first chapter. No, I must keep to my own style and go on in my own way; and though I may never succeed again in that, I am convinced that I should totally fail in any other.[177]

However, Mr Clarke's well-meant intervention had one happy result in the inspiring of the *Plan of a Novel according to hints from various quarters*, a light-hearted little piece which goes straight back to the lively literary criticisms of Jane's early burlesques.[178]

This renewal of interest in burlesque was no doubt one of the reasons which led to the recovery at this time of the early work *Susan*, which had now languished unpublished at Crosby's for the last thirteen years. Once the manuscript was safely bought back, it must have given both Jane and Henry a good deal of satisfaction to inform this tardy publisher that the work he had so long neglected was by the author of the highly regarded *Pride and Prejudice*.

FIVE

Death Untimely

Not many letters remain to record the last months of Jane Austen's life. Those that do, show remarkable courage and resilience for a woman embarked on a slow process of dying.

On 21st April, she was writing to Caroline, reporting the death of their elderly relative, Miss Elizabeth Leigh. Evidently, Charles's daughter Cassy was staying at Chawton again, and she had been busy. "Cassy has had great pleasure in working this—whatever it may be—for you, I believe she rather fancied it might do for a quilt for your little wax doll, but you will find a use for it if you can I am sure."[1] The following Saturday was Alton Fair and the ninth birthday of Frank's eldest girl, Mary Jane. Her aunt hoped that Caroline would be able to celebrate the double event with them. For domestic reasons, it was not really convenient for the Chawton ladies to include Mary with Caroline and her father in this short visit. The careful wording Jane uses to convey this message shows that sister-in-law Mary was still regarded as inclined to be difficult—"We are almost ashamed to include your Mama in the invitation, or to ask *her* to be at the trouble of a long ride for so few days as we shall be having disengaged, for we *must* wash before the GM Party come & therefore Monday would be the last day that our House could be comfortable for her; but if she does feel disposed to pay us a little visit & you could *all* come, so much the better. We do not like to invite her to come on wednesday, to be turned out of the house on Monday."[2] Nothing could be more tactful than that.

We do not know whether the little girls enjoyed Alton Fair together, but in May, Cassy was taken to Steventon to stay with Uncle James, Aunt Mary, and her cousin Caroline, while her aunts travelled on to spend three weeks in Cheltenham. It seems very likely that Jane's indifferent health was the reason for this visit, as Cheltenham was well known for its spa, and

Jane did not care for Bath. Certainly, when she and Cassandra paid a call at Kintbury on their return, the Fowle family had the impression that her health was failing, and Caroline records that Mary Jane Fowle told her: "Aunt Jane went over the old places, and recalled old recollections associated with them, in a very particular manner . . . as if she never expected to see them again".[3]

On 23rd June, brother Charles's birthday, Jane writes an affectionate letter to Anna, who had given his daughter Cassy a book. "She was quite delighted to see it. I do not know when I have seen her so much struck by anybody's kindness as on this occasion. Her sensibility seems to be opening to the perception of great actions."[4] No doubt under the influence of her grandmother and aunts, Cassy's behaviour was improving, and from now on she no longer features as "that puss".

In July, Mary was seriously ill, and in spite of their occasional differences, Jane writes to her nephew Edward with much concern, "We have been wanting very much to hear of your mother, and are happy to find she continues to mend, but her illness must have been a very serious one indeed.—When she is really recovered, she ought to try a change of air and come over to us."[5] In fact, the change of air was had at Cheltenham where Cassandra returned in September, this time with Mary and young Caroline.

Jane was writing to Edward during an unusually quiet period. Cassandra, Frank, and Martha Lloyd were all in London, Frank's wife was spending some time with her family, and little Cassy had rejoined her Aunt Harriet Palmer and sisters for a holiday at Broadstairs. Jane was alone in the house with her mother and Frank's little girl, Mary Jane. Edward, now in his last year at school, was home from Winchester for the summer holidays:

We saw a countless number of postchaises full of boys pass by yesterday morng—full of future heroes, legislators, fools, and villains . . . You will not pay us a visit yet of course; we must not think of it. Your mother must get well first, and you must go to Oxford and *not* be elected; after that, a little change of scene may be good for you, and your physicians I hope will order you to the sea, or to a house by the side of a very considerable pond. Oh! it rains again; it beats against the window. Mary Jane and I have been wet through once already today; we set off in the donkey-carriage for Farringdon, as I wanted to see the improvements Mr. Woolls is making, but we

M

were obliged to turn back before we got there, but not soon
enough to avoid a pelter all the way home. We met Mr Woolls
—I talked of its being bad weather for the hay, and he returned
me the comfort of its being much worse for the wheat.[6]

This is the first mention in the letters of the donkey carriage
which had been provided for Mrs Austen, but which was to
become increasingly useful to Jane herself when she became
so quickly tired by walking. The soaking and the gloomy
weather would not have helped her, but she must have been
grateful for a spell of quiet in the busy household, for she
finished Persuasion in August, and she wanted to make a start
on the revisions to Susan, which underwent the transitional
title of Catherine, before finally becoming the work we now
know as Northanger Abbey.

Jane had no idea that by now three of her novels had been
published in France. Sense and Sensibility had been freely
translated by Mme Isabelle de Montolieu the previous year
under the title Raison et Sensibilité, ou Les Deux Manières
d'Aimer. In 1816 appeared Le Parc de Mansfield, ou Les Trois
Cousines, and La Nouvelle Emma, ou les Caractères Anglais du
Siècle. These were the only translations of her works to appear
in her lifetime, and there was, of course, no question of any
copyright or foreign-rights fees. It seems strange that Pride and
Prejudice was not included, perhaps because in the opinion of
the influential Mme de Stael, whom Jane had declined or was
too shy to meet in London, it was "vulgaire".[7] The translations
were poor, and it was probably as well their originator was not
to see them.

Edward's visit to the "house by a very considerable pond"
came sooner than his aunt expected, for a week later, she was
writing to Caroline, "Edward's visit has been a great pleasure
to us. He has not lost one good quality or good Look, & is only
altered in being improved by being some months older than
when we saw him last. He is getting very near our own age,
for we do not grow older of course."

Caroline had been at work again and had submitted her
effort to her critical aunt. "I am particularly glad to find you
so much alive upon any topic of such absurdity, as the usual
description of a Heroine's father.—You have done it full
justice—or if anything be wanting, it is the information of the
venerable old Man's having married when only Twenty-one,
& being a father at Twenty-two."[8]

All James's children wanted to write, and first Anna, then

Caroline, and finally in September, Edward, who was to be her first biographer, all sought their aunt's advice. "Edward is writing a Novel—we have all heard what he has written—it is extremely clever; written with great ease & spirit;—if he can carry it on in the same way, it will be a first-rate work, & in a style, I think, to be popular. Pray tell Mary how much I admire it.—And tell Caroline that I think it is hardly fair upon her & myself, to have him take up the Novel line. . . ." Jane is writing to Cassandra, now staying at Cheltenham, and shocked by the three guineas a week her sister was being charged for her lodgings there. She reports that Henry "is decided for Orders &c.—I have written to him to say that after this week, he cannot come too soon.—I do not really expect him however immediately; they will hardly part with him at Gm. yet."[9] Edward, still involved in his court case, and so much the poorer because of Henry's failure, must indeed have been a generous-hearted brother.

Her next letter on the 8th is full of the usual plans and arrangements for family visits. Sometimes it was in the nature of a jigsaw puzzle with too many pieces trying to fit so many guests into a small house. Luckily, the Great House nearby was currently empty for any overflow. Mrs Frank Austen was expecting her seventh child, and Jane remarks frankly, "Mrs. F. A. seldom either looks or appears quite well.—Little Embryo is troublesome I suppose." She had spent a pleasant day with them at Alton, "venison quite right, children well-behaved, & Mr. & Mrs. Digweed taking kindly to our charades, and other games."[10]

Both Mrs Frank and Mrs Digweed were having servant problems; Mrs Frank suffering from the lack of a housemaid, and Mrs Digweed parting with "both Hannah and old cook; the former will not give up her lover, who is a man of bad character; the latter is guilty only of being unequal to anything."[11]

Ben Lefroy had walked over with his brother Edward, recently returned from France. "We found him very agreeable. He is come back from France, thinking of the French as one could wish—disappointed in everything."[12] These insular views were confirmed by Henry's old servants, Mme Bigeon and her daughter Mme Perigord, who had also been visiting their home country and, not surprisingly in the year after Waterloo, spoke of "France as a scene of general poverty and misery: no money, no trade, nothing to be got but by the innkeepers".[13]

In this letter, Jane gives expression to a feeling of frustration which must often have swept over her, and will be echoed by every woman who has ever tried to combine housekeeping with any form of creative work. "I enjoyed Edward's company very much, as I said before, & yet I was not sorry when Friday came. It had been a busy week, and I wanted a few days quiet and exemption from the thought and contrivancy which any sort of company gives. . . . Composition seems to me impossible, with a head full of joints of mutton and doses of rhubarb."[14] The doses of rhubarb were no doubt a feature of Mrs Austen's careful regime.

For the first time, it is plain that Jane's health had been giving rise to serious concern: "Thank you, my back has given me scarcely any pain for many days. I have an idea that agitation does it as much harm as fatigue, and that I was ill at the time of your going from the very circumstance of your going."[15]

On what was to be her last birthday, Jane wrote to Edward. He was a lucky nephew to receive such a wise and humorous letter, and it is fortunate that the youngsters to whom she wrote so generously appreciated their aunt's letters sufficiently to preserve them. "I give you Joy of having left Winchester.— Now you may own, how miserable you were there; now, it will gradually all come out—your crimes and your miseries— how often you went up by the Mail to London and threw away fifty guineas at a tavern, and how often you were on the point of hanging yourself. . . ."[16] Henry and Charles were staying at Chawton, and in spite of their recent troubles, both brothers were at present in good health, "And they are each of them so agreeable in their different way, and harmonize so well, that their visit is thorough enjoyment".[17] By now, Cassandra was at home again to take charge of the housekeeping.

Uncle Henry writes very superior sermons. You and I must try to get hold of one or two, and put them into our Novels. . . . By the bye, my dear Edward, I am quite concerned for the loss your mother mentions in her letter; two chapters and a half to be missing is monstrous! It is well that *I* have not been to Steventon lately, and therefore cannot be suspected of purloining them: two strong twigs & a half towards a nest of my own, would have been something. I do not think however that any theft of that sort would be really very useful to me. What should I do with your strong, manly, spirited sketches, full of variety and glow? How could I possibly join them on to the little bit (two inches wide) of ivory on which I work with so fine a brush, as produces little effect after much labour?[18]

Although there is a hint of Jane Austen's customary irony in this statement, it indicates that she was critically alive to her self-imposed limitations, and that she consciously aspired to the delicacy and accuracy of a miniaturist. It also underlines her awareness of the need for much labour to produce her own particular effects. *Persuasion* was completed, but she had already rewritten one chapter, and no doubt planned a great deal more revising and polishing before committing her new novel for publication.

At the turn of the year, there is a seasonal letter to Anna, thanking her for a turkey, and then the New Year of 1817 opens with a note of good wishes to Cassy, with all the words written backwards by her "Etanoitceffa Tnua Enaj."[19]

Another niece, Caroline this time, received a letter from her aunt on 23rd January. She reported on Edward's visit, and carried on with her task of reviewing his novel and Caroline's own. About her health, Jane writes optimistically, "*I* feel myself getting stronger than I was half a year ago, & can so perfectly well walk to Alton, *or* back again, without the slightest fatigue that I hope to be able to do both when Summer comes."[20] The distance between the two places is a little under two miles.

She had been spending a few days with Frank and his family at Alton, "& though the Children are sometimes very noisy & not under such Order as they ought & easily might, I cannot help liking them & even loving them, which I hope may be not wholly inexcusable in their & your affectionate Aunt".[21]

A charming postscript reveals that Jane still enjoyed her piano. "The Piano Forté often talks of you;—in various keys, tunes, & expressions I allow—but be it Lesson or Country Dance, Sonata or Waltz, *you* are really it's constant Theme. I wish you cd come and see us, as easily as Edward can."[22] Her letters to Caroline are particularly understanding, and have the unique and pleasing quality of a wiser and older person speaking to one much younger already as an equal.

Jane's next letter of 24th January to Alethea Bigg was prompted by a current scarcity of mead, for in a postscript she reveals: "The real object of this letter is to ask you for a receipt, but I thought it genteel not to let it appear early. We remember some excellent orange wine at Manydown, made from Seville oranges, entirely or chiefly, & should be very much obliged to you for the receipt, if you can command it within a few weeks." She is still optimistic about her health, "I think I understand my own case now so much better than I did, as to be able by care to keep off any serious return of illness. I am more & more convinced that *bile* is at the bottom of all I have suffered, which makes it easy to know how to treat myself."[23] Another invalid in the family now was James, who was to die two years later in his mid-fifties. He and his youngest sister were the two unfortunate exceptions in this remarkably long lived family.

There is more news of Edward, "He grows still, and still improves in appearance, at least in the estimation of his aunts, who love him better and better, as they see the sweet temper and warm affections of the boy confirmed in the young man." While Anna "has not been so well or so strong or looking so much like herself since her marriage as she is now". But Jane's deepest concern at the moment was for Henry's debut at Chawton in his latest and last role as a clergyman. "I shall be very glad when the first hearing is over. It will be a nervous hour for our pew, though we hear that he acquits himself with as much ease and collectedness, as if he had been used to it all his life."[24] No doubt on this occasion, the least nervous Austen in the church was Henry.

A month later, Fanny Knight again takes the centre of the stage, and Jane writes: "You are inimitable, irresistible. You are the delight of my life . . . You can hardly think what a pleasure it is to me to have such thorough pictures of your heart. Oh, what a loss it will be when you are married!"

The present candidate for Fanny's affections was Mr J. Wildman of Chilham Castle, but he too was to be disappointed: "I do wish you to marry very much, because I know you will never be happy till you are; but the loss of a Fanny Knight will be never made up to me. . . ."[25]

Two of Fanny's brothers, Henry and William, had been staying at Chawton, and had met with approval. There was news of cousin Anna, who with her husband had walked over to hear Uncle Henry preach, "she looked so pretty, it was quite a pleasure to see her, so young and so blooming and so innocent, as if she had never had a wicked thought in her life. . . ."[26]

Fanny's Aunt Sophia, Mrs Deedes, had added once more to her enormous family (already numbering eleven nine years earlier), "Good Mrs Deedes!—I hope she will get the better of this Marianne, & then I wd recommend to her & Mr D. the simple regimen of separate rooms.—"[27]

Apparently Fanny still sighed after the rejected John Plumtre, and her aunt admonishes her in terms that would have been perfectly applicable to the Emma who fancied herself in love with Frank Churchill: "Do not speak ill of your sense merely for the gratification of your fancy.—Yours is sense which deserves more honourable treatment. You are *not* in love with him; you never *have* been really in love with him."[28]

Emma is again recalled in the next letter, also addressed to Fanny, which speaks of the death of old Mrs Milles, whose daughter had been one of the sources of inspiration for Miss Bates. "I am sorry & surprised that you speak of her as having little to leave, & must feel for Miss Milles . . . if a material loss of income is to attend her other loss.—Single Women have a dreadful propensity for being poor—which is one very strong argument in favour of Matrimony. . . ."[29]

Aunt Jane prophesies: "Do not be in a hurry; depend on it, the right Man will come at last . . . who will so completely attach you, that you will feel you never really loved before.— And then, by not beginning the business of Mothering quite so early in life, you will be young in Constitution, spirits, figure & countenance, while Mrs Wm Hammond is growing old by confinements & nursing."[30]

Other members of the family "growing old by confinements and nursing" were Frank's wife, due to be confined again in April, "& is by no means remarkably Large for her",[31] and young Anna, who had just weaned her second daughter, Julia, and whose looks made her aunt suspicious. As it happened, Anna was either not pregnant this time or miscarried, but her family of six daughters and one son was probably only thus limited by the early death of her husband when Anna was thirty-six. Jane's exclamation—"Poor Animal, she will be worn out before she is thirty.—I am very sorry for her.— Mrs Clement too is in that way again. I am quite tired of so many Children.—Mrs Benn has a 13th"[32] can leave little doubt that she would have been a warm supporter of birth-control and sensible family planning.

To Fanny, Jane confided that " 'Miss Catherine' is put upon the shelf for the present, and I do not know that she will ever come out; but I have a something ready for publication, which may, perhaps, appear about a twelvemonth hence."[33] Her estimate of another twelve months before the publication of

Persuasion indicates the need she felt for further polishing. She does not mention the new work she had had in hand since January, the fragment of a novel we know as *Sanditon*.

She reports on her health: "I am got tolerably well again, quite equal to walking about and enjoying the air, and by sitting down and resting a good while between my walks, I get exercise enough. I have a scheme, however, for accomplishing more, as the weather grows spring-like. I mean to take to riding the donkey."[34]

The next day, she wrote to Caroline, with more literary criticism for her, encouragement for Edward, and thanks to Mary for the gift of a Ham and some "seacale".[35] Frank had been to town with his eldest daughter, Mary Jane, and Mrs Frank had spent the week of his absence at Chawton, with a different child with her every day—a complicated plan which must have taken some arranging, and entailed a good deal of fuss and upheaval, quite unsuitable for a household with an invalid in its midst. Possibly, this was one of the contributory reasons for the fact that apparently Jane added nothing further to *Sanditon* after 18th March.

The manuscript of *Sanditon* as it has become known, although there is also a suggestion that it was intended to call it *The Brothers*, now rests in the library of King's College, Cambridge.[36] It is a first draft, heavily corrected, and dated from 17th January to 18th March 1817. The work is divided into twelve chapters, but there are no paragraphs, and it has the air of being written fast to keep pace with the speed of composition.

Surprisingly, since it was written so close to the end of Jane Austen's life, the piece is full of vigour and vitality. The themes introduced are various: first, as topical now as then, land speculation and property development; the contrast between the old practice of land management and the new; the economics of development; tourism; hypochondria; romanticism; seduction; and charity. There is no evidence here of mental fatigue or loss of ideas.

It is a fascinating, funny, somewhat bewildering piece as it stands, partly because of its pace, and partly because it is not clear which direction it is to take. But one aspect must be particularly noted.

For most of her adult life, Jane Austen had suffered at close quarters from her mother's hypochondria, or at least excessive preoccupation about her health. Even during her own last illness, before she was forced to take to her bed, she rested uncomfortably on three chairs, leaving the sofa free for her mother, whose accustomed place it was. The arrangement considerably bothered the twelve-year-old Caroline: "I wondered and wondered—for the real sofa was frequently vacant, and *still* she laid in this comfortless manner—I often asked her how she *could* like the chairs best—and I suppose I worried her into telling me the reason of her choice—which was, that if ever she used the sofa, Grandmama would be leaving it for her, and would not lie down, as she did now, whenever she felt inclined—"[37]

In Mr Woodhouse, Jane Austen had drawn one of the most gently ironic portraits of an imaginary invalid in English literature. His eldest daughter Isabella, with her concern for the proper preparation of "a basin of nice smooth gruel, thin, but not too thin", and "those little nervous head-aches and palpitations"[38] from which she was never entirely free anywhere, in spite of giving birth to five healthy children, was clearly following in her father's halting footsteps. Another worrier about her health was young Mary Musgrove in *Persuasion*, whose sore throats were always much worse than anyone else's, and who feared being "seized of a sudden in some dreadful way, and not able to ring the bell"![39]

But at this point in her life, when at a comparatively early age, with her talent at its height, and recognition and some more material rewards beginning to come her way, Jane Austen realized she was in serious danger of dying, she treated the subject of hypochondria in a vein of broad humour. It is one of the most courageous performances in English literature, which must arouse admiration for both Jane Austen the woman and the writer. Few are brave enough to mock at illness in the face of death.

Here for example, is Mr Arthur Parker describing his state of health: "*I* am very nervous.—To say the truth Nerves are the worst part of my Complaints in *my* opinion. My Sisters think me Bilious, but I doubt it.—" "You are quite in the right, to doubt it as long as you possibly can, I am sure.—" "If I were Bilious, he continued, you know Wine wd disagree with me, but it always does me good.—The more Wine I drink (in Moderation) the better I am.—I am always best of an Eveng."[40]

Other elements of emerging importance in this fragment are literary romanticism, an air of mystery, and a feeling for locality, in particular for the bright freshness of the sea, which, by this time, Jane Austen probably realized she might never see again.

With all the imperfections that must exist in the first draft of an author whose habitual method of working entailed constant revision, *Sanditon* remains entertaining and rewarding. At the end of her career, it represents a new beginning: visual description plays a more important part; the delicate irony is still there, but a broader vein of humour looks forward to Dickens; and the mysterious element points the way to the works of Wilkie Collins.

In her next letter to Fanny on 23rd March, Jane says, "Do not be surprised at finding Uncle Henry acquainted with my having another ready for publication. I could not say No when he asked me, but he knows nothing more of it.—You will not like it, so you need not be impatient. You may perhaps like the heroine, as she is almost too good for me."[41]

This time, her bulletin on her health has provided some of the clues which have enabled Sir Zachary Cope to make a probable diagnosis of her complaint. "I certainly have not been well for many weeks, and about a week ago I was very poorly. I have had a good deal of fever at times, and indifferent nights; but am considerably better now and am recovering my looks a little, which have been bad enough—black and white and every wrong colour. I must not depend upon being ever very blooming again. Sickness is a dangerous indulgence at my time of life."[42]

Together with the description of the onset, the progress, and the climax of Jane's illness, this has led Sir Zachary Cope to the conclusion that she was suffering from Addison's disease of the suprarenal capsules (two small glands situated one on each side of the body close to the corresponding kidney), characterized by anaemia, weakness, and discolouration of the skin, with periods of recession, but usually fatal within a year. Sir Zachary suggests that the disease was susceptible of being influenced by mental shock, such as Henry's illness and bankruptcy. It was not identified by Dr Addison until the mid 1850s.[43]

On 24th March, Jane felt herself strong enough to take her first ride and "liked it very much. I went up Mounter's Lane, and round by where the new cottages are to be, and found the exercise and everything very pleasant. . . ."[44]

Three days later, she was answering a letter from Caroline, who was still busy writing: "I like Frederick and Caroline better than I did, but must still prefer Edgar and Julia. Julia is a warm-hearted, ingenuous, natural Girl, which I like her for; —but I know the word *Natural* is no recommendation to you."

Jane concludes what was to be her last letter to Caroline: "you must try to get me quiet, mild days, that I may be able to go out pretty constantly.—A great deal of Wind does not suit me, as I have still a tendency to Rheumatism. In short I am a poor Honey at present. . . ."[45]

Mr James Leigh Perrot, whose health had been causing anxiety for some while, died on 28th March. In spite of the loss he had sustained in Henry's bankruptcy, he was still a wealthy man. The Austens' only expectation of any inheritance had always been from Uncle Leigh Perrot, who at least it was felt could be depended upon to do something substantial for his sister. Between them, the Austen ladies had a very modest income, and Jane in particular yearned for them to have money of their own, and independence.

But when the will was read, it proved a terrible disappointment. His houses at Scarlets and Bathwick and their contents, his lands in the parish of Wargrave, and £10,000 were left to his wife and her heirs. The remainder of the property was left in trust to James Austen, with the income going to Aunt Leigh Perrot during her life. This trust was to cease with her death, and apart from the sum of £6,000 to be shared equally among the Austen nieces and nephews, with the exception of the unfortunate George, the remainder of the property was left to James Austen. There was no mention at all of old Mrs Austen. Since the will was made in 1811, it appears she had cried wolf too often, and her brother had been convinced she was bound to predecease him. In fact, she lived another ten years until 1827, and Aunt Leigh Perrot survived until 1836. The major beneficiary, therefore, was to be James's son and Jane's biographer, Edward, who was also the residual legatee under his great-aunt's will.

Because of her weakness, the effect of this bad news on Jane was disastrous, yet she retained sufficient sense of proportion to disapprove of the violence of her own reaction. On 6th April, she wrote to thank Charles for an affectionate letter. "A few days ago my complaint appeared removed, but I am ashamed to say that the shock of my Uncle's Will brought on a relapse, & I was so ill on friday & thought myself so likely to be worse that I could not but press for Cassandra's returning with Frank after the Funeral last night, which she of course did, & either her return, or my having seen Mr Curtis, or my Disorder's chusing to go away, have made me better this morning. I live upstairs however for the present & am coddled. I was the only one of the Legatees who has been so silly, but a weak Body must excuse weak Nerves." It is much to her credit that old Mrs Austen bore "the forgetfulness of *her* extremely well".[46] Aunt Leigh Perrot had been truly devoted to the husband who had loved her so long and faithfully, and had been grateful for Cassandra's sympathetic company. She was "poor Woman! so miserable at present (for her affliction has very much increased since the first) that we feel more regard for her than we ever did before".[47]

It must have been about this time that young Caroline paid what was to be a farewell visit to her aunt. She had been expecting to spend a few days at Chawton while her parents were away, but since Aunt Jane was so ill, she went instead to Anna at Wyards. The day after her arrival, she and Anna walked over to Chawton, and were invited to see Aunt Jane in her room.

She was in her dressing gown and sitting quite like an invalide in an arm chair—but she got up, and kindly greeted us—and then pointing to seats which had been arranged for us by the fire, she said: "There's a chair for the married lady, and a little stool for you, Caroline."—It is strange, but those trifling words are the last of hers that I can remember—for I retain *no* recollection *at* all of what was said by anyone in the conversation that of course ensued.

I was struck by the alteration in herself.—She was very pale—her voice was weak and low and there was about her, a general appearance of debility and suffering; but I have been told that she never *had* much actual pain—

She was not equal to the exertion of talking to us, and our visit to the sick room was a very short one—Aunt Cassandra soon taking us away—I do not suppose we stayed a quarter of an hour; and *I* never saw Aunt Jane again—[48]

On 27th April, Jane Austen made her simple will, apart from two legacies of £50 to Henry and Eliza's faithful servant Mme Bigeon, leaving everything to "my dearest sister Cassandra".[49]

By 22nd May, when Jane replied to a letter from Anne Sharpe, it had been decided that she must go to Winchester to be under the care of Mr. Lyford. She had suffered her worst attack ever. Cassandra and Martha Lloyd were to go with her.

How to do justice to the kindness of all my family during this illness is quite beyond me!—Every dear Brother so affectionate & so anxious! and as for my Sister!—Words must fail me in any attempt to describe what a Nurse she has been to me. Thank God! she does not seem the worse for it *yet*, & as there was never any sitting-up necessary, I am willing to hope she has no after-fatigues to suffer from. I have so many alleviations & comforts to bless the Almighty for!—My head was always clear, & I had scarcely any pain; my cheif sufferings were from feverish nights, weakness and Langour.—This Discharge was on me for above a week, & as our Alton Apoth^y did not pretend to be able to cope with it, better advice was called in. Our nearest, *very good*, is at Winchester, where there is a Hospital & capital Surgeons, & one of them attended me, & *his* Applications gradually removed the Evil.[50]

The sixteen-mile journey to Winchester was to be accomplished in James's carriage, and Jane describes herself as a "very genteel, portable sort of an Invalid".[51] Their lodgings in College Street had been engaged by their old friend, Mrs Heathcote, the former Miss Elizabeth Bigg, who might have been Jane's sister-in-law. The youngest Miss Bigg, Alethea, was not to be in Winchester, having been "frisked off like half England into Switzerland".[52]

Sadly she concludes, "if I live to be an old Woman, I must expect to wish I had died now; blessed in the tenderness of such a Family, & before I had survived either them or their affection.—You would have held the memory of your friend Jane too in tender regret I am sure.—But the Providence of God has restored me—& may I be more fit to appear before him when I *am* summoned, than I shd have been now!"[53]

As her letter to Edward of 27th May reports, she performed the journey with very little fatigue, and was happy with their comfortable lodgings. Her brother Henry and William Knight had ridden with them on horseback, and Jane had been distressed for them as the day was so wet. Mrs Heathcote was a constant visitor, William and Henry were again expected, and Charles Knight was to come in for breakfast when he was released from the Winchester school sickroom. Although she gave an optimistic report of her health, nonetheless, Jane's last paragraph to Edward sounds a note of farewell. "God bless you my dear Edward. If ever you are ill, may you be as tenderly nursed as I have been, may the same blessed alleviations of anxious, sympathising friends be yours: and may you possess, as I daresay you will, the greatest blessing of all, in the consciousness of not being unworthy of their love. *I* could not feel this."[54]

There is one last letter to an unknown correspondent, which was quoted—and censored—by Henry in his *Biographical Notice*. It is a touching mixture of bravery, humour, and resignation.

My attendant is encouraging, and talks of making me quite well. I live chiefly on the sofa, but am allowed to walk from one room to the other. I have been out once in a sedan-chair, and am to repeat it, and be promoted to a wheel-chair as the weather serves. On this subject I will only say further that my dearest sister, my tender, watchful, indefatigable nurse, has not been made ill by her exertions. As to what I owe to her, and to the anxious affection of all my beloved family on this occasion, I can only cry over it, and pray to God to bless them more and more.

There follows a characteristic note from Henry, which presumably alludes to the Leigh Perrot Will.

(She next touches with just and gentle animadversion on a subject of domestic disappointment. Of this the particulars do not concern the public. Yet in justice to her characteristic sweetness and resignation, the concluding observation of our authoress thereon must not be suppressed.)
"But I am getting too near complaint. It has been the appointment of God, however secondary causes may have operated. . . .
You will find Captain—— a very respectable, well meaning man, without much manner, his wife and sister all good humour and obligingness, and I hope (since the fashion allows it) with rather longer petticoats than last year."[55]

Henry gives some idea of his sister's ordeal during the brief remainder of her life.

She supported, during two months, all the varying pain, irksomeness, and tedium, attendant on decaying nature, with more than resignation, with a truly elastic cheerfulness. She retained her faculties, her memory, her fancy, her temper, and her affections, warm, clear, and unimpaired, to the last. Neither her love of God, nor of her fellow creatures flagged for a moment. She made a point of receiving the sacrament before excessive bodily weakness might have rendered her perception unequal to her wishes. She wrote whilst she could hold a pen, and with a pencil when a pen was become too laborious. The day preceding her death she composed some stanzas replete with fancy and vigour.[56]

These verses are dated, "Written at Winchester on Tuesday the 15th July 1817," which was St Swithin's day, and it is hard to believe that Jane Austen could have concentrated on such a light hearted production just two days before her death.

> When Winchester races first took their beginning
> It is said the good people forgot their old Saint
> Not applying at all for the leave of St Swithin
> And that William of Wykham's approval was faint . . .[57]

Yet, Jane Austen had been writing throughout most of her life, and although she may merely have been copying verses composed earlier, it is not impossible that for her the most reliable means of escaping from her anxiety and pain lay in the putting together of words.

By this time, Mrs James had arrived to help Cassandra with the nursing. In this sort of situation, she was at her best, and Jane was now able to appreciate her good qualities and forget the rest. She thanked her particularly, and added: "You have always been a kind sister to me, Mary".[58]

On Thursday morning, a letter arrived from Fanny Knight, one of the "kind, amusing letters", she had continued to write to cheer her aunt in her illness. Cassandra cut the seal and gave it to her sister. Jane read it with pleasure, passed it to Cassandra, and they discussed its contents "not uncheerfully". Clearly, Cassandra had no idea the crisis was so near, for immediately after dinner that day, she went out to do an errand for her sister. When she returned, Jane was just recovering from a bout of faintness and oppression, and able to give Cassandra a quiet account of her symptoms. Shortly after six, she was seized by a similar attack.

> "She felt herself to be dying about half-an-hour before she became tranquil and apparently unconscious. During that half-hour was her struggle, poor soul! she said she could not tell us what she suffered, though she complained of little fixed pain. When I asked her if there was anything she wanted, her answer was she wanted nothing but death, and some of her words were 'God grant me patience, pray for me, oh, pray for me!' Her voice was affected but as long as she spoke she was intelligible."[59]

Dr Lyford had been sent for, and arrived in time to give her something to allay her suffering:

She was in a state of quiet insensibility by seven o'clock at the latest. From that time till half-past four, when she ceased to breathe, she scarcely moved a limb, so that we have every reason to think, with gratitude to the Almighty, that her sufferings were over. A slight motion of the head with every breath remained till almost the last. . . . There was nothing convulsed or which gave the idea of pain in her look; on the contrary, but for the continual motion of the head she gave me the idea of a beautiful statue, and even now in her coffin, there is such a sweet, serene air over her countenance as is quite pleasant to contemplate.[60]

With her younger sister, Cassandra had shared the joys, the griefs, the pleasures, the leisure, and the labour of her whole life. Yet she was able to write:

I *have* lost a treasure, such a sister, such a friend as never can have been surpassed. She was the sun of my life, the gilder of every pleasure, the soother of every sorrow; I had not a thought concealed from her, and it is as if I had lost a part of myself. I loved her only too well—not better than she deserved, but I am conscious that my affection for her made me sometimes unjust to and negligent of others; and I can acknowledge, more than as a general principle, the justice of the Hand which has struck this blow. . . .[61] Never was human being more sincerely mourned by those who attended her remains than was this dear creature. May the sorrow with which she is parted with on earth be a prognostic of the joy with which she is hailed in heaven![62]

Like her sister, Cassandra Austen was a Christian Stoic.

Jane Austen the woman had died, but the writer lived on. There were still two books unpublished, not as ready for the press as their author would have wished, but as Henry Austen, who acted as his sister's literary executor, was well aware, far too good to be left on the shelf, as Jane herself had hinted might be the fate of *Miss Catherine*.

In December 1817, *Northanger Abbey*, the new title for which Henry had aptly chosen, and *Persuasion* were published together in four volumes, prefaced by Henry's short but influential *Biographical Notice*. It was a most important work, containing as it did, Jane Austen's first and last completed novels, and the first published clues to her identity and character.

For the whole family, Cassandra in particular, this publication must have caused much pride and much pain. There was no Jane now to collect opinions, and eagerly await the news of sales, but there were reviews. The first to appear was that in the *British Critic*, dated March 1818.

Besides providing a criticism of Jane Austen's last published works, the article also served as an obituary. Among much praise along the lines laid down by Walter Scott, faults were found. "In imagination, of all kinds, she appears to have been extremely deficient; not only her stories are utterly devoid of invention, but her characters, her incidents, her sentiments, are obviously all drawn exclusively from experience." Curiously, it is stated, she "never dips her pen in satire".

As B. C. Southam has said, "the novels of Jane Austen called for a freedom of response which her audience, private readers and critics alike, were not yet ready to give. In particular . . . contemporary readers were not yet ready to accept her disconcerting account of the ways and values of their own society."[63]

Of the two works, *Northanger Abbey* received the most praise and attention, a preference also maintained in the "trifling notice" in the *Gentleman's Magazine* of July 1818. *Northanger Abbey* springs directly from Jane Austen's juvenile works. It presents a burlesque and criticism of certain aspects of the Gothic novel and the novel of sensibility, and a statement about the adverse effects on susceptible minds of too much reading of such works. The problem is treated humorously but seriously and is much the same as that preoccupying moral authorities today, but in connection with novels of pornography, violence, and the productions of Enid Blyton.

Jane Austen's genius has contrived to blend all this convincingly with a charming version of that favourite romantic subject—a young girl's entry onto the stage of the world. Of all these fictional young girls, Catherine Morland is one of the most sturdy, innocent, honest, and likeable, and it is not surprising that the much more sophisticated kind and witty Henry Tilney falls in love with her. Catherine's "moral assault course" begins at Bath and ends at Northanger Abbey. In the course of it, a romantic girl is schooled into becoming a young woman seriously and sensibly in love.

The first half of the novel provides plenty of opportunity for comment on the Bath social scene. One of the principal activities for young people at Bath was the dancing, which for Jane Austen, a lover of dancing herself, was always to have a good deal of significance as an initial rite and essential part of courtship. Henry Tilney takes it even further.

N

" 'I consider a country-dance as an emblem of marriage. Fidelity and complaisance are the principal duties of both; and those men who do not chuse to dance or marry themselves, have no business with the partners or wives of their neighbours.' "[64]

Northanger Abbey is a light-hearted book and the dancing here is light-hearted, but as David Daiches so vividly reminds us: "It is a stately dance on the lawn—but all around are the dark trees, the shadows. And if you do not dance well, if you have not been able by the end of the day, to secure a permanent partner with whom to walk off the lawn, you are left, when the sun sets, alone amid the shadows. We are never allowed to forget that possibility, never allowed to forget what a serious business this dancing is. One false step can be fatal."[65]

In the second half of the novel, when Catherine arrives at Northanger Abbey, the Gothic theme comes to the fore, and the heroine's imagination runs away with her to the extent of suspecting that her host, General Tilney, has in some way or other done away with his wife. It is Henry, the one hero of her works who comments throughout in the authentic tones of Jane Austen herself, who demonstrates to the girl who adores him how foolish she is being: " 'Consult your own understanding, your own sense of the probable, your own observation of what is passing around you—Does our education prepare us for such atrocities? Do our laws connive at them? Could they be perpetrated without being known, in a country like this, where social and literary intercourse is on such a footing; where every man is surrounded by a neighbourhood of voluntary spies, and where roads and newspapers lay everything open? Dearest Miss Morland, what ideas have you been admitting?' "[66]

Yet, although she had allowed herself to dramatize, Catherine has been right to believe that the General's character is not all it should be. For suddenly disappointed in his estimate of her expectations, he bundles her off home on the flimsiest pretext, to travel for the first time in her seventeen years by postchaise and alone. Most miserable of all, she must leave without a word of explanation to Henry.

Catherine returns home a very different girl from the careless young creature who set forth for Bath with such high expectations three months earlier. She has learned judgment of character, relative values, self-reliance, and she is in love. Expectedly, Henry Tilney soon arrives to put everything right and give the novel its appropriate ending of a happy marriage. Perhaps *Northanger Abbey* must be considered Jane Austen's slightest novel, but it is highly typical of its author, and has great deftness and charm.

Today it can only seem strange that *Persuasion*, the favourite novel of so many, should have been shortly dismissed in the *British Critic* review as "a much less fortunate performance.... It is manifestly the work of the same mind, and contains parts of very great merit; among them, however, we certainly should not number its *moral*, which seems to be, that young people should always marry according to their own inclinations and upon their own judgment. . . ."[67] If this is, indeed, the moral of the novel, it is one of which few people would dare to disapprove today.

Just as it is tempting to discern a portrait of the young Jane Austen in Elizabeth Bennet, so many people seek a likeness of the older Jane in Anne Elliot. At this point, it is perhaps worth considering how very different from each other are the heroines who give life and individuality to each of the six novels. All are living, credible, well-rounded characters, with minds and spirits very much their own, each creating the special atmosphere of the novels they dominate: ingenuous Catherine; passionate, poetical Marianne and reasonable, sensitive Elinor; witty, vivacious Elizabeth; frail, conscientious Fanny; brilliant bossy Emma, and finally the more mature, self-contained, elegant little figure of Anne.

No doubt in each of these curiously familiar girls are embodied some of the characteristics of their author. Apart perhaps from Fanny Price, they are none of them "pictures of perfection".[68] To Anne Elliot, Jane Austen has given her own love of the sea and everything connected with the navy; her preference for the country and dislike of Bath, her readiness to sit back and play the piano for the others when her own dancing days seem to be over; the more controlled irony of her later years; her keen-sighted vision and apprehension of social values; her quiet competence and capability; and her balanced outlook in which the scales are weighted more in favour of reason than romance. Most of all, the reader likes to hope that when Anne Elliot speaks up so passionately for enduring love and constancy, she is voicing the beliefs of her author.

With the possible exception of Catherine Morland's, the family backgrounds of Jane Austen's heroines can hardly be described as ideal. The Dashwood girls have lost their father, and their mother is an affectionate but impractical romantic incapable of giving them sensible guidance. The Bennet family has an egregiously foolish mother with a deplorable sense of values, and an intelligent father, who except for his favourite Lizzie, appears to have cast himself in the role of Pontius Pilate. Fanny Price is removed from her own careless improvident family to the household at Mansfield Park, where Lady Bertram vaguely slumbers, Sir Thomas is dignified and aloof, and the effective direction is given by the detestable Mrs Norris. Instead of a parent to look after her, self-willed Emma Woodhouse, whose mother died when she was young, is herself in charge of that sickly, self-centred, elderly child, her father. Like Emma, Anne Elliot has also lost her mother, and her father is "a foolish spendthrift baronet, who had not had principle or sense enough to maintain himself in the situation in which Providence had placed him",[69] and is a heartless, selfish snob. Her godmother, Lady Russell, although well-meaning and good-hearted, is also a snob, and goes far towards wrecking Anne's life by advising against her romantic youthful engagement to Frederick Wentworth.

Throughout the whole of her life Jane Austen was totally immersed in her family, but much as she loved her own, her family portraits cannot fail to raise doubts about her happiness within this situation. In all her invented families, she displays an acute awareness of the part played by the generation gap, and in spite of her natural conservatism and perhaps because of her essential optimism, invariably she comes out on the side of youth.

When *Persuasion* opens, with its brilliantly ironic evocation of her father, the best part of Anne's "moral assault course" is already in the past, and only the final lap remains to be run. By now, Anne knows her rejection of Wentworth to have been utterly wrong, and she consciously tries to prevent her life from being governed only by regrets. But unlike Jane Austen, Anne is about to be presented with a second chance, for Frederick, now Captain Wentworth, is to enter her life again. When he does so, Anne is resigned, and Captain Wentworth, now wealthy and a good match, is resentful. Seeking a very different spirit from his pliant first love, he appears to be courting Louisa Musgrove, a wilful girl whom he regards as a "character of decision and firmness".[70]

It is in the famous scene at Lyme Regis that Captain Wentworth realizes the debit side of a strong willed nature, when insisting on being "jumped" for a second time from the Upper

Cobb, Louisa "fell on the pavement on the Lower Cobb, and was taken up lifeless!"[71]

The Cobb, the breakwater which gives Lyme Regis its sheltered harbour, has been altered since Jane Austen saw it. But although some critics have tended to belittle this famous accident, even today, most young Amazons would think twice before precipitating themselves from top to bottom of any of the existing flights of steps into the sturdiest pair of arms. The steps are steep and the Upper Cobb is some six feet higher than the lower. Louisa's flight may have been less dangerous, but even so, the possibility of a serious injury resulting from her reckless action remains a real one.

Anne's quiet capability in this crisis, the only one to keep her head when all about are losing theirs, cannot fail to promote her value at the expense of Louisa's. Moreover, the sea breezes have restored the bloom and freshness of youth to her very regular, very pretty features, and Captain Wentworth has observed another gentleman, who is in fact her cousin, her father's heir, and the novel's anti-hero, William Walter Elliot, clearly admiring her.

From this moment, it is only a question of time before Anne and Wentworth are reunited. The plot is complicated by the possibility of Anne's marriage to William Elliot, approved by Lady Russell, when Anne is briefly tempted by the idea of returning as mistress of her old home at Kellynch; perhaps as Jane Austen was once tempted by the prospect of becoming mistress of Manydown.

But Mr Elliot's true character is soon to be revealed by Anne's old friend, Mrs Smith. For most readers, Mrs Smith's narration of her life-story and her revelation of Mr Elliot's callous behaviour, is unconvincing; just as is Elliot's final elopement with Mrs Clay, that cunning lady still of child-bearing age who threatens to marry Sir Walter and thus jeopardise his inheritance. Clearly, had she been in good health and followed her customary practice, Jane Austen must have revised or rewritten these sketchy sequences, just as she did that of Anne and Captain Wentworth's final reconciliation.

The cancelled first version of this scene has its own merits, but Jane Austen's instinct rightly urged her to revise it, to give the additional interest of the lively bustling scenes at the White Hart Inn, when Anne is overheard by her lover making the beautiful statement that finally reunites them.

" 'We certainly do not forget you, so soon as you forget us. It is, perhaps, our fate rather than our merit. We cannot help ourselves. We live at home, quiet, confined, and our feelings prey upon us. . . . All the privilege I claim for my own sex (it is not a very enviable one, you need not covet it) is that of loving longest, when existence or when hope is gone.' "[72]

In *Mansfield Park*, Jane Austen had enjoyed inserting references to her brother Charles's gift of topaz crosses, and to some of Frank's ships. In *Persuasion*, it seems that the handy and resourceful Captain Harville was based on the character of Frank, and certainly he thought so. Captain Benwick, another nautical character, was Jane Austen's first portrayal of the newly fashionable romantic, which she was to develop with broader humour in Sir Edward Denham in *Sanditon*. She was observing new trends up to the end.

In spite of the symbolic value she always attached to matrimony, *Persuasion* is one of the few Austen novels to depict in the union of Captain Wentworth's sister and her husband, Admiral and Mrs Croft, a happy marriage of equal partners. As for Anne, she was "tenderness itself, and she had the full worth of it in Captain Wentworth's affection. His profession was all that could ever make her friends wish that tenderness less; the dread of a future war all that could dim her sunshine. She gloried in being a sailor's wife, but she must pay the tax of quick alarm for belonging to that profession which is, if possible, more distinguished in its domestic virtues than in its national importance."[73]

When she wrote that passage, Jane Austen must have temporarily forgotten the home life of the great Lord Nelson.

The great strength of *Persuasion* is the subtlety of the characterization of Anne, which pervades the novel from start to finish. Captain Wentworth is also drawn with great conviction, and his vigorous character is well contrasted with Anne's fineness and delicacy. Physically attractive, immensely warmhearted, impulsive, confident, courageous, Wentworth is also honest, honest enough to recognize the part played in his long estrangement from Anne by his own hurt pride and obstinacy.

It would be wrong to leave this brief discussion of *Persuasion* without reference to a subject which must be especially relevant to her last completed work—Jane Austen's attitude to death. She has often been criticized for her attack in this novel on nice Mrs Musgrove's sentimental mourning for her admittedly scapegrace sailor son, "whom nobody alive had cared for".

"Personal size and mental sorrow have certainly no necessary proportions. A large bulky figure has as good a right to be in deep affliction, as the most graceful set of limbs in the world. But, fair or not fair, there are unbecoming conjunctions, which reason will patronize in vain,—which taste cannot tolerate,—which ridicule will seize.''[74]

Certainly, the reference to Mrs Musgrove's figure may well seem unkind and irrelevant, a return to the younger, tarter Jane Austen, but this "tough rationality", as D. W. Harding rightly terms it,[75] in the face of death, was an attitude which she had always maintained, both in her novels and in her letters. Just as she disliked hypocrisy in every branch of life, so she had no taste for extravagance of grief, or the sentimental recollection of the characters of the deceased.

It would be misleading to draw any conclusions from the absence, frequently remarked, of moving death scenes or references to God in the novels of Jane Austen. With the rigorous limitations she imposed on her material, it is not likely she would have regarded either subject suitable for the atmosphere of her social comedies. But her prayers, her letters after the death of her father and of Elizabeth Austen, and her courage in the face of death's approach, leave no doubt of her own firm belief in the reality of God, the teaching of the Christian church, and the existence of an afterlife. She felt no need to discuss such great questions in her correspondence with her sister. For both of them, these were indisputable facts, and perhaps there is never need for discussion when there is calm acceptance, without fear or doubts.

The opening passages of Jane Austen's last novel, written so near the end of her life, are set in that beautiful but sad time of year, the autumn. Symbolically, it ends with the spring and the beginning of a particularly hopeful marriage. In spite of the sombre and bitingly critical judgments to be found in her work, it cannot be doubted that her vision was ultimately hopeful, and that she had faith in progress and improvement both for the individual and for society.

Jane Austen's quiet but assured place in English literature took many years to assume the importance that is granted it today. For a long while after her death, she remained the favourite of a small elite. Her works were first reprinted by Bentley in 1833, and subsequently in 1866, 1869, and 1878–9. By this time, her reputation was steadily gaining ground, and a great deal of interest in the woman as well as the writer had been created by the publication of her nephew's *Memoir* in 1870. In 1884, Lord Brabourne, Jane's great nephew, and the eldest son of her favourite niece, Fanny, published his edition of the *Letters of Jane Austen*, with critical remarks, which contained many letters additional to those printed by Edward. Like *Emma*, this work was distinguished by a royal dedication, this time to Queen Victoria. In whatever spirit she perused them, it is pleasant to recall that the Queen "so highly appreciated the works of Jane Austen" that Lord Brabourne was "emboldened" to ask permission to dedicate to her Majesty his two interesting volumes.[76]

From this time onward, critical and other writing on Jane Austen and her work steadily increased in quality and volume, and today every aspect of her art is under the scrutiny of a growing number of perceptive critics on both sides of the Atlantic and never has her reputation stood higher. But apart from the specialized world of literary criticism, Jane Austen's chief strength is that she caught and continues to hold generations of readers.

In doing so, she has triumphantly succeeded in what, there can be little doubt, were her primary intentions: to entertain, to make her readers laugh, and to make them think. Even she may not have realized how powerfully her works were pervaded by her own individual charm and magic as a writer. The same charm and magic that she possessed as a woman, which was revealed so movingly by one of her young nephews: "his visits to Chawton after the death of his aunt Jane, were always a disappointment to him. From old associations he could not help expecting to be particularly happy in that house; and never till he got there could he realize to himself how all its peculiar charm was gone. It was not only that the chief light in the house was quenched, but that the loss of it had cast a shade over the spirits of the survivors."[77]

Fortunately, for we who are privileged only to know Jane Austen the writer, enhanced by the bracing dash of acidity her family preferred to forget, the "peculiar charm" lives on.

Notes

Abbreviations:

Memoir: A Memoir of Jane Austen, J. E. Austen-Leigh with *Persuasion* in the Penguin English Library, 1971

Life: Jane Austen, Her Life and Letters, W & R. A. Austen-Leigh, Smith Elder & Co. London, 1913

Brabourne: Letters of Jane Austen, Edward Lord Brabourne, Richard Bentley & Son, London, 1884

Letters: Jane Austen's Letters to her sister Cassandra and Others, ed. R. W. Chapman, Oxford University Press, 2nd ed. 1969

A.P.: Austen Papers, 1704–1856, ed. R. A. Austen-Leigh, Spottiswoode Ballantyne & Co. Ltd., 1942

M.W.: Minor Works, ed. R. W. Chapman & B. C. Southam, Oxford University Press, 1972

All quotations from the novels have been reprinted by permission of Penguin Books from the editions of the Penguin English Library. For the convenience of the reader, after the references to quotations from Brabourne, the relevant number in the Oxford edition of the *Letters*, or in some cases the page number, has been added in brackets.

1 PRELUDE

1 *Cornhill*, No. 973, Winter 1947–48.
2 *M.W.*, p. 453.
3 *Biographical Notice*, Henry Austen with *Northanger Abbey*, Penguin English Library, 1974
4 *Memoir*, p. 339.
5 *Memoir*, p. 390.
6 *Life*, p. 300.
7 R. W. Chapman, *Jane Austen*, Oxford University Press, 1948, p. 97.
8 *Emma*, Chap. 18, p. 164.
9 *A.P.*, p. 32.
10 *Life*, p. 5.
11 *Memoir*, p. 276.
12 *Memoir*, p. 286.
13 *Life*, p. 15.
14 E. G. Selwyn, *Jane Austen's Clergymen*, Report, Jane Austen Society, 1959.
15 *Memoir*, p. 281.
16 William Cowper, *The Task*, II ll. 409–414.
17 *Memoir*, p. 277
18 *A.P.*, p. 56.
19 *A.P.*, p. 70.
20 *A.P.*, 75.
21 *A.P.*, p. 325
22 *A.P.*, p. 102.
23 *A.P.*, p. 100.
24 *Life*, p. 48.
25 *Life*, p. 23.
26 *Life*, p. 26.
27 *Sense and Sensibility*, Chap. 26, p. 176.

28 *Life*, p. 47.
29 J. H. & Edith Hubback, *Jane Austen's Sailor Brothers*, John Lane, 1906.
30 *A.P.*, p. 123.
31 *A.P.*, p. 125.
32 *A.P.*, p. 156.
33 *A.P.*, p. 133.
34 *A.P.*, p. 131.
35 *Life*, p. 60.
36 *A.P.*, p. 145.
37 *A.P.*, p. 139.
38 *A.P.*, p. 146.
39 *Letters*, No 27.
40 *A.P.*, p. 148.
41 *A.P.*, p. 150.
42 *Life*, p. 70.
43 *Memoir*, p. 331.
44 Joyce M. S. Tompkins, *The Popular Novel in England*, Methuen, 1969.
45 Brabourne, vol. I, p. 178 (14)
46 *M.W.*, p. 4.
47 *M.W.*, p. 9.
48 *M.W.*, p. 7.
49 *M.W.*, p. 5.
50 *M.W.*, p. 13.
51 *M.W.*, p. 33.
52 *M.W.*, p. 48.
53 W. H. Auden, *Collected Longer Poems*, Faber & Faber, 1968, "Letter to Lord Byron", Random House Inc. in USA.
54 *M.W.*, p. 72.
55 B. C. Southam, *Jane Austen's Literary MSS*, Oxford University Press, 1964, pp. 3, 24.
56 *M.W.*, p. 77.
57 *M.W.*, p. 86.
58 *M.W.*, p. 97.
59 *M.W.*, p. 100.
60 *M.W.*, p. 102.
61 *M.W.*, p. 108.
62 *M.W.*, p. 120.
63 *M.W.*, p. 121.
64 *M.W.*, p. 138.
65 *M.W.*, p. 138.
66 *Northanger Abbey*, Chap. 14, p. 123.
67 *M.W.*, p. 141.
68 *M.W.*, p. 140.
69 *M.W.*, p. 142.
70 *M.W.*, p. 144.
71 *M.W.*, p. 146.
72 *M.W.*, p. 147.
73 *M.W.*, p. 148.
74 A. Walton Litz, *Jane Austen, A Study of her Artistic Development*, Chatto & Windus, 1965, Oxford University Press in USA.
75 *M.W.*, p. 189.
76 *M.W.*, p. 192.
77 *M.W.*, p. 194.
78 *M.W.*, p. 220.
79 *M.W.*, p. 230.
80 *M.W.*, p. 201.
81 *M.W.*, p. 205.
82 B. C. Southam, *Jane Austen's Literary MSS*, Oxford University Press, 1964.
83 *M.W.*, p. 175.
84 *M.W.*, p. 246.
85 *M.W.*, p. 6.
86 *Northanger Abbey*, Chap. 3, p. 49.
87 *M.W.*, p. 93.
88 *Sense and Sensibility*, Chap. 3, p. 51
89 *M.W.*, p. 298.
90 *Sense and Sensibility*, Chap. 2, p. 46.
91 *A.P.*, p. 144.
92 *A.P.*, p. 142.
93 Elizabeth Jenkins, Report, Jane Austen Society, 1965.
94 *A.P.*, p. 321.

2 THE YEARS OF PROMISE

1 William Wordsworth, *The Prelude*, XI, l. 108.
2 Edna Nixon, *Mary Wollstonecraft, Her Life and Times*, J. M. Dent, 1971.
3 Virginia Woolf, "Two Women" in *Collected Essays IV*, Hogarth Press, 1966, Harcourt Brace Jovanovich in USA.
4 Joyce M. Tompkins, *The Popular Novel in England*, Methuen, 1969.
5 John Gore, Introduction, *Semi-Attached Couple* by Emily Eden, Elkin Mathews & Marrot, 1928.

6 Virginia Woolf, "The Niece of an Earl" in *Collected Essays I*, The Hogarth Press, 1966, Harcourt Brace Jovanovich in USA.

7 V. S. Pritchett, *George Meredith and English Comedy*, Chatto & Windus 1970, Alfred A. Knopf Inc. in USA.

8 R. W. Chapman, *Jane Austen*, Oxford University Press, 1948, p. 92.

9 Harold Nicolson, Report, Jane Austen Society, 1956.

10 H. W. Garrod, "Jane Austen: A Depreciation", in *Essays by Divers Hands*, Royal Society of Literature, Oxford University Press, 1928.

11 E. M. Forster, *Times Literary Supplement*, 10th November 1932.

12 Marvin Mudrick, *Jane Austen, Irony as Defense and Discovery*, University of California Press, 1968.

13 Brabourne, vol. I, p. 253 (29).

14 Brabourne, vol. I, p. 159 (10).

15 *Letters*, No 27.

16 B. C. Southam ed. *Jane Austen, The Critical Heritage*, Routledge & Kegan Paul, 1968, Barnes & Noble in USA.

17 *Biographical Notice*, Henry Austen, *Northanger Abbey* Penguin English Library, p. 31.

18 *Memoir*, p. 330.

19 *Life*, p. 68.

20 Brabourne, vol. I, p. 143 (6).

21 *Letters*, No 25.

22 Brabourne, vol. I, p. 127 (1).

23 Brabourne, vol. I, p. 126 (1).

24 Brabourne, vol. I, p. 131 (2).

25 Brabourne, vol. I, p. 132 (2).

26 Brabourne, vol. I, p. 163 (11).

27 A.P., p. 154.

28 A.P., p. 156.

29 A.P., p. 228.

30 A.P., p. 157.

31 Brabourne, vol. I, p. 148 (7).

32 Brabourne, vol. I, p. 140 (5).

33 Brabourne, vol. I, p. 147 (7).

34 A.P., p. 155.

35 A.P., p. 160.

36 A.P., p. 168.

37 A.P., p. 230.

38 A.P., p. 159.

39 *Letters*, No 77.

40 *Life*, p. 96.

41 *Letters*, No 14.

42 *Letters*, No 8.

43 Brabourne, vol. I, p. 164 (11).

44 Brabourne, vol. I, p. 164 (11).

45 *Letters*, No. 81.

46 Brabourne, vol. I, p. 155 (9).

47 Brabourne, vol. I, p. 158 (10).

48 Brabourne, vol. I, p. 165–6 (11).

49 Brabourne, vol. I, p. 165 (11).

50 Brabourne, vol. I, p. 166 (11).

51 Brabourne, vol. I, p. 170 (12).

52 Brabourne, vol. I, p. 172 (13).

53 Brabourne, vol. I, p. 173 (13).

54 Brabourne, vol. I, p. 174 (13).

55 Report, Jane Austen Society, 1972.

56 Brabourne, vol. I, p. 185 (15).

57 Brabourne, vol. I, p. 196 (17).

58 Brabourne, vol. I, p. 194 (17).

59 Brabourne, vol. I, p. 197 (17).

60 Brabourne, vol. I, p. 200 (18).

61 Brabourne, vol. I, p. 186 (15).

62 Brabourne, vol. I, p. 193 (17).

63 *Pride and Prejudice*, Chap. 41, p. 259.

64 Brabourne, vol. I, p. 208 (19).

65 Brabourne, vol. I, p. 211 (20).

66 Brabourne, vol. I, p. 216 (21).

67 Brabourne, vol. I, p. 210 (19).

68 Brabourne, vol. I, p. 217 (21).

69 Brabourne, vol. I, p. 214 (20).

70 Brabourne, vol. I, p. 219 (21), p. 222 (22).

71 Brabourne, vol. I, p. 162 (10).

72 Brabourne, vol. I, p. 293 (37).

73 *Letters*, No 44.

74 Brabourne, vol. II, p. 35 (60).

75 A.P., p. 241

76 A.P., p. 185.

77 A.P., p. 195.

78 A.P., p. 206.

79 A.P., p. 210.

80 A.P., p. 209.

81 Brabourne, vol. I, p. 234 (23).

82 Brabourne, vol. I, p. 238 (24).

83 Brabourne, vol. I, p. 240 (24).

84 *Letters*, No 25.

85 *Letters*, No 25.

86 *Memoir*, p. 316 (26).

87 *Letters*, No 28.

88 *Letters*, No 44.
89 *Letters*, No 28.
90 Brabourne, vol. I, p. 242 (27).
91 *Letters*, No 27.
92 *Letters*, No 28.
93 E. M. Forster, *Times Literary Supplement*, 10th Nov., 1932.
94 Brabourne, vol. I, p. 236 (24).
95 Brabourne, vol. I, p. 244 (27).
96 *Letters*, No 28.
97 *Letters*, No 28.
98 *Life*, p. 155.
99 *Life*, p. 155.

3 A TIME OF DISAPPOINTMENT

1 Brabourne, vol. I, p. 249 (29).
2 Brabourne, vol. I, p. 254 (29).
3 Brabourne, vol. I, p. 254 (29).
4 Brabourne, vol. I, p. 259 (30).
5 Brabourne, vol. I, p. 263 (31).
6 Brabourne, vol. I, p. 276 (33).
7 *Letters*, No 29.
8 *A.P.*, p. 175.
9 Brabourne, vol. I, p. 275 (33).
10 *Sense and Sensibility*, Chap. 5, p. 60.
11 Brabourne, vol. I, p. 278 (35).
12 Brabourne, vol. I, p. 281 (35).
13 Brabourne, vol. I, p. 285 (36).
14 *Letters*, No 36.
15 Brabourne, vol. I, p. 288 (36).
16 Brabourne, vol. I, p. 291 (37).
17 Brabourne, vol. I, p. 293 (37).
18 Brabourne, vol. I, p. 293 (37).
19 *Letters*, No 38.
20 *Letters*, No 38.
21 *Letters*, No 38.
22 *Letters*, No 38.
23 *Letters*, No 38.
24 *A.P.*, p. 175.
25 *Life*, p. 93.
26 Q. D. Leavis, *A Selection from Scrutiny*, compiled by F. R. Leavis, Cambridge University Press, 1968, "A Critical Theory of Jane Austen's Writings".
27 H. W. Garrod, Jane Austen: *A Depreciation* in *Essays by Divers Hands*, Royal Society of Literature, Oxford University Press, 1928.
28 Elizabeth Jenkins, *Jane Austen*, Gollancz, 1968.
29 Mary Lascelles, *Jane Austen and her Art*, Oxford University Press, 1937.
30 R. W. Chapman, *Jane Austen*, Oxford University Press, 1948.
31 Yasmine Gooneratne, *Jane Austen*, Cambridge University Press, 1970.
32 B. C. Southam, *Jane Austen's Literary MSS*, Oxford University Press, 1964.
33 *Letters*, No 40.
34 *Life*, p. 173.
35 *Persuasion*, Chap. 11, p. 117.
36 *Letters*, No 43.
37 *Letters*, No 39.
38 *Letters*, No 39.
39 *Letters*, No 39.
40 *Letters*, No 39.
41 *M.W.*, p. 440.
42 *Letters*, No 40.
43 *Letters*, No 41.
44 *A.P.*, p. 233.
45 *A.P.*, p. 235.
46 *Letters*, No 43.
47 *Letters*, No 43.
48 *Letters*, No 43.
49 *Letters*, No 43.
50 *Letters*, No 44.
51 Brabourne, vol. I, p. 299-300 (45)
52 Brabourne, vol. I, p. 302 (45).
53 Brabourne, vol. I, p. 305 (46).
54 Brabourne, vol. I, p. 311 (47).
55 Brabourne, vol. I, p. 250 (29).
56 Brabourne, vol. I, p. 372 (54).
57 *A.P.*, p. 245.
58 Brabourne, vol. I, p. 300 (45).
59 *Letters*, No 140.
60 *Letters*, No 49.
61 Brabourne, vol. I, p. 329 (50).
62 Brabourne, vol. I, p. 318 (48).
63 Brabourne, vol. I, p. 319 (48).
64 Brabourne, vol. I, p. 323 (49).
65 William Cowper, *The Task*, VI, ll. 147-151.
66 Brabourne, vol. I, p. 325 (49).
67 *Memoir*, p. 337.
68 *Memoir*, p. 326.
69 Brabourne, vol. I, p. 324 (49).

70 *Letters*, No 51.
71 *Letters*, No 51.
72 *Letters*, No 52.
73 *Letters*, No 52.
74 Brabourne, vol. I, p. 361–2 (53).
75 Brabourne, vol. I, p. 348 (51).
76 Brabourne, vol. I, p. 363 (53).
77 Brabourne, vol. I, p. 352 (52).
78 Brabourne, vol. I, p. 368 (54).
79 Brabourne, vol. I, p. 357 (52).
80 Brabourne, vol. I, p. 359 (53).
81 Brabourne, vol. I, p. 371 (54).
82 *Letters*, No 52.
83 Brabourne, vol. I, p. 360 (53).
84 Brabourne, vol. I, p. 373 (54).
85 *Letters*, No 99.1.
86 Brabourne, vol. II, p. 7 (55).
87 Brabourne, vol. II, p. 16 (56).
88 Brabourne, vol. II, p. 18 (57).
89 Brabourne, vol. II, p. 18 (57).
90 Brabourne, vol. II, p. 22 (58).
91 Brabourne, vol. II, p. 24 (58).
92 Brabourne, vol. II, p. 21 (58).
93 Brabourne, vol. II, p. 30 (59).
94 Brabourne, vol. II, p. 33 (60).
95 Brabourne, vol. II, p. 48 (62).
96 Brabourne, vol. II, p. 43 (61).
97 Brabourne, vol. II, p. 74 (66).
98 Brabourne, vol. II, p. 50 (62).
99 Brabourne, vol. II, p. 51 (62).
100 Brabourne, vol. II, p. 51 (62).
101 Brabourne, vol. II, p. 41 (61).
102 Brabourne, vol. II, p. 37 (60).
103 Brabourne, vol. II, p. 40 (61).
104 Brabourne, vol. II, p. 41 (61).
105 Brabourne, vol. II, p. 47 (62).
106 Brabourne, vol. II, p. 50 (62).
107 Brabourne, vol. II, p. 49 (62).
108 Brabourne, vol. II, p. 47 (62).
109 Brabourne, vol. II, p. 61 (64).
110 Brabourne, vol. II, p. 71 (65).
111 Brabourne, vol. II, p. 47 (62).
112 Brabourne, vol. II, p. 63 (64).
113 Brabourne, vol. II, p. 68 (65).
114 Wendy Hinde, *Canning*, Collins, 1973.
115 Brabourne, vol. II, p. 76 (66).
116 P. B. Shelley, "Julian and Maddalo", l.449.
117 Brabourne, vol. II, p. 54 (63).
118 Brabourne, vol. II, p. 57 (63).
119 Brabourne, vol. II, p. 62 (64).
120 Brabourne, vol. II, p. 68 (65).
121 Brabourne, vol. II, p. 267 (133).
122 Brabourne, vol. II, p. 68 (65).
123 *A.P.*, p. 160.
124 Brabourne, vol. I, p. 357 (52).
125 *Mansfield Park*, Chap. 46, p. 428.
126 *Letters*, No 67.

4 THE YEARS OF FULFILMENT

1 *Letters*, No 68.
2 Caroline Austen, *My Aunt Jane Austen*, Jane Austen Society, 1952.
3 *Memoir*, p. 375.
4 Virginia Woolf, "Personalities", *Collected Essays II*, Hogarth Press, 1966, Harcourt Brace Jovanovich in USA.
5 *Letters*, No 69.
6 Brabourne, vol. II, p. 90 (70).
7 Brabourne, vol. II, p. 97 (71).
8 Brabourne, vol. II, p. 94 (70).
9 Brabourne, vol. II, p. 98 (71).
10 Brabourne, vol. II, p. 101 (72).
11 Brabourne, vol. II, p. 114 (74).
12 *Letters*, Note 291.
13 *Life*, p. 254.
14 R. W. Chapman, *Jane Austen*, Oxford University Press, 1948, p. 157.
15 *Letters*, No 81.
16 Malcolm Bradbury, "Jane Austen's Emma" in *Emma, A Casebook*, ed. David Lodge, Macmillan, 1968.
17 Tony Tanner, Introduction, *Sense and Sensibility*, Penguin English Library, 1969.
18 Tony Tanner, Introduction, *Sense and Sensibility*, Penguin English Library, 1969.
19 *A.P.*, p. 250.
20 *Letters*, No 74.1.
21 *Letters*, No 74.1.
22 *Letters*, No 78.
23 *Letters*, No 75.
24 *Letters*, No 75.
25 *Letters*, No 76.
26 *Letters*, No 76.
27 *Letters*, No 77.
28 *Letters*, No 78.

29 *Letters*, No 78.1.

30 B. C. Southam ed. *Jane Austen,
    The Critical Heritage*, Rout-
    ledge & Kegan Paul, 1968,
    Barnes & Noble in USA.

31 R. W. Chapman, *Jane Austen*,
    Oxford University Press, 1948,
    p. 171.

32 *Pride and Prejudice*, Chap. 1,
    p. 51.

33 *Pride and Prejudice*, Chap. 29,
    p. 196.

34 *Pride and Prejudice*, Chap. 59,
    p. 385.

35 *Pride and Prejudice*, Chap. 51,
    p. 329.

36 *Pride and Prejudice*, Chap. 11,
    p. 102.

37 *Pride and Prejudice*, Chap. 7,
    p. 79.

38 B. C. Southam ed. Charlotte
    Brontë on Jane Austen, *Jane
    Austen, The Critical Heritage*,
    Routledge & Kegan Paul, 1968,
    Barnes and Noble in USA.

39 *Letters*, No 81.

40 *Letters*, No 79.

41 *Letters*, No 79.

42 Brabourne, vol. II, p. 143 (80).

43 Brabourne, vol. II, p. 141 (80).

44 *Letters*, No 81.

45 J. H. and Edith Hubback, *Jane
    Austen's Sailor Brothers*, John
    Lane, 1906.

46 *Letters*, No 81.

47 Brabourne, vol. II, p. 145 (82).

48 Brabourne, vol. II, p. 147 (82).

49 Brabourne, vol. II, p. 149 (82).

50 Brabourne, vol. II, p. 151 (82).

51 Brabourne, vol. II, p. 152 (82).

52 Brabourne, vol. II, p. 157 (83).

53 Brabourne, vol. II, p. 150 (82).

54 Brabourne, vol. II, p. 155 (83).

55 Brabourne, vol. II, p. 160 (84).

56 Brabourne, vol. II, p. 161 (84).

57 Brabourne, vol. II, p. 167 (84).

58 *Letters*, No 85.

59 Brabourne, vol. II, p. 175 (86).

60 *Letters*, No 85.

61 *Letters*, No 85.

62 Brabourne, vol. II, p. 169 (86).

63 Brabourne, vol. II, p. 196 (89).

64 Brabourne, vol. II, p. 172 (86).

65 Brabourne, vol. II, p. 172 (86).

66 Brabourne, vol. II, p. 215 (91).

67 Norman Page, *The Language of
    Jane Austen*, Basil Blackwell,
    1972.

68 Brabourne, vol. II, p. 170 (86).

69 Brabourne, vol. II, p. 179 (87).

70 Brabourne, vol. II, p. 179 (87).

71 Brabourne, vol. II, p. 186 (87).

72 Brabourne, vol. II, p. 173 (86).

73 Brabourne, vol. II, p. 181 (87).

74 Brabourne, vol. II, p. 185 (87).

75 Brabourne, vol. II, p. 191 (88).

76 Brabourne, vol. II, p. 190 (88).

77 Brabourne, vol. II, p. 196 (89).

78 Brabourne, vol. II, p. 199 (89).

79 Brabourne, vol. II, p. 201 (90).

80 Brabourne, vol. II, p. 203 (90).

81 *Letters*, No 85.

82 *Letters*, No 89.

83 Brabourne, vol. II, p. 205 (90).

84 Brabourne, vol. II, pp. 211, 209
    (91).

85 Brabourne, vol. II, p. 207 (90).

86 Brabourne, vol. II, p. 207 (90).

87 Brabourne, vol. II, p. 209 (91).

88 Brabourne, vol. II, p. 212 (91).

89 Brabourne, vol. II, p. 214 (91).

90 *Letters*, No 92.

91 *Letters*, No 92.

92 *Letters*, No 92.

93 *Letters*, No 92.

94 Brabourne, vol. II, p. 222 (93).

95 Brabourne, vol. II, p. 222 (93).

96 Brabourne, vol. II, p. 222 (93).

97 Brabourne, vol. II, p. 225 (93).

98 Brabourne, vol. II, p. 227 (93).

99 Brabourne, vol. II, p. 230 (93).

100 Brabourne, vol. II, p. 231 (94).

101 Brabourne, vol. II, p. 229 (93).

102 Brabourne, vol. II, p. 232 (94).

103 Brabourne, vol. II, p. 232 (94).

104 *M.W.*, p. 431.

105 Kingsley Amis, *What Became
    of Jane Austen?*, Jonathan Cape,
    1970: E. G. Selwyn, *Jane
    Austen's Clergymen*, Report
    Jane Austen Society, 1959:
    Elizabeth Bowen, *Jane Austen
    and Charm*, Report Jane Austen
    Society, 1969: Marvin Mudrick,
    *Jane Austen, Irony as Defense
    and Discovery*, Princeton, 1952:
    Tony Tanner, Introduction,

Mansfield Park, Penguin English Library, 1966.

106 *Mansfield Park*, Chap. 48, p. 448.
107 *Mansfield Park*, Chap. 13, p. 150.
108 *Mansfield Park*, Chap. 25, p. 248.
109 *Mansfield Park*, Chap. 39, p. 384.
110 *Mansfield Park*, Chap. 46, p. 428.
111 *Mansfield Park*, Chap. 39, pp. 382–3.
112 *Mansfield Park*, Chap. 48, p. 455.
113 *Memoir*, p. 336.
114 *Letters*, Note on Letter 95, p. 387.
115 *Letters*, No 95.
116 *Letters*, No 98.
117 *Letters*, No 98.
118 Brabourne, vol. II, p. 312 (100).
119 Brabourne, vol. II, p. 313 (100).
120 Brabourne, vol. II, pp. 315, 316 (101).
121 Brabourne, vol. II, p. 317 (101).
122 Brabourne, vol. II, p. 317 (101).
123 *Letters*, No 107.
124 Brabourne, vol. II, p. 313 (100).
125 *Letters*, No 107.
126 *Letters*, No 124.
127 Brabourne, vol. II, p. 235 (96).
128 *Life*, p. 302.
129 Brabourne, vol. II, p. 235 (96).
130 Brabourne, vol. II, p. 239 (97).
131 Brabourne, vol. II, p. 241 (99).
132 Brabourne, vol. II, p. 243 (99).
133 *Letters*, No 99.1.
134 *Letters*, No 99.1.
135 *Cornhill*, No 973, Winter 1947–48.
136 *Letters*, No 103.
137 *Letters*, No 103.
138 Brabourne, vol. II, p. 285 (106).
139 *Letters*, No 105.
140 Brabourne, vol. II, pp. 286–7 (106).
141 Brabourne, vol. II, p. 290 (106).
142 Brabourne, vol. II, p. 288 (106).
143 *Letters*, No 106.
144 Brabourne, vol. II, p. 289 (106).
145 Carola Oman, *Britain Against Napoleon*, Faber & Faber, 1942.
146 Alfred Cobban, *History of Modern France*, vol. 2, Pelican Original, 1972.
147 J. H. and Edith Hubback, *Jane Austen's Sailor Brothers*, John Lane, 1906.
148 Elizabeth Jenkins, *Jane Austen and Wyards*, Report, Jane Austen Society, 1958.
149 Brabourne, vol. II, p. 324 (110).
150 *Letters*, No 111.
151 *Letters*, No 111.
152 *Letters*, No 111.
153 *Life*, p. 310.
154 *Letters*, No 112.
155 *Letters*, No 114.
156 *Memoir*, p. 351 (113).
157 *Memoir*, p. 351 (113a).
158 *Letters*, No 115.
159 Brabourne, vol. II, p. 250 (116).
160 Brabourne, vol. II, p. 250 (116).
161 Brabourne, vol. II, p. 254 (117).
162 Brabourne, vol. II, p. 256 (117).
163 *Letters*, No 117.
164 Brabourne, vol. II, p. 259 (118).
165 Brabourne, vol. II, p. 260 (118).
166 *Letters*, No 119.
167 *Memoir*, p. 352 (120).
168 *Letters*, No 120a.
169 B. C. Southam ed. *Jane Austen, The Critical Heritage*, Routledge & Kegan Paul, 1968, Barnes & Noble in USA.
170 *M.W.*, p. 436.
171 *Memoir*, p. 375.
172 *Emma*, Chap. 1, p. 37.
173 E. F. Shannon, Jnr, from "Emma, Character and Construction", 1956, in *Emma, A Casebook*, ed David Lodge, Macmillan, 1968.
174 *A.P.*, p. 263.
175 *Life*, p. 333.
176 *Letters*, No 126a.
177 *Memoir*, p. 354 (126).
178 *M.W.*, p. 428.

5 DEATH UNTIMELY

1 *Letters*, No 128.
2 *Letters*, No 128.1.
3 Caroline Austen, *My Aunt Jane Austen*, Jane Austen Society, 1952, p. 14.
4 Brabourne, vol. II, p. 326 (129).
5 *Memoir*, p. 377 (130).
6 *Memoir*, p. 378 (130).
7 R. W. Chapman, *Jane Austen*, Oxford University Press, 1948.

B. C. Southam ed. *Jane Austen, The Critical Heritage*, Routledge & Kegan Paul, 1968, Barnes & Noble in USA.

8 *Letters*, No 131.

9 *Letters*, No 132.

10 Brabourne, vol. II, pp. 263-4 (133).

11 Brabourne, vol. II, p. 265 (133).

12 Brabourne, vol. II, p. 265 (133).

13 Brabourne, vol. II, p. 266 (133).

14 Brabourne, vol. II, p. 266 (133).

15 Brabourne, vol. II, p. 264 (133).

16 *Memoir*, pp. 379-380 (134).

17 *Memoir*, pp. 379-380 (134)

18 *Memoir*, pp. 379-380 (134).

19 *Letters*, No 136.

20 *Letters*, No 137.

21 *Letters*, No 137.

22 *Letters*, No 137.

23 *Letters*, No 139.

24 *Letters*, No 139.

25 Brabourne, vol. II, pp. 290-291 (140).

26 Brabourne, vol. II, p. 294 (140).

27 *Letters*, No 140.

28 Brabourne, vol. II, p. 295 (140).

29 *Letters*, No 141.

30 *Letters*, No 141.

31 *Letters*, No 141.

32 *Letters*, No 142.

33 Brabourne, vol. II, p. 297 (141).

34 Brabourne, vol. II, p. 298 (141).

35 *Letters*, No 141.1.

36 B. C. Southam, *Jane Austen's Literary MSS.*, Oxford University Press, 1964.

37 Caroline Austen, *My Aunt Jane Austen*, Jane Austen Society, 1952.

38 *Emma*, Chap. 12 pp. 127, 125.

39 *Persuasion*, Chap. 5, p. 64.

40 *M.W.*, p. 415.

41 Brabourne, vol. II, p. 300 (142).

42 Brabourne, vol. II, p. 300 (142).

43 Sir Zachary Cope, *Jane Austen's Last Illness*, Report, Jane Austen Society, 1964, reprinted from the British Medical Journal, 18th July 1964.

44 Brabourne, vol. II, p. 303 (142).

45 *Letters*, No 143.

46 *Letters*, No 144.

47 *Letters*, No 144.

48 Caroline Austen, *My Aunt Jane Austen*, Jane Austen Society, 1952, p. 14.

49 *Letters*, p. 519.

50 *Letters*, No 145.

51 *Letters*, No 145.

52 *Letters*, No 145.

53 *Letters*, No 145.

54 *Memoir*, p. 386 (146).

55 *Biographical Notice*, Henry Austen with *Northanger Abbey*, Penguin English Library, 1974 pp. 34, 30.

56 *Biographical Notice*, Henry Austen with *Northanger Abbey*, Penguin English Library, 1974 p. 30.

57 *M.W.*, p. 451.

58 *Memoir*, p. 387.

59 Brabourne, vol. II, p. 334 (513).

60 Brabourne, vol. II, p. 336 (513).

61 Brabourne, vol. II, p. 334 (513).

62 Brabourne, vol. II, p. 339 (517).

63 B. C. Southam ed. *Jane Austen, The Critical Heritage*, Routledge & Kegan Paul, 1968, Barnes & Noble in USA.

64 *Northanger Abbey*, Chap. 10, p. 94.

65 David Daiches, *A Study of Literature*, quoted in Howard S. Babb, *Jane Austen's Novels, The Fabric of Dialogue*, Archon Books, 1967, Ohio University Press, 1962.

66 *Northanger Abbey*, Chap. 24, p. 199.

67 B. C. Southam ed. *Jane Austen, The Critical Heritage*, Routledge & Kegan Paul, 1968, Barnes & Noble in USA.

68 *Letters*, No 142.

69 *Persuasion*, Chap. 24, p. 250.

70 *Persuasion*, Chap. 10, p. 110.

71 *Persuasion*, Chap. 12, p. 129.

72 *Persuasion*, Chap. 23 pp. 236, 238.

73 *Persuasion*, Chap. 24, p. 253.

74 *Persuasion*, Chap. 8, p. 92.

75 D. W. Harding, Introduction, *Persuasion*, Penguin English Library, 1971, p. 21.

76 Brabourne, vol. I, Dedication.

77 *Memoir*, p. 333.

Principal Characters

AUSTEN, REV. GEORGE, 1731–1805. Rector of Steventon and Deane, Jane Austen's father.

AUSTEN, CASSANDRA, (née Leigh), 1739–1827. m. George Austen 1764, Jane Austen's mother.

AUSTEN, REV. JAMES, 1765–1819. Jane Austen's eldest brother, m. (1) 1792 Anne Mathew by whom he had one daughter Jane Anna Elizabeth, (2) 1797 Mary Lloyd who was the mother of Jane Austen's first biographer, James Edward, and Caroline, author of *My Aunt Jane Austen*

AUSTEN, EDWARD, 1768–1852. The lucky brother adopted by the Knight family. He inherited the Godmersham and Chawton estates and from 1812 was known as Edward Knight. m. 1791 Elizabeth Bridges by whom he had eleven children, including Jane's favourite niece, Fanny.

AUSTEN, HENRY, 1771–1850. Jane Austen's favourite brother and literary advisor—soldier, banker, and priest. m. 1797 Eliza, Comtesse de Feuillide.

AUSTEN, CASSANDRA ELIZABETH, 1773–1845. Jane Austen's much loved older sister, with whom she shared the closest relationship of her life.

AUSTEN, FRANCIS WILLIAM, 1774–1865. The elder of the sailor brothers. m. 1806 Mary Gibson. After the death of his first wife, in 1828 he married Martha Lloyd, the sister of his brother James's second wife and one of Jane Austen's dearest friends. Perhaps the model for Captain Harville in *Persuasion*.

AUSTEN, CHARLES JOHN, 1779–1852. The younger sailor brother, who presented his sisters with a topaz cross each with his first prize money, thus inspiring a famous incident in *Mansfield Park*. m. (1) 1807 Frances Palmer (2) 1820, her sister Harriet Palmer.

o

AUSTEN, JANE ANNA ELIZABETH, 1793–1872 Known as Anna, daughter of Jane Austen's eldest brother, James, by his first wife. m. 1814 Ben Lefroy, was herself an aspiring novelist.

AUSTEN, JAMES EDWARD, 1798–1874. Only son of Jane Austen's eldest brother James, always referred to as Edward and from 1837 known as Austen-Leigh. His aunt's first biographer, he published the *Memoir* in 1870.

AUSTEN, CAROLINE MARY CRAVEN, 1805–1880. Youngest daughter of Jane Austen's eldest brother, James. Interested herself in writing, she left invaluable memories of her favourite aunt in *My Aunt Jane Austen*.

AUSTEN, FANNY CATHERINE, 1793–1882. Eldest daughter of Edward Austen, later Knight, and Jane Austen's favourite niece. m. 1820 Sir Edward Knatchbull Bt.

AUSTEN, ELIZA, 1761–1813. Only daughter of the Rev. George Austen's sister, Philadelphia Hancock. m. (1) 1781, Jean Capotte, Comte de Feuillide, who was guillotined in 1794. (2) 1797 Henry Austen. Warren Hastings's goddaughter, she had one child, always in bad health, by her first husband, Hastings, 1786–1801.

BIGEON, MADAME, The devoted servant of the Comtesse de Feuillide and after her death of Henry Austen, to whom Jane Austen left £50.

BIGG, ALETHEA, 1777–1847. The youngest daughter of Lovelace Bigg Wither of Manydown, sister of Harris.

BIGG, CATHERINE, b. 1773. Sister of Harris Bigg Wither. m. 1808 Rev. Herbert Hill, uncle of the Poet Laureate, Robert Southey. Her son Herbert was to marry Southey's daughter Bertha.

BIGG, ELIZABETH, 1773–1855. Sister of Harris Bigg Wither. m. 1798 Rev. William Heathcote, who died in 1802. In 1814, she moved to the Close, Winchester, with her sister Alethea, and was one of Jane Austen's last visitors.

BIGG-WITHER, HARRIS, 1781–1833. Heir to Manydown, Hants, who proposed marriage to Jane Austen in 1802, was accepted, and overnight, rejected. m. 1804 Anne Frith.

BLACKALL, REV. SAMUEL, 1771–1842. A rather luke-warm suitor of Jane Austen.

BRIDGES, REV. BROOK EDWARD, 1779–1825. Brother of Jane's sister-in-law, Elizabeth, wife of Edward. Possibly he made an unsuccessful proposal of marriage to Jane Austen. *m.* 1809 Harriet Foote.

BRIDGES, ELIZABETH, 1773–1808. Daughter of Sir Brook Bridges Third Baronet, *m*, Edward Austen 1791.

BRIDGES, FANNY LADY, d. 1825. Mother of Edward Austen's wife, Elizabeth, lived at Goodnestone Farm.

BRYDGES, SIR SAMUEL EGERTON, 1762–1837. Brother of Jane Austen's friend Mrs Lefroy, and author of the novel *Arthur Fitz-Albini*.

CLARKE, REV. JAMES STANIER, 1765(?)–1834. Chaplain to the Prince Regent at the time of the publication of *Emma*, which was dedicated to the Prince.

COOKE, REV. SAMUEL, 1741–1820. Vicar of Great Bookham who married Cassandra Leigh, first cousin of Mrs George Austen, and was Jane Austen's godfather.

COOPER, JANE, d. 1798. Daughter of Mrs George Austen's sister, and school fellow of Jane and Cassandra Austen. *m.* 1792 Captain, later Admiral Sir Thomas Williams. Tragically killed in a fall from a light horse carriage.

COOPER, REV. EDWARD, 1770–1835. Only son of Mrs George Austen's sister, Jane. Brother of Jane above. *m.* 1793 Caroline Isabella Lybbe Powys. Rector Hamstal-Ridware, Staffs, author several volumes of sermons.

DIGWEED, HARRY, 1771–1848. Tenant of Steventon Manor, perhaps an admirer of Jane Austen. *m.* 1808 Jane Terry, lived at Alton near the Austens at Chawton. Other Digweed brothers were the Rev. James of Dummer, and William who stayed at Steventon after Harry's removal.

EGERTON, THOMAS. Jane Austen's first publisher.

FOWLE, ELIZABETH, 1768–1839. Middle daughter of Rev. Nowes Lloyd. *m.* Rev. Fulwer Craven Fowle, Vicar of Kintbury.

FOWLE, REV. THOMAS, 1766–1796. Rector of Allingham. Pupil of Rev. George Austen, later engaged to Jane's sister Cassandra. He died of yellow fever on a voyage to the West Indies.

GIBSON, MARY, d. 1823. First wife of Francis Austen.

HADEN, CHARLES THOMAS, 1786–1824. The surgeon of Sloane Street who treated Henry Austen. An admirer of Jane Austen and her niece Fanny, who in their turn, greatly admired him.

HANCOCK, PHILADELPHIA, 1730–1792. Sister of Rev. George Austen. m. 1753 Tysoe Saul Hancock in India. Mother of Eliza, Comtesse de Feuillide.

HASTINGS, WARREN, 1732–1818. The great first Governor General of India, whose impeachment trial was closely followed by the Austen family, who rejoiced at its outcome. He was the generous godfather of Eliza Hancock, Comtesse de Feuillide, and an early admirer of Jane Austen's novels.

KNATCHBULL, REV. DR WYNDHAM, 1786–1868. A young man whom Jane Austen thought might 'do' for her favourite niece Fanny. But she married his elder widowed brother, Sir Edward, Ninth Baronet, in 1820.

KNIGHT, MRS CATHERINE, 1753–1812. Widow of Edward Austen's benefactor, Thomas Knight of Godmersham, who later lived at White Friars near Canterbury, and always retained her affection for Edward and his family.

LEFROY, MRS ANNE, 1749–1804. Sister of Sir Samuel Egerton Brydges. m. 1778 Rev. Isaac Peter George Lefroy. Her son Ben was to marry Jane Austen's eldest niece, Anna. She died tragically in a fall from her horse on Jane Austen's birthday.

LEFROY, REV. BENJAMIN, 1791–1829. Youngest son of Jane Austen's good friend Anne Lefroy, who married her niece Anna in 1814.

LEFROY, THOMAS LANGLOIS, 1776–1869. Nephew of Rev. Isaac Lefroy, with whom Jane flirted in a "most profligate and shocking" way in the winter of her twentieth year.

LEIGH, ELIZABETH, d. 1816. Sister of Rev. Thomas Leigh, cousin to Mrs George Austen, and Cassandra's godmother.

LEIGH, REV. THOMAS, d. 1813. Rector of Adlestrop, Gloucestershire, Mrs George Austen's cousin. Succeeded to Stoneleigh estates in 1806.

LEIGH PERROT, JAMES, d. 1817. Wealthy brother of Mrs George Austen. m. Jane Cholmeley, resided at Scarlets, Berks, and Bath.

LEIGH PERROT, JANE, 1744–1836. Wife of Jane Austen's uncle James Leigh Perrot, who in 1799 was unjustly involved in a case of shoplifting. By no means a family favourite.

LLOYD, MARTHA, d. 1843. Eldest daughter of Rev. Nowes Lloyd. Jane Austen's close and elegant friend who became in 1828 her brother Frank's second wife.

LLOYD, MRS MARTHA, d. 1805. Daughter of Hon. Charles Craven. m. 1763 Rev. Nowes Lloyd. Her three daughters, Martha, Elizabeth, and Mary, were close friends of Jane and Cassandra Austen.

LLOYD, MARY, d. 1843. Youngest daughter of Rev. Nowes Lloyd. m. 1797 Jane Austen's eldest brother James. Mother of James Edward and Caroline.

LYFORD, GILES KING, 1764–1837. The surgeon of Winchester who attended Jane Austen in her last illness, a relative of the Basingstoke father and son doctors John and Charles Lyford who looked after Mrs George Austen.

MILLES, MRS CHARLES, 1723–1817, and her daughter Molly, who perhaps inspired the creation of Mrs and Miss Bates.

MOORE, REV. GEORGE. Eldest son of John, Archbishop of Canterbury, who married Harriot Mary Bridges, sister of Edward Austen's wife, Elizabeth.

MURRAY, JOHN, 1778–1843. Jane Austen's second publisher.

PALMER, FRANCES AND HARRIET. The sisters from Bermuda who were the first and second wives of Charles Austen.

PAPILLON, REV. JOHN RAWSTON, 1801–37. Rector of Chawton.

PEARSON, MARY. Daughter of Sir Richard Pearson, officer of Greenwich Hospital, whom Henry Austen courted before his marriage to his cousin Eliza.

PLUMTRE, JOHN, 1791–1864. An anxious and unsuccessful suitor for the hand of Fanny Knight.

SACREE, SUSANNA, 1761–1851. The faithful nursemaid at Godmersham.

SHARPE, ANNE. A former governess at Godmersham, with whom Cassandra and Jane Austen maintained a continuous friendship. She was one of Jane's last correspondents before her death.

STENT, MRS. Mrs Lloyd's companion, and perhaps another who helped to inspire the creation of Miss Bates.

TILSON, JAMES. Henry Austen's partner in the ill-fated banking firm of Austen, Maude, and Tilson.

WALTER, PHILADELPHIA, d. 1834. Daughter of William Hampson Walter, half brother of the Rev. George Austen. *m.* George Whitaker. A frequent and rather tart correspondent of Eliza, Comtesse de Feuillide.

WALTER, WILLIAM HAMPSON, d. 1798. Rev. George Austen's half brother, father of Philadelphia.

Reading List

The following were among the works consulted during the preparation of this book. Obviously they vary tremendously both in content and quality, but each one has made some contribution both to my book and my own picture of Jane Austen, woman and writer, for which I am grateful.

Allen, W. *The English Novel*, Phoenix, 1954

Amis, Kingsley, *What Became of Jane Austen?*, Jonathan Cape, 1970

Austen, Caroline, *My Aunt Jane Austen*, Jane Austen Society, 1952

Austen, Henry, *Biographical Notice*, in *Northanger Abbey*, Penguin English Library, 1974

Austen, Jane, *Sense and Sensibility*, Introduction by Tony Tanner, Penguin English Library, 1969

Austen, Jane, *Pride and Prejudice*, Introduction by Tony Tanner, Penguin English Library, 1972

Austen, Jane, *Mansfield Park*, Introduction by Tony Tanner, Penguin English Library, 1972

Austen, Jane, *Emma*, Introduction by Ronald Blythe, Penguin English, Library 1973

Austen, Jane, *Northanger Abbey*, Introduction by Anne Henry Ehrenpreis, Penguin English Library, 1974

Austen, Jane, *Persuasion*, Introduction by D. W. Harding, Penguin English Library, 1971

Austen, Jane, *Minor Works*, ed. R. W. Chapman & B. C. Southam, Oxford University Press, 1972

Austen, Jane, *Jane Austen's Letters to her Sister Cassandra and Others*, Oxford University Press, 1969

Austen-Leigh, Emma, *Jane Austen and Bath*, Spottiswoode, Ballantyne & Co., 1939

Austen-Leigh, J. E., *A Memoir of Jane Austen*, with *Persuasion*, Penguin English Library, 1971

Austen-Leigh, Mary, *James Edward Austen Leigh, A Memoir*, privately printed, 1911

Austen-Leigh, Mary, *Personal Aspects of Jane Austen*, 1920

Austen-Leigh, R. A., *Jane Austen and Lyme Regis*, Spottiswoode & Ballantyne, 1941

Austen-Leigh, R. A., *Jane Austen and Southampton*, Spottiswoode & Ballantyne, 1949

Austen-Leigh, R. A., *Austen Papers, 1704–1856*, Spottiswoode & Ballantyne, 1942

Austen-Leigh, W. & R. A., *Jane Austen, Her Life and Letters*, Smith Elder & Co., 1913

Babb, Howard S., *Jane Austen's Novels, The Fabric of Dialogue*, Archon Books, 1967

Bateson, F. W., *The Scholar-Critic*, Routledge & Kegan Paul, 1972

Brabourne, Edward Lord, *Letters of Jane Austen*, Richard Bentley & Son, 1884

Bradley, A. C., *Jane Austen*, in Essays and Studies by Members of the English Association, 11 (1911)

Briggs, Asa, *The Age of Improvement*, Longmans, 1959

Brophy, Bridget, *Don't Never Forget*, Jonathan Cape, 1966

Brown, Helen, *Jane Austen*, Duckworth, 1939

Bradbrook, Frank W., *Jane Austen and her Predecessors*, Cambridge University Press, 1966

Bradbury, Malcolm, *Possibilities*, Oxford University Press, 1973

Bryant, Arthur, *The Age of Elegance*, Collins, 1950

Burrows, J. F., *Jane Austen's Emma*, Sydney University Press, 1968

Bush, Douglas, *Jane Austen*, Macmillan, 1975

Cecil, Lord David, *Jane Austen*, Cambridge University Press, 1936

Chapman, R. W., *Jane Austen*, Oxford University Press, 1948

Cobban, Arthur, *History of Modern France*, Pelican Original, 1972

Craik, Wendy A., *Jane Austen in her Time*, Nelson, 1969

Craik, Wendy A., *Jane Austen, The Six Novels*, Methuen, 1965

Daiches, David, *The Novel and the Modern World*, University of Chicago Press, 1939

Daiches, David, *Literary Essays*, Oliver & Boyd, 1956

Eden, Emily, *Semi-Attached Couple*, Introduction by John Gore, Elkin, Mathews & Marrot, 1928

Forster, E. M., *Times Literary Supplement*, 10 November 1932

Forster, E. M., *Abinger Harvest*, E. Arnold & Co., 1953

Freeman, Jean, *Jane Austen in Bath*, Jane Austen Society, 1969

Freeman, Kathleen, *T'Other Miss Austen*, Macdonald, 1956

Garrod, H. W., *Jane Austen: A Depreciation* in *Essays by Divers Hands*, Royal Society of Literature, Oxford University Press, 1928

Gooneratne, Yasmine, *Jane Austen*, Cambridge University Press, 1970

Gorer, Geoffrey, *The Danger of Equality and other Essays*, The Cresset Press, 1966

Harding, D. W., *Regulated Hatred: An Aspect of the Work of Jane Austen*, Scrutiny VIII, 1940

Hill, Constance, *Jane Austen, Her Home and Her Friends*, John Lane, 1902

Hinde, Wendy, *Canning*, Collins, 1973

Hodge, Jane Aiken, *The Double Life of Jane Austen*, Hodder and Stoughton, 1972

Hubback, J. H. & Edith, *Jane Austen's Sailor Brothers*, John Lane, 1906

Jane Austen Society, *Annual Reports*, 1949–1974

Jenkins, Elizabeth, *Jane Austen*, Gollancz, 1968

Johnson, R. Brimley, *A New Study*, with Leonie Villard, *A French Appreciation*, Routledge, 1924

Kaye-Smith, Sheila, & Stern, G. B., *Talking of Jane Austen*, Cassell, 1944

Kennedy, Margaret, *Jane Austen*, Arthur Barker, 1950

Lascelles, Mary, *Jane Austen and Her Art*, Oxford University Press, 1939

Leavis, F. R., *The Great Tradition*, Chatto & Windus, 1948

Leavis, Q. D., *Fiction and the Reading Public*, Chatto & Windus, 1932

Leavis, Q. D., *A Critical Theory of Jane Austen's Writings in A Selection from Scrutiny*, Cambridge University Press, 1968

Lerner, Laurence, *The Truth Tellers*, Chatto & Windus, 1967

Litz, A. Walton, *Jane Austen, A Study of her Artistic Development*, Chatto & Windus, 1965, Oxford University Press in USA

Lodge, David, ed. *Emma, A Casebook*, Macmillan, 1968

Mansell, Darrel, *The Novels of Jane Austen*, Macmillan, 1973

Maugham, W. S., *Ten Novels and their Authors*, William Heinemann Ltd., 1954

Mews, Hazel, *Frail Vessels*, Athlone Press, 1969

MacKinnon, Sir Frank, *Grand Larceny, The Trial of Jane Leigh Perrot*, Oxford University Press, 1937

Mitton, Q. E., *Jane Austen and her Times*, Methuen, 1905

Moore, George, *Avowals*, Constable, 1919

Mudrick, Marvin, *Jane Austen, Irony as Defense and Discovery*, University of California Press, 1968

Neill, S. Diana, *A Short History of the English Novel*, Jarrolds, 1951

Nixon, Edna, *Mary Wollstonecraft, Her Life and Times*, J. M. Dent, 1971

O'Connor, Frank, *The Mirror in the Roadway*, Hamish Hamilton, 1957

Oman, Carola, *Britain Against Napoleon*, Faber and Faber, 1942

Page, Norman, *The Language of Jane Austen*, Basil Blackwell, 1972

Phillips, Kenneth A., *Jane Austen's English*, André Deutsch, 1970

Pinion, Francis B., *A Jane Austen Companion*, Macmillan, 1973

Pollock, Walter H., *Jane Austen: Her Contemporaries and Herself*, Longmans Green & Co., 1899

Priestley, J. B., *The Prince of Pleasure*, Sphere Books, 1971

Pritchett, V. S., *George Meredith and English Comedy*, Chatto & Windus, in USA, Alfred A. Knopf, Inc., 1970

Rhydderch, David, *Jane Austen, Her Life and Art*, Jonathan Cape, 1932

Richards, I. A., *Practical Criticism*, Routledge & Kegan Paul, 1964

Roth, Barry, & Weinsteiner, Joel, *An Annotated Bibliography of Jane Austen Studies, 1952–1972*, University of Virginia, 1973

Southam, B. C., *Jane Austen's Literary MSS*, Oxford University Press, 1964

Southam, B. C., ed. *Critical Essays on Jane Austen*, Routledge & Kegan Paul, 1968

Southam, B. C., ed. *Jane Austen, The Critical Heritage*, Routledge & Kegan Paul, 1968, Barnes & Noble in USA

Stowell, H. E., *Quill Pens and Petticoats*, Wayland, 1970

Sutherland, James, *English Satire*, Cambridge University Press, 1962

Thomas, C. Linklater, *Jane Austen, A Survey*, Horace Marshall, 1929

Tompkins, Joyce M. S., *The Popular Novel in England*, Methuen, 1969

Trilling, Lionel, *The Opposing Self*, Secker and Warburg, 1955

Watt, I., *The Rise of the Novel*, Chatto & Windus, 1957

Women in Print, George Allen & Unwin, 1972

Woodworth, Mary K., *The Literary Career of Sir Samuel Egerton Brydges*, Basil Blackwell, 1935

Woolf, Virginia, *Collected Essays*, Vols: I, II, IV, Hogarth Press, 1966, Harcourt Brace Jovanovich in USA

Wright, Andrew H., *Jane Austen's Novels*, Chatto & Windus, 1953

Index